PRAISE FOR THE BOOK

This book has been reviewed by number of technology professionals across the world. Some of their comments are listed as follows,

"This is one among the best books in the field of Automation testing. This smartly demonstrates a nice blend of automation tools and its efficiency. A must read for testing professionals for enriching their proficiency and mastering the automation world"

Satyadip Das, Test manager, Lloyds Banking Group

"Those want to jump start their carrier in automation testing. This book is a bible for them to guide and lead the life in a systematic manner."

Arul Velan, Wipro technologies

"Very much helpful for those who are new to automation testing, Detailed explanation with Perfect Practical Coverage. What else you need to jumpstart in the globe of Software Automation !!"

Altamash Khan, Senior Test Engineer, Wipro Technologies

"This book provides practical insight into the world of Software Testing.

Very Concise, and just filled with Excellent Information."

Anku Jain, Senior Test Engineer, Wipro Technologies

"Automation Testing - Doesn't only means that you save some time. It just more than saving the time, it gives a life to the system to function on its own."

Sathya Narayanan, Wipro Technologies

"Future belongs to those, who believe in the beauty of their dreams. And this book will surely help you in guiding your way towards Automation testing."

Pratiksha Kadam, Senior Software Engineer, Wipro Technologies.

"In celebration of the release software automation testing i appreciate your dedication and hard work.you deserve to be proud on your achievement. May your future efforts be equally successful and rewarding.Thanks for Releasing software automation testing"

Raman Sharda

"Encyclopedia of all automation tools !!"

Raghavendra mesta, Wipro Technologies

"This will be definitely helpful for all the current automation test engineers and upcoming automation test engineers. All the best"

Greeni Hari, Wipro Technologies

"hope it is easy understandable by everyone"

Jagan Kanniappan, Accenture

"Great effort by the author! It is a step by step guide which aims at making sure anybody can do automation be it selenium or any other tool. I would say this book is a wonderful package available in market right now, just go for it."

Shweta Bhat, Wipro Technologies

"book is really helpful in understanding core of automation testing, a great guide that is useful in planning test strategy and fit right into product management"

Ishwar Singh, Consultant, Deloitte

"Let the 'Software Automation Testing' - be helpful to all the testing professionals to explore the unexpected."

Neenu Ratheesh, Wipro Technologies

"This book will be a great help for anyone to learn about Test automation frameworks, use as an effective reference guide to select and use various automation tools. This book is another solid contribution from Narayanan Palani to help anyone to develop and become an expert in automation testing"

Libin Jose Mannala, Wipro Technologies

"Automation testing is the current and future approach for the robotic systems.This book from such an experienced and thoughtful person Mr. Narayanan will sure help the budding techies to enhance as an expert"

Arun Kumar, Technical Lead, Wipro Technologies

"Automation testings is more than enough for a smart tester to sustain in smart world.This book enlightenes the way to achieve it in the crazy labyrinth of test automation techniques."

Sumayya Nej, Wipro Technologies

"Time is Power and Money, and thats exactly why Automation Testing has an important role in the software industry. It is the solution to maximize the effectiveness, efficiency and coverage of software testing. Automation Testing reduces the work force as well as the time for repetitive tests from days to hours with improved accuracy. Identification of the right automation tool is critical to ensure the success of the project."

-Neethu Joseph

"Great book. This book is for people who want to know in depth of selenium Web Driver concepts. And also the topics has been explained in detail which will be very useful for the people who want to start a new career or for cracking interviews. This is a must buy!"

Dinesh Balaji, Test Automation Specialist, USBANK

"Automated tests can run fast and frequently, which is cost-effective for software products with a long maintenance life."

Rahul Bhat

It is fantastic book! If your organization is interested in having a mature automated testing process, you need this book. I already recommended it to all friends on mine and got very good reply. I would recommend it to anyone who already has or planning to automate their testing practices. Thank you for the great work!

Rohan Vakharia

" 'Software Automation Testing' presents a test automation methodology which is practical, useful, and complete, encompassing the state of the art of test automation as it stands right now.

If your organization is interested in having a mature automated testing process, you need this book.

It will guide you throughout the entire process from thinking about standards to implementing and maintaining them.

Also, it guides readers through each step in the planning, selection, and implementation process to assure that automated software testing will be developed in a systematic manner. Bon Apprentissage!"

Anjana Nambron, Wipro Technologies

"Automation Testing has gained more prominence in recent times because of the Software Industry rapidly evolving where functionalities of an Mobile App or a Web App has to be tested and certified thoroughly within a short span of time. This book will help the young job seekers in understanding on the processes, Methodologies adopted by different Companies having a wide range of Automation Practices and Frameworks."

Sriharsha Karanth

"Keep up the good work going on.. as always the way you do. It will help everyone to know when exactly automation testing can be used and how useful it will be by saving time..."

Vijayalakshmi N Savanth, Wipro Technologies

"I know you are dynamic and interesting Blog writer. Nice to see you as a good author. You are brilliant person and we are expecting soon to read the revealing secrets of the Software Automation Testing... Your abstract tells - Sample Projects to download and practice on specific chapters !!! This would be helpful for advanced and all levels of Testing professionals."

Vijeyasekaran Kbd

"With growing trends of companies rapidly moving towards automation testing, having automation skills are no more considered just a "good to have skill". IT professionals who wants to have a career in automation testing, this book is a great start to kick off as Narayanan Palani has explained in detail the fundamentals of automation. This book is a great guide to learn automation."

Rajavarman Rajendran, Test Specialist, USBANK

"This book is really helpful for people who want to grow in the testing domain. Everything is explained in very easy language. A book highly recommended for testers."

Soma Mazumder, Wipro Technologies

"Automation testing is very important in every Project testing life-cycle. Through automation we can achieve more test case in less time.So it is both cost effective and also help to achieve the stringent time lines. This book will be an eye-opener for job seekers in the above field, to achieve their goals and also to optimize their performance."

Sunit Roy, Consultant, Capgemini

"This book will surely encompass all corners of testing a to zee...it will be beneficial for all testers irrespective of what profile they are into... people Looking for transitioning from manual to automation will get the most..."

Shubham Joshi

"it will be beneficial for all testers irrespective of what profile they are into...people Looking for transitioning from manual to automation will get the most..."

Karthik Manoharan, Senior Analyst, Wipro Technologies

"Good"

Krishnamurthy Chinnasamy,
Finance Manager, Britannia Industries Limited

"Very nice Narayanan."

Kothandan Sivalingam,
Quality Analyst, Dupont sustainable solutions L & D

"Clear and easy to understand! congrats"

Kamalbharathi Murugesan,
South Plainfield, New Jersey

"I, as a professional Automation Tester often fall in situations where we need to take call on what automation solution to employ for a project that would be most effective and efficient at the same time. But it is hard to take such decisions with limited insight and knowledge of the available tools for automated testing in the market today. The book here by Narayanan provides a panoramic view into these tools, thus empowering the reader to take more educated decisions to provide better automation test solutions."

Sohag Satpati

"Software automation testing - secrets revealed follows a job oriented testing process that can make anyone industry ready. Keep up the good work & all the best!"

Mitha SR Nair, BA, Wipro Technologies

Software Automation Testing

-Secrets Revealed!

Narayanan Palani

How to Automate Software Applications using

Selenium Web Driver using Java, Selenium Web Driver using Dot Net, Selenium IDE, AutoIT, Cucumber, Specflow, BDD, TDD, Jenkins, NUnit, ReportUnit, XSLT Reporting, Maven, Jason Phantom Ghost Driver, TestNG, JUnit, Ant, Eclipse, Team Foundation Server, *Visual Studio, HP Unified Functional Testing (formerly Quick Test Professional), Ranorex, IBM Rational Functional Test, Excel VBA Automation, Excel Objects Automation, SOA Testing-SOAP UI Automation, ETL Testing and SQL Testing for Agile-Continuous Integration*

with

Sample Projects to download and practice on specific chapters!

Very first book in the market on Machine Learning Technology of Automation Testing

First published in 2016 by

BecomeShakespeare.com

Wordit Content Design & Editing Services Pvt Ltd
Quest Offices, C38/39,
Parinee Crescenzo Building,
Bandra Kurla Complex, Bandra East,
Mumbai 400 051, India
T: +91 8080226699

ISBN 978-93-83952-95-3

Preface

Why this book?

This book best describes on how to use automation tools to build the frameworks for most wanted test automation job! Effectively a solid book to get an interview call for automation tester role; Also this book is a best fit for college students to study as part of Software Testing course as 'Junior Test Analyst', 'Automation Tester', 'Developer in Test' are the most wanted job in IT Industry!

Who is this book for?

This book is intended to be of most help to software testing professionals who are working in functional testing projects and interested to step into automation testing assignments as beginners. The target audience for this book includes:

- potential and recent purchasers of test automation tools
- those who already have a test automation experience and interested to know advanced automation testing solution for continuous integration
- anyone who is building in house test automation, security tools
- test tool vendors
- technical managers who want to insure that automation testing projects provides benefits

- management consultants and domain consultants and
- college students who intend to get a job in IT as a junior test analyst.

What this book talks about?

How to Automate Software Applications using Selenium Web Driver using Java, Selenium Web Driver using Dot Net, Selenium IDE,Cucumber,Specflow,BDD,TDD,Jenkins,NUnit,ReportUnit, XSLT Reporting, TestNG, JUnit, Ant, Eclipse, Team Foundation Server, Visual Studio, HP Unified Functional Testing (formerly Quick Test Professional), Ranorex, IBM Rational Functional Test, Excel VBA Automation, Excel Objects Automation, SOA Testing-SOAP UI Automation, ETL Testing and SQL Testing for Agile-Continuous Integration with Sample Projects to download and practice on specific chapters!

About Author

AMBITION

Narayanan Palani is keen in sharing the technical knowledge for those starting out a career in Software Testing or even for those with few years of testing experience. He is endorsed by Tech City UK as an exceptional talent/world leader in digital technology. His aim is to reduce the unemployment of developed countries like United Kingdom and developing countries like India by training the graduate students and jobseekers through his technical books. This book is the culmination of six years of research and effort in this field.

He can be reached at https://www.linkedin.com/in/narayananpalani

QUALIFICATIONS

Author is one of the world leading test automation professional with technical masters (Master of Science-Software Engineering) from Birla Institute of Technology and Science-Pilani and management masters (ExecMBA full time) from KJ Somaiya Institute of Management Studies and Research-Mumbai. Number of industry wide accepted International Certifications he acquired and respective bodies are listed as follows:

Software Automation Testing

HP Accredited Integration Specialist

HP

Wipro certified in Web Testing

Wipro

Wipro certified in MiLK Plus Certification in Quality Center v9

Wipro

HP Accredited Integration Specialist in Application Security

HP

ISTQB Certified Tester Foundation Level

International Software Testing Qualification Board, ISEB, BCS

IBM Certified Specialist in Requirements Management with Use case

IBM August 2011

ITIL Foundations

EXIN December 2013

IBM Certified Solution Designer - Rational Functional Tester for Java

IBM October 2008

IBM Certified Solution Designer - Rational Performance Tester

IBM January 2009

IBM Certified Specialist - Rational AppScan Standard Edition

IBM August 2010

IBM Certified Specialist – Rational Test Management and Robot v2003

IBM October 2008

Prince2 Project Management Foundations

AXELOS Global Best Practice License 4944123.20281955 May 2014

ISTQB Certified Tester Advanced Level TEST MANAGER

ISTQB - International Software Testing Qualifications BoardJuly 2015

RECOMMENDATIONS

Author's work has been appreciated and recommended across corporate industries. Some of them are listed here as reference:

"Narayanan is a dynamic personality and his writings are crisp, vivid and easy to understand. He is always inspiring!"

— Ruchir Shukla, Area Business Manager, housing.com

"Narayanan is a specialised automation testing specialist in designing the test automation frameworks using Selenium Webdriver, TestNG and Ant. Especially his selenium framework of automation using Selenium Reusable Libraries, XSLT Reports, JUnit, Ant Build, Object Libraries, Screenshot Utilities, Cross Browser Driver tests are dynamic and most important for any testing projects. When you talk about an Exceptional Talent in the IT industry especially in QA and Automation test, then you talk about Narayanan Palani."

— Olufemi Ade-Olusile, worked indirectly for Narayanan

"I have worked on some projects in Narayanan Palani's team and he was my Trainer in automation testing also, before I was getting into projects. He made excellent trainer as well as Test Manager. He is very determinant, inquisitive and keen on upgrading his skills consistently. His interest and knowledge in Software Testing are unbelievable! Saying 'Aiming to King of all' would better suit him rather saying 'Jack of all'. He is an unmissable employee for any company! I am sure he would go places and wish him good luck! :-)"

— Jeyabala George, reported to Narayanan

"Mr. Narayanan Palani has many certifications related to software testing that I won't be able to write all of them. In my view he is one of the most talented test lead/trainer around. I have had the great opportunity to learn from him as he has vast knowledge in software testing and capable of solving issues at any time. He has also complete knowledge of manual and automation testing including Selenium IDE, Selenium RC, Selenium WebDriver and Eclipse platform. He is a team key role player and wonderful motivator. I have learned many things from him and I would not have been a complete tester without his kind help and support. I would like to personally thank him for being my mentor and help me to be where I am now. I would like to mention some of his excellent skills out of many, those are as follows: Principles of Testing SDLC and STLC Static Testing Tools Support for Testing Dynamic Testing Techniques SQL Testing Test Design Techniques-Test Scenarios/ Test Cases Defect Management System Testing, Regression Testing OOPs and Java Programming concepts Test Automation-Selenium, Cucumber, Frameworks Selenium IDE Actions, Asserts, Assesors Selenium WebDriver TestNG Annotations and Data Providers Creating Test Suit with TestNG I wish him best of luck Regards Aminul"

— Aminul Islam, reported to Narayanan

"Narayanan is very experienced and knowledgeable in software testing. He has lots to offer in automation testing and can deal with complex projects. His extensive knowledge in testing tools and methodologies ensures quality work, and timely delivery. He is a great person to work with."

— Swati Kundu, reported to Narayanan

"Great Personality.Hard worker. Incredible Knowledge in Software Testing Q.A/Analyst. (Selenium IDE, Selenium Webdriver, Firebug, QTP, Load runner, Team Foundation Server, Junit Framework, TestNg, Cucumber, Jenkins, Versa Test Automator,

HP Performance Center, JMeter, Web Logic, JIRA ADMIN and AGILE, SOAP UI, Hudson Continuous integration, Subversion and Maven, Any question u ask him he has answer for it. Great person who has tremendous knowledge he has. I strongly believe that he will be one of the gem in testing world in near future."

— Mahender Molige, reported to Narayanan

"One of the greatest professional in the market. He has a Incredible talent and a further extendable knowledge in the Software Testing. Great personality and fun person to be with. I have gained so much just to be next to him in the latest Testing QA project at VICAPRI_GLOBAL I don't need to say much just take a look on his profile and you see how great talent professional he is"

— Ulisses Bezerra Da Silva, reported to Narayanan

"Narayanan is without a doubt the number one Executive Technical Coach for software testing I have come know in the country. I am proud to have been a part of his testing sessions as it was a great time to work with him on test design using tools like Selenium, test execution and defect management."

— Shawn Sibamba, reported to Narayanan

"I had the pleasure of working with Narayanan in a few eCommerce projects. I found Narayanan to be dedicated, has good ideas and approaches to testing, and takes ownership of tasks assigned to him. Narayanan would be an asset to any companies."

— Shirley Ong, managed Narayanan

"Success is the result of perfection, hard work, learning from failure, loyalty, and persistence which I saw in him. He is like a river where all near by him will be getting good out of it. Truly, he has made an everlasting impression on us. He does not tolerate fights in our team. He is an attentive listener and an approachable personality.

In today's world everyone is out to pursue their own success but he is a true leader who cares for the team. Individual contributor, Methodical, organized and very creative. His ability to connect people and willing to carry people along with his growth, inspire the team with innovative ideas and presentation skills are amazing. He has a great meter to measure each individual capacity and where they can continue to grow.

He has made everyone to grow and expand our skills without limits. I will recommend Narayanan Palani, So called Mr. Software Testing for any company and for any creative and responsible role."

— Karthikeyan Sadaiyappan, managed Narayanan indirectly

"Narayanan is very endowed and fanatical worker. He strongly deserves the word Commitment in both Career and Studies and the Word Loyalty in Personal behaviour with Others. Wish you to get all the Success Brother!"

— Aneesh Sharmila Jaffarullah Khan, Student, Birla Institute of Technology and Science, worked directly with Narayanan at Wipro Technologies

"Narayanan Palani is a very intelligent and great team player. He makes it is point to help his collegues and team members. He is a dedicated and process oriented person."

— Shashank Welankar, Project Manager, Wipro Technologies, managed Narayanan at Wipro Technologies

"Narayan is extremely intelligent and very strong in technical and Testing skills...."

— shuchi sinha, Software Engineer, Accenture Technology Solutions, was with another company when working with Narayanan at Wipro Technologies

"Narayan Palani, has a Great vision. He has the thirst for gaining knowledge. He has done quite a lot of Certifications. And moreover he is a good human being. Hope he continues to have a Great life ahead."

— Karthik Prabhakar, Student Computer applications, Wipro Technologies, worked with Narayanan at Wipro Technologies

"Hard working creative guy with good managerial skills, who analyses the things in different angles."

— Mohammad Rafi Shaik, R&D Engineer, Ramakrishna Electro Components India Pvt. Ltd., was with another company when working with Narayanan at Wipro Technologies

"He is a very experienced guy in his field."

— Kirandas Haridasan, Software Engineer, Wipro Technologies, worked with Narayanan at Wipro Technologies

"I met Narayanan in Wipro. We worked together in a project related to Banking domain. I found that Narayanan has a great capacity to learn new technologies very fast. He owns various technical certifications and has proved his working knowledge in the project. In short, he is an all rounder."

— Rajeev Gaur, Senior Software Engineer, Wipro Technologies, worked directly with Narayanan at Wipro

"I got to meet Narayanan while Teaching at the WASE Program and have known him for over 2 years. He strikes me as one who displays great initiative, integrity, a concern for colleagues and sense of the 'common good'. Has good potential for leadership positions."

— Saijee Rao Tammineedi, Consulting Trainer, CDS India, advised Narayanan at Birla Institute of Technology and Science

"A live wire. Promising gentleman with great commitment and conviction even during his under graduation course of study. Happy to see him soaring up in his career. I am sure he will achieve far greater heights. An invaluable asset to his family, friends and company. Wish him all the best in all his future endeavours."

— Ibrahim Khaleel, Professor, The New College, Chennai, India, taught Narayanan at The New College

Table of Contents

Dedicated to,

Holy Navabrindhavana Saints[1]

****

Padmanabham Kaveendram cha Vaagheesam Vyaasarajakam,

Raghuvaryam Sreenivasam, Ramatheertham Thaithaiva Cha,

Shri Sudeendram Cha Govindam Navavrundavanam Bhaje

****

---

[1] The nine sacred saints, in their order are (the periods given in bracket are the period during which they headed the Mathwa peeta):

Sri Padmanabha Theerthar, the prime sishya of Sri Madhvacharyar (1317-1324)

a) Sri Jaya Theerthar (1365-1388)

b) Sri Raghu Variyar, Guru of Raghothama Theerthar whose Brindhavan is at Thirukkoyilur near Thiruvannamalai (1502-1537)

Sri Kaveendhra Theerthar (1392-1398)

Sri Vaageesa Theerthar (1398-1406)

Sri Vyasaraja Theerthar (1447-1539), Raja guru of Krishna Deva Raya and the next avatar of Brhalatha and the earlier avatar of Sri Raghavendhra

Sri Srinivasa Theerthar (1539-1564)

Sri Rama Theerthar (1564-1584)

Sri Suseendhra Theerthar, Ragavendhra swami's guru (1614-1623)

Sri Govindha Odeyar (1534)

About Editor

Special Thanks to Mr.Sibbi Maruthu, Automation Testing Progam Manager of Cognizant Technology Solutions for the extensive review of this book and providing guidance from the beginning of the career of author as a strong mentor!

https://www.linkedin.com/pub/sibbi-maruthu/23/419/242

About Project Manager

My sincere thanks to Rinky Gopalani for the extensive hard work and dedication in managing this complete project of 'book making' and delivering the whole content to your beautiful hands!

Introduction

Software Testing is growing rapidly into automation as an exclusive specialised industry and the need of development experience and tools knowledge is enormous to sustain in testing profession! Tool based testers are migrated to core automation testers over a period of time with different tool experiences. The agile based projects brought the need for testers with strong development background hence automation testers are migrated to 'Developer in Test' roles to categories as a test specialist who is good at coding background.

This book brings the essence of automation basics in different topics varies from Selenium Web Driver to Excel VBA Test Automation-so that the target audience can be benefited with knowledge across the automation possibilities.

How to get benefited from this book

Automation Test Frameworks are explained in the beginning of the chapters which will help in understanding the types of frameworks used across the organizations.

Set of questions provided at the end of the chapter related to Automation Framework Types-which are open questions and unanswered! The main reason is to keep this questions open and go through rest of the chapters. So the readers surely get the answer to these questions when the chapters are understood and relevant open source projects are practiced in parallel.

Note: These questions remain open when the practice is not good enough. It is suggested to practice available projects online to move to next chapters which will help in building the skill-set and get benefited maximum from the book in parallel.

Immediate chapters are talking about how to select automation tools for the projects based on the nature of each tools.

When testers are contributing to automation test projects the key factors differentiating them from others are: Test Estimation, Test Environments, Cost Estimation, Time Estimation, Test Schedule Compression Techniques, Function Point Based Test Estimation, Delphi Test Estimation Technique, Automation Return on Investment, Automation Test Scheduling.

After discussing key foundations of automation tests, main topics of automation tools discussed such as Selenium IDE, Selenium Web Driver using Java/TestNG/Ant and Selenium Web Driver using Dot Net/Cucumber. Reason being, Selenium Web Driver using Specflow and C++ is an emerging field within BDD and TDD. This has been detailed in respective sections and moved towards other famous automation tools such as HP UFT, Excel VBA Automation and IBM RFT (Rational Functional Test).

Since Cucumber is an emerging BDD tool in testing domain, this has been elaborated in an exclusive section. Along with Cucumber BDD, SOA tools such as SOAP UI also detailed to give basics on how to automate when the GUI is not available! This is irrelevant topic in this book to discuss specifically at sections of SOA, ETL domains-but the reason SOAP UI is discussed is mainly on the job market needs!

Knowing SOAP UI and ETL basics increases the possibilities to get good job profile in quick span of time. So these sections are briefly explained along with sample test strategy, test plan and test cases of functional testing.

Automation testing book explaining about functional testing is not new and it is always good to refer the foundations of functional/ manual testing by sample documentations. Importantly the basics of functional testing are provided through the sample test plan, test cases which will be helpful to build the fundamentals while practicing the automation framework.

Test Automation Framework

As a first step in test automation, it is important to learn how to build an automation framework hence this chapter explains from basic on how to build an open source framework for testing

A test automation framework act as a Software developed to test the actual Automation Framework! Set of practices, assumptions and concepts are used to design automation frameworks using testing tools which are used for automation testing. The main benefit of automation framework is to provide better reusability of test scripts. This is possible only if the automation framework is designed to help faster development of test scripts for new testing cycles, flexibility in adapting the product changes, comfort in training new comers to understand the framework and mainly the maintenance of automation framework once developed!

Test Automation Framework Maintenance:

Developing a test automation framework with open source tools such as Selenium, Test NG, Ant and Jenkins to have web browser automation testing is simply great! But this framework should support the maintenance of test data exclusively from excel sheets! So it is important to extend the framework with the help of Read_XLS.jar to read and write the excel from automation framework during test execution.

Types of Automation Test Frameworks:

Linear Scripting

Keyword Driven Testing

Structured Driven Testing

Data Driven Testing

Hybrid Automation Framework

Agile Continuous Integration Automation Framework

Famous wide used automation frameworks and test automation tools are:

Automation Framework using Selenium Web Driver, JUnit, TestNG, Ant and Jenkins

Excel Automation Framework using HP UFT

Excel VBA Automation Frameworks

Web services (REST/SOAP) Automation Frameworks

Definition

Set of assumptions, concepts, methods and workflows that constitute a work platform and best practice that provide complete support for automated Automation Framework testing and maintenance.

This includes script organization, documentation, coding standards &instructions, version control and unit test of the test scripts.

Key SFERMS Benefits – Stable, Flexible, Extensible, Reusable, Maintainable, Scalable

Following are some of the key elements in which frameworks are assessed against:

Usability

Automation Framework usability can be described as how effectively new test analysts/SME (Subject Matter Expert) can use, learn, or control the system. Some questions to ask yourself to determine usability might be:

Is there a UI metaphor (Driver Script) that I am using to help users adapt?

(for example, the 'Eclipse' is a metaphor for Selenium)

If a new test analyst takes responsibility over the test automation scripts, the amount of knowledge required on the sub systems and dependable software such as Eclipse IDE (for Selenium Web Driver using JAVA), .Net (for Selenium Web Driver using C#) or any Driver Scripts which run their Automation Engine (such as UFT, Selenium) in the backend to produce results.

> Best Practice:
>
> It is always a best practice to use an exclusive usability document to use the actions such as Web launch, User Login, Driver Script Launch; Additional to this document, Library Functions Specification document should be designed to list the reusable libraries designed as part of the project-Sibbi Maruthu, Automation Test Program Manager

Are the most common operations streamlined to be performed quickly?

Actions such as Web Launch, User Login, Driver Script Launch are taken into consideration on how quick the automation framework is. Especially Rational Function Test need test configurations to be completed first in order to run the test scripts in Test Execution. Flexible tools like Selenium IDE look forward for assertions and assessors to be incorporated manually in the test script. Based on how quick these operations are performed in the test design, the overall test strategy get affected on the test automation projects.

Can new test users quickly adapt to the Automation Framework without help? (is it intuitive?)

If Subject Matter Experts learn the automation framework, it should be user friendly and straight forward in user interactions rather than code amendments which is complex for any new test users such as fresh test talents. What would be the ideal hands-on training required for the framework and how long it takes to master in the tool are the key aspects of looking at it. While discussing on the training, it is also important to look at the test framework document on how extensive it has been documented. If the documentation is not in place, this could be one of the primary cause of automation framework failures over a period of time in agile testing projects.

Do validation and error messages make sense?

An excellent automation framework is judged based on how effective the errors are handled and the measures are taken into capture the maximum possible issues during test execution. Taking screenshots are not the only test deliverable as part of automation. The match between expected and actual results has to be proved with the help the test inputs and outputs. Thus validation check against the test results should result the need derived from Test Requirements. If the test results doesn't match to the needs of testable requirements, though the automation tool run the test scripts, it doesn't serve the purpose of test objective.

Maintainability (Flexibility / Testability)

The definition of maintainability implies how brittle the code is to change. As a result, I tie the terms flexibility and testability into the overall maintainability of a project.

Does the entire team understand the code base or does knowledge islands exist?

Is the code thoroughly regression tested?

Can modifications to the project be done in a timely manner?

> Best Practice
>
> Automation scripts, functional library, other test scripts can be externally controlled with different files which can be easy to maintain file model as any update to the functional library in future will affect only specific files and rest of the framework remain reusable!

Scalability

Scalability is the ability for your program to gracefully meet the demand of stress caused by increased usage. In short, ensuring your program doesn't slow or bust when pounded by more users than you originally anticipated.

What is your current peak load that you can handle?

How many database records can create until critical operations slow down?

Is the primary scaling strategy to "scale up" or to "scale out" — that is, to upgrade the nodes in a fixed topology, or to add nodes?

Availability (or Reliability)

How long the system is up and running and the Mean Time Between Failure (MTBF) is known as the availability of a program.

How long does the system need to run without failure?

What is the acceptable length of time for the system to be down?

Can down times be scheduled?

Extensibility

Are there points in the system where changes can be made with (or without) program changes?

Can the database schema flex to accommodate change?

Does the system allow Inversion of Control (IoC)?

Can end users extend the system (scripts, user defined fields, etc)?

Can 3rd party developers leverage your system?

Security

The measure of system's ability to resist unauthorized attempts at usage or behavior modification, while still providing service to legitimate users.

Does the system need user or role based security?

Does code access security need to occur?

What operations need to be secured?

How will users be administered?

Portability

Portability is the ability for your application to run on numerous platforms. This is can include actual application hosting, viewing, or data portability.

Can the data be migrated to other systems?

For web applications, which browsers does your web app support?

Which operating systems does your program run on?

The above questions are kept open and unanswered purposefully the readers has to keep these questions in mind when going through further chapters in test automation. So these questions will be helpful in identifying answers for your own projects at the particular test environment. The next chapter help in understanding the types of famous automation tools and their classifications.

Automation Tool Selection-Know How

Earlier chapter on automation framework has been left with some open questions to get answered by referring rest of the sections. This section explains about the comparison between two important automation tools and their differences.Especially this is a sample comparison between UFT and Selenium only as there are very important tools discussed in this book which are not included as part of comparison such as Selenium IDE, AutoIT, Cucumber, Specflow, BDD, TDD, Jenkins, NUnit, ReportUnit, XSLT Reporting, Maven, Jason Phantom Ghost Driver, TestNG, JUnit, Ant, Eclipse, Team Foundation Server, *Visual Studio, HP Unified Functional Testing (formerly Quick Test Professional), Ranorex, IBM Rational Functional Test, Excel VBA Automation, Excel Objects Automation, and SOA Testing-SOAP UI Automation.*

Important tools in test automation are always compared to find out the best among them -so the right tool is picked every time before automating the test projects. As an example, Selenium and UFT are provided here with comparison elements:

FEATURES	SELENIUM (IDE/WEB DRIVER/GRID)	UNIFIED FUNCTIONAL TESTING
License	Open source and free of cost	Licensed and very Expensive.
Framework	Integrate with Selenium, Eclipse, Maven, Ant, Jenkins, Hudson, TestNG, JUnit, SVN, XSLT Reports	Integrate with HP ALM (Application Life Cycle Management)

FEATURES	SELENIUM (IDE/WEB DRIVER/GRID)	UNIFIED FUNCTIONAL TESTING
Continuous Integration	Possible through Jenkins, Hudson, Cruise Control	Possible through HP ALM, Jenkins
Script Creation Time	High	Low
Image Based Tests	Need Extensions like SIKULI	Possible
Application support	Web applications only.	Client server applications (like built in TCL/TK and PowerBuilder)
Browser support	Supports IE, Firefox, Opera, Safari, etc.	Supports only IE and Firefox.
Operating System/ Platform	Windows PC, MAC, UNIX platforms.	Windows Platform only.
Object Oriented Language support and Scalability	Supports Java, .Net, Perl, PHP, Python, C# and Ruby.	Supports VBScript or JavaScript.
Usage	Needs a quite Expertise.	Easy to learn.
Technical support	No official technical support.	Good technical support via phone, mail, web forum.
Test Development Environment	Test scripts can be developed in various IDEs like Eclipse, Visual Studio, TFS (Team Foundation Server), Net beans, etc.	Developed only in QTP.
Support for File Upload	Not available	Supports all kinds of File upload
Database Applications	Not so convenient.	Very well with Database applications.
Report Generation	Integration with Jenkins can give good reporting.	Quality Center has built-in dashboards.

Reference: "Comparative Study of Automated Testing Tools: Selenium and Quick Test Professional." by S.Rajeevan, B.Sathiyan

Test Requirements

Earlier sections talked about framework and comparison between automation tools. The next step is to understand how the framework has to be constructed technically. But strong fundamentals on test requirements, test plans, scenarios, test cases are required in order to proceed on automation essentials. So this chapter basically explains on testing basics as a pre-requisite.

Requirements are any statement describing functionality that is expected of the system. It is always needed in order to be able to design test and it is also important to understand that it can be introduced at any level. The more details in the requirement, results in an easier test scenarios. Although a set of requirement can be provided it can never be complete or as testable as required.

An example of a requirement is that a customer should be able to place orders online or cancel online order. This would be classified as a high level requirement. In order to deal with this requirement we have go through the concept of scenarios.

The requirements always to be needed to design a test. The statement that describing any behavior or any functionality that someone expects from the system. Requirements can be come on level of details. The more requirements for us is easier to test because we know that Requirements are never be complete and never be testable.

Requirements are illustrations that describe what is expected of the system, it's always important that before you move to the next step of software testing, you need to understand what is expected of the system in the requirements document.

Please refer the Sample Test Requirement section to understand how testable requirements look and how to derive the scenarios from the requirements.

Test Plans

Master Test Plan contains set of important project details on testing activities such as Summary, Test Items, Environment, References, Comprehensive Assessment, Identification of Intermittent issues, Summary of Results, Evaluation, Limitations, Summary of Activities and Approvals

Refer the sample test plan section for detailed section specific examples.

Test Scenarios

Sometimes the requirements may not be elaborative or complete; this could simply be because, for every requirement, there may be several or multiple ***scenarios*** expected to give similar results, these attributed to conditions that may happen along the line of production.

The system needs to be tested on these multiple scenarios in order to increase the chances of having a more reliable and efficient system free from errors, which is the ultimate target of the project as well as the software testing team. This also helps in having a much more predictable system.

Test Cases

In order to make sure that the scenarios are tested from one scenario to another scenario in a systematic way, the team needs to come up with ***test cases***, were all scenarios will be tested individually. Each case will be tested according to what has been specified in the requirement document e.g the conditions associated with a particular test case such as a pre-condition and post condition which is the expected outcome.

These groups of test cases with similar requirements are bundled up in one to create a ***test set***. A test set is a group of test cases that require the same steps to be executed. And they are executed by creating ***a test script***; these can be done for both manual and automated testing.

Formula for test case: **Input + pre-condition -> Post – conditions + output**

Test cases are means in which we test the scenarios. For each scenario we have a number of test cases. Each test case consist of a set of inputs that are going to be fed to the system and pre-condition are all conditions that exist before a test case

For example:

<u>Pre-conditions:</u> all facts about the input e.g. card used, order has not been cancelled, card is still valid etc.

Input =order number

<u>Post –conditions:</u> output = confirmation message e.g. order has been cancelled. As a result of order cancellation card has been refunded with correct amount.

Refer to the sample test cases section for the detailed test cases with each columns with example test cases.

Agile Scrum Based Testing-Continuous Integration

Basic sections of this book explained about automation framework, basics on test requirements etc. But the main reason to learn automation is to implement in most challenging life cycles such as Agile based Continuous Integration. So the following section drives through the fundamentals on Scrum based Agile Testing.

Scrum is described as an iterative and incremental agile software development framework for managing product development. Scrum focuses on delivering the requirement on time as well as responding to emerging requirements promptly.

- Scrum makes everything visible and allows clients to experience each part of the development
- It also helps in keeping track of project development
- Help keep up with time to avoid extra costs that come with additional development time.
- Scrum allows you to see problems in good time in order to make necessary adjustments before it's too late.

Why do we need Scrum?

When we are planning to develop a software, we don't know what will happen in few weeks' time so it becomes difficult to keep track of the project progress. Delays in project development causes additional cost to the project as you will need additional development time. This will upset the client.

Scrum helps to keep track of the project progress and allows the team to know exactly what's going on and where adjustments are required to finish the project on time. Similarly Automation Frameworks such as BDD are built from the beginning when the backlogs are constructed in step1 below.

Step 1 – Create a Product backlog

The backlog contains all features that the client would like to have including their dream system and imagination, but that does not mean everything will be included in the project. These features converted to Cucumber based .feature files in automation frameworks (still the automation scripts are not ready- so the scripts status in step1 would be pending)

Step 2 – Estimate and prioritize

Once the product backlog is ready, product owner estimates the timescale for the amount of work required for each feature providing the total amount of work involved for the release backlog.

Product owner then prioritize the features, most important on the top of the list and less important goes on the bottom of the list. He then picks the features that will be on the release and creates a release backlog.

Step3 – Sprint

Sprint is a short duration milestone that allows team to prepare chunk of the project to get in to ship ready state. Sprint generally is ranged between 3 to 30 days depending on the product release backlog. A project usually includes several sprints.

At the beginning of the Sprint, a team will have Sprint Planning Meeting where product owner and team decides what will be done. They select the features which are on highest priority from the release backlog.

Sprint Planning Meeting has two parts

1) Team and product owner to decide which features to develop
2) The team plans out the sprint

The selected backlog features are assigned in to the sprint backlog and are assigned to different team members. Each team member in automation framework assigned to list of .feature files in BDD (refer BDD section) design their automation scripts to get ready.

Everyday team meets for short meeting which is called Daily Scrum. Each team member answers three questions during the scrum meeting.

1) What have you done on this project since the last daily scrum meeting?
2) What do you plan on doing on this project between now and the next scrum meeting?
3) What stands in your way to meet your commitments to this sprint and this project?

The purpose of the daily scrum is to discuss the progress of the sprint and address any issues that might cause delays in the project.

In the sprint, the team must complete the feature/task, that was defined for that sprint. Bugs that are related to the features on the backlog should also be fixed.

At the each completion of sprint, team arranges Sprint Review meeting. In this meeting the team presents what was developed during this sprint to the product owner and other stakeholders.

This meeting helps to decide what the team should do next. This also helps the client as client can see the progress of the project and can provide a feedback. This prevents the risk of developing features that the client didn't ask for and also in case of a delay in the development process, the sprint will not be completed on time. This means project is running behind the schedule and something needs to be done.

Therefore it is important to monitor the progress of each sprint with burn down chart. This is the best way to monitor the progress and it gives the best visibility of the project. Burn down chart gives day by day progress report and remaining work on the sprint.

Scrum is a simple and effective way to have control over your development process. It ensures that things go according to plan.

Test Estimation

Earlier chapter discussed about Sprint based Agile Testing; This chapter will help in understanding how important the estimation for automation projects. Due to incorrect estimation, large automation projects led to expensive failures in the history. So this chapter illustrates the details about how to estimate any test automation assignment.

Projections of Testing Project based on the testing process, data, extracts are basically derived from test estimation using various test estimation techniques. Time and resources required for testing and number of estimations required for business have been calculated before initiating the testing activities.

Test effort, duration, Infrastructure, resources, required expertise, tools and need for test environments are estimated and analysed as part of test estimation.

Test effort

Amount of time required to write the test scenarios, review of test scenarios, write test cases, test case review, test data preparation, test execution time, defect tracking time, backup time on each test execution cycle due to environment issues, number of test environment and systems required.

Duration

Schedule for Test Design (Scenario, Test Cases, Test Data, Test Script Preparation on Test Automation), Schedule for Smoke

Test, Schedule for Test Execution, Schedule for Test Reports and Sign-off

Resources

Number of test resources required for functional (manual, automation) and non functional tests (performance, penetration, usability tests)

Tools

Required tools for test management, test case management, test configuration management, test automation, defect reporting tool, test report tool

Test Environments

Smoke Test Needs(Environment Shakedown Tests/Environment Readiness Test), Number of test environment required, Number of systems required in each test environment and their code versions.

Cost Estimation

A cost estimate is the approximation of the cost of a testing program, project, or operation such as change request testing. It has a single total value along with set of component values as part of testing assignment.

Famous cost estimation techniques in the testing projects are classified as top down method, bottom up method, Analogues and parametric test estimation

Top-Down Test Estimation

Efforts are estimated at task level such as cost of test case preparation, test execution etc. Individual work items as part of the testing project has been taken into consideration. This estimation starts from main modules and stepping into downstream of the components and estimate the cost involved in each component.

This means, calculation of the test project duration and the cost by comparing it with the set of existing projects which were successful.

It is a fast and easy approach comparing to other estimation models and the only negative factor is that the bottleneck cases are not taken into consideration such as test environment downtime, poor quality of test design etc.

Bottom-Up Test Estimation

Each low level components of testing project are classified and taken into consideration and step 1. When the test estimation is completed for each component, the sum of whole test estimation is calculated for the entire project. Each test resource availability, entry and exit time between the test cycles are also taken into consideration. If a test specialist involved in test design of cycle 1 and test execution of cycle 3, respective amount of duration included as part of the estimation. So the resource identification, task dependencies between the resources, details on when the task has to be completed and what is the dependency with other test cycles are mapped with detailed for each test cycle.

This method is a best approach only when the resources are available from the beginning of project initiation or at least at the time of test estimation. Also test plan should be ready to refer for bottom up test estimation as the plan derives the tasks on each test cycle and test items. So it is difficult to perform bottom up test estimation in the early stages of the STLC (Software Testing Life Cycle).

Analogues Test Estimation

When the project details are not completely available and the dynamic projects such as continuous integration oriented agile projects are estimated with the help of expert judgement and existing project statistics. In analogues estimation technique, the actual duration and effort vary drastically as the initial estimation is derived with the help of judgements on key factors such as resource availability, test cycle duration etc. Often it has been proved that the estimation derived from this technique is less accurate. But it is one of the fastest technique to provide test estimations. It is not suitable for Agile based sprint cycles as the most of the sprint projects are dynamic and this has to be estimated accurately to avoid the pitfalls and failures. This is a proven successful technique for change requests and any testing for small needs.

Parametric Test Estimation

Scalable cost per unit are estimated as part of parametric test estimation based on the statistical data available from the earlier projects.

Cost per line of code for automation project, Cost per hour of automation test execution are some of the key calculations in this method. This is most relevant test estimation technique for test automation as the LOC (Line of Code) Estimation is highly recommended.

Time Estimation

Duration of test cycles, test resources availability and the time required to complete the test activities are calculated as part of test time estimation process.

CPM (Critical Path Method), CCM (Critical Chain Method), Resource Levelling, PERT (Program Evaluation and Review Techniques) and Monte Carlo Simulation are some of the famous techniques used as part of the test estimation methods for testing projects.

Critical Path Method (CPM)

The critical path calculates the longest path of activities to the end of the testing project; So the highly critical path where the earliest and shortest time in each activity can start and finish without extending the project is highly important. The visibility into the critical path allows test managers to prioritize the activities and take appropriate actions to meet the schedule.

Critical Chain Method (CCM)

The fundamental idea of CCM is CPM with the key difference in resource limitation. By adding resource limitation to the calculation, this estimation differs from Critical Path Method. If the test resource is extended in Sprint 1 of the Agile Project and not available in Sprint 2 and available only for Sprint 3, this has to be taken as a constraint while calculating the CPM. Adding duration buffers by introducing alternative test resource to testing project schedules to protect the targeted finish date from slippage is a key factor while calculating the time required for the test cycle.

Resource Levelling on CPM

Changing and amending the test schedule in order to mitigate the risks and changes over the test project is part of Resource Levelling for testing project estimates. Resolving over-allocation of the resources and conflicts over test cycles on test resources are adjusted and amended in order to meet the deadlines of the test projects.

Test Schedule Compression Techniques

As a result of test schedule analysis, test teams may identify a need to compress the test schedule. Schedule compression shortens the test project duration in order to meet schedule deadlines without reducing the project scope for testing the application.

Crashing Compression Technique

Crashing involves either adding test resources or increasing work(e.g: daily test execution) hours (overtime, weekends) to shorten task duration. Shorter test durations typically result in higher task costs, so project teams must determine, prior to crashing, whether the total costs savings is enough to justify the higher costs for the allocated testing project. Crashing almost always requires cost increases because it usually necessitates new tasks and activities such as test design, execution and reporting. Crashing is a controversial technique because adding test resources can increase project complexity or risk and may ultimately have a negative impact on the test schedule. Crashing does not involve reducing test project scope or eliminating project tasks mentioned in the test plan.

Fast Tracking Compression Technique

Fast tracking is a schedule compression technique in which test project phases or activities usually conducted sequentially are performed in parallel to reduce the overall test duration. If possible sprints run parallel in order to reduce the total duration of the agile testing project. Extra care must be taken to make sure that parallel work does not create additional work or increase risk in the testing activities such as defect reporting. Fast tracking frequently results in increased complexities in test dependencies, so additional test project controls must be implemented to ensure ongoing and accurate insight into test schedule performance.

Program Evaluation and Review Techniques (PERT)

Probabilistic time estimation is followed to calculate the estimate in order to get the realistic test estimation. The most pessimistic duration, most likely duration and most optimistic duration are taken into consideration to derive at probabilistic test estimation.

PERT: (P + 4M + O) / 6
Standard Deviation of a testing task using PERT: (P – O) / 6
Variation of a testing task using PERT: ((P – O) / 6)2

P: The most pessimistic duration
M: The most Likely duration
O: The most Optimistic duration

Monte Carlo Simulation

Set of computational algorithm used to get random sampling data to obtain numerical results of test estimation. So this technique is used mostly using software applications.

Test Estimation Flow Chart

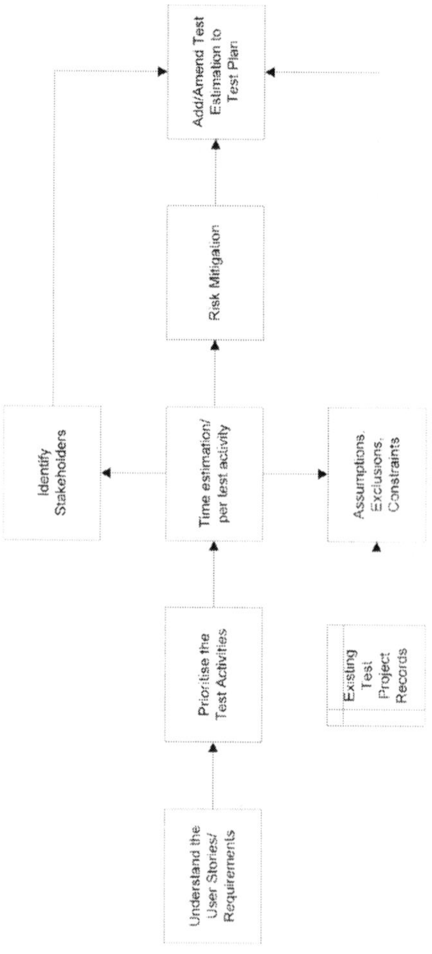

Function Point Based Test Estimation

Units of measurement in this method is known as Function Points (FP) and this is calculated for the size of the software functionality.

Following five types are taken as Function Points:
External Inputs: Automation Test Data Sheets
External Outputs: Excel Sheets and Test Outputs to extract test records
External Inquires: SQL Queries/ Set of actions requested to validate the test
Internal Logical Files: Logs, screenshot, build and other logical files of automation framework
External Logical Files: Driver Scripts (to interact with automation test engines)

Development of Automation Framework- Function Point Calculation:
Use the following formula to calculate the development project function point count.
DFP = (UFP + CFP) * VAF
Where:
DFP is the development of Automation Framework function point count
UFP is the unadjusted function point count
CFP is the function points added by the conversion unadjusted function point count
VAF is the value adjustment factor

Enhancement of Automation Framework Function Point Calculation:

Use the following formula to calculating the size for enhancement projects.

EFP = [(ADD + CHGA + CFP) * VAFA] + (DEL* VAFB)

Where:

EFP is the enhancement of Automation Framework function point count.

ADD is the unadjusted function point count of those functions that were added by the enhancement project.

CHGA is the unadjusted function point count of those functions that were modified by the enhancement of Automation Framework. This number reflects the functions after the modifications.

CFP is the function point count added by the conversion.

VAFA is the value adjustment factor of the application after the enhancement of Automation Framework.

DEL is the unadjusted function point count of those functions that were deleted by the enhancement of Automation Framework.

VAFB is the value adjustment factor of the application before the enhancement of Automation Framework.

Case Study on Automation Framework FP Analysis:

Using the following table for function point weightings:

Factors	Weights		
	Simple	Average	Complex
Number of user inputs (Number of Excel Sheets for user inputs)	3	4	6
Number of user outputs (Test extracts as Excel Files)	4	5	7
Number of user inquiries (SQL Scripts used to extract search results in Automation Framework)	3	4	6
Number of files (Application Under Test)	7	10	15
Number of external interfaces (Driver scripts used to interact with different systems and automation engine)	5	7	10

A system being developed has the following characteristics:

Number of user inputs	10 (simple)
Number of user outputs	7 (simple)
Number of user inquiries	3 (average)
Number of files	6 (average)
Number of external interfaces	1 (complex)

Solution:

Basic Count	Function Types	Weight	Total
10 simple	inputs	10 * 3	30
7 simple	Outputs	7 * 4	28
3 average	Inquiries	3 * 4	12
6 average	Logical files	6 * 10	60
1 complex	Interface	1 * 10	10
		Unadjusted Total	**140**

Constructive Cost Model (COCOMO)
Effort and schedule are estimated by analysing line of code in this COCOMO model.

Case Study on a Sample Test Automation Framework:

COCOMO models include 3 automation framework development types:
Organic: relatively small automation teams develop familiar types of framework in an in-house environment. Most personnel have previous experience on similar automation tools (Effort: $PM=2.4\ (KDSI)^{1.05}$; Schedule: $TD=2.5\ (PM)^{0.38}$))
Embedded: the automation project may require new tool and technology, unfamiliar algorithms, or an innovative new method for solving the problem of test automation (Effort:$PM=3.0\ (KDSI)^{1.12}$ Schedule: $TD=2.5\ (PM)^{0.35}$)
Semi-detached: having a mixture between organic and embedded types (Effort: $PM=3.6\ (KDSI)^{1.20}$ Schedule: $TD=2.5\ (PM)^{0.32}$)

Where,
PM = person-month (man-month)
KDSI = delivered source instructions, in thousands
TD = number of months estimated for framework development

COCOMO Calculation

Assuming an organic type project with an estimated size = 132, 000 lines of code.

Effort: PM = $2.4(128)^{1.05}$ = 392 person-months

Productivity: 132, 000 DSI / 392 PM = 336 DSI/PM
Schedule: TD = TD=2.5 $(PM)^{0.38}$ = 24 months
Avg. Staffing: 392 PM / 24 months = 16 FSP

Where,

FSP = full-time-equivalent staff person

Collective Test Estimation Technique

Automation Leads discuss with stakeholders of the project and get the single outcome as test estimation. Project Managers, Business Analysts, Developers are usually involved in this discussion to contribute inputs on the test estimation.

Sample Test Estimation on Automation Framework Development:

Number	Action Items	Estimated Hours
	Environment Readiness	
1	Test Environment Setup to perform Automation Test	3
2	Automation Test Engine Installation	2
3	Network Connectivity Check	1
	Data Gathering Stage	
4	Object Data Collection	20
5	Understanding the Functionality	30
6	Automation Test Scenario/Test Case Review	2
	Tools Analysis Stage	
7	Object Recognition	3
8	Tool Usability Comparison	5
9	Features Testability	5

Number	Action Items	Estimated Hours
10	Tool Support-Framework Compatibility Analysis	5
	Sample Framework Design Stage	
11	Library Architecture Design	20
12	Data Mapping Design	20
13	Driver Script Design	20
14	Utility Script Design	20
	Total Automation Framework Development Hours	**156**

Delphi Test Estimation Technique

Test Manager acts as moderator and collect the estimations from experts confidentially.

Once the estimations are taken from each stakeholder of test automation, he or she takes average of the estimates and update to the test plan as automation test estimate.

Sample Delphi Test Estimation on Automation Framework Development:

Number	Action Items	(Average) Estimated Hours
	Environment Readiness-From Environment Managers	
1	Test Environment Setup to perform Automation Test	3
2	Automation Test Engine Installation	2
3	Network Connectivity Check	1
	Data Gathering Stage-From Data Architect/Test Leads	
4	Object Data Collection	20
5	Understanding the Functionality	30
6	Automation Test Scenario/Test Case Review	2
	Tools Analysis Stage-From Automation Lead	
7	Object Recognition	3
8	Tool Usability Comparison	5

Number	Action Items	(Average) Estimated Hours
9	Features Testability	5
10	Tool Support-Framework Compatibility Analysis	5
	Sample Framework Design Stage-From Automation Lead/Automation Test Analysts	
11	Library Architecture Design	20
12	Data Mapping Design	20
13	Driver Script Design	20
14	Utility Script Design	20
	Total Automation Framework Development Hours	**156**

Automation Return on Investment

Initial Cost to Automate (ICA)

Cost of licenses required for automation tools and cost for developing automation scripts are known as ICA

E.g: £1000 per test cycle

Number of Test Cycles (NTC)

Total number of test cycles planned for test automation

E.g: Six Sprint Cycles are planned as part of the Agile Project (NTC: 6)

Manual Test Cost Per Test Cycle (MTCPTC)

Average hourly rates of manual test analysts*total number of hours is calculated as MTCPTC
Along with the hourly rates, additional costs like virtual server/ hardware costs and opportunity costs are included as part of MTCPTC
E.g: £25*350=£8750 for first test cycle
Automation Test Cost Per Test Cycle (ATCPTC)
Average hourly rates of automation test analysts*total number of hours is calculated as ATCPTC

Along with the hourly rates, additional costs like automation test machine/hardware costs and opportunity costs are included as part of ATCPTC
E.g: £27.8*350=£9750 for first test cycle

Maintenance Time of the Automation Framework for the next Test Cycle (MTAF)
Approximately 5% to 25% are the average maintenance time for any well developed automation frameworks for long running test projects. This has to be calculated as part of MTAF
E.g: 10% (which is 35 hours) for the first test cycle

Multiply the difference between MTCPTC and ATCPTC &Sum it over the number of test cycles (yield)
This calculation provide the execution cost difference for test cycles

ROI=(Total benefit derived from test automation/Total Cost of Test Automation)
ROI={NTC [(MTCPTC-ATCPTC)+MTAF]-ICA}/ICA

Calculations:
Note: Assuming that the efforts required for manual testing and automation testing are getting reduced from Sprint 3 onwards.

Test Cycle	Return on Investment
Sprint 1	(1*((8750-9750)+35)-1000)/1000
Sprint 2	(2*((8750-9750)+30)-1000)/1000
Sprint 3	(3*((2750-3750)+35)-1000)/1000
Sprint 4	(4*((1750-750)+35)-1000)/1000
Sprint 5	(5*((1750-750)+35)-1000)/1000
Sprint 6	(6*((1750-750)+35)-1000)/1000

Final Positive ROI in Sprint 4:

Test Cycle	Return on Investment
Sprint 1	-1.965
Sprint 2	-2.94
Sprint 3	-3.895
Sprint 4	3.14
Sprint 5	4.175
Sprint 6	5.21

As per the ROI calculation, the return gets added to the project only when the automation is implemented successfully for the first three sprints and moved on to fourth sprint.

Automation Test Scheduling

This section explains on how to schedule the automation and functional activities for the test project. This will help in scheduling the projects later in tools such as Hudson or Jenkins.

When the automation test pack is getting designed, the most important decision is to plan on Test Scheduling of those Automated Test Scripts. The objective of test automation is to reduce the amount of time spent in Regression Testing. Following are some of the strategies which can be implemented into automation projects:

Activity List

Set of Test Scripts can be listed as part of activity list and executed based on the satisfied criteria like most of the test scripts should be scheduled based on the pre-conditions and post conditions. So the continuation of the script execution can be maintained till the end.

Example1:

In the below list, Test 9A and 9B are parallel tests. So they get completed in 3 hrs time where as all other tests can start executed only when the previous tests are completed (not necessary that the pre-condition tests have to be passed)

Pre-Condition	Activity List	Duration
Environment Set-up	Sanity Test	1 Hr
Sanity Test	Regression Tests 1	2Hrs
Regression Tests 1	Regression Tests 2	2Hrs
Regression Tests 2	Regression Tests 3	2Hrs
Regression Tests 3	Regression Tests 4	2Hrs
Regression Tests 4	Regression Tests 5	2Hrs
Regression Tests 5	Regression Tests 6	2Hrs
Regression Tests 6	Regression Tests 7	2Hrs
Regression Tests 7	Regression Tests 8	2Hrs
Regression Tests 8	Regression Tests 9A	3 Hrs
Regression Tests 8	Regression Tests 9B	
Regression Tests 9A & 9B	Regression Tests 10	1 Hr

Example 2:

In the below example, tests are listed based with the priorities where Critical is the top priority followed by High, Medium and the bottom priority is Low. When the project required only important tests to be executed, 2 Critical and 4 High priority tests can be executed in order to complete the test execution.

Pre-Condition	Activity List	Priority
Environment Set-up	Sanity Test	Critical
Sanity Test	Regression Tests 1	High
Regression Tests 1	Regression Tests 2	Medium
Regression Tests 2	Regression Tests 3	Medium
Regression Tests 3	Regression Tests 4	High
Regression Tests 4	Regression Tests 5	Medium
Regression Tests 5	Regression Tests 6	Low
Regression Tests 6	Regression Tests 7	High
Regression Tests 7	Regression Tests 8	Medium
Regression Tests 8	Regression Tests 9A	High
Regression Tests 8	Regression Tests 9B	
Regression Tests 9A & 9B	Regression Tests 10	Critical

Bar Chart

The best representation of automation test execution scheduling is possible through Bar Charts when multiple Automation Testers are involved in the test project.

Example1

Below table shows the number of days of the tests completed and remaining number of days to test the application in a sample project.

Task	**Start Date**	**Completed Days**	**Remaining Days**	**Lead Contact**
Sanity Tests	11/19/07	10	0	Rajavarman
Regression Tests 1	11/19/07	20	0	Jagan
Regression Tests 2	11/19/07	30	0	Karthick
Regression Tests 3	12/01/07	25	35	Siva
Regression Tests 4	01/15/08	0	15	Robin H.
Regression Tests 5	02/01/08	0	160	Jessica S.
Regression Tests 6	04/15/08	0	140	Pete P.
Regression Tests 7	08/30/08	0	20	Robin H.
Regression Tests 8	09/15/08	0	10	Jessica S.
Regression Tests 9	10/20/08	0	10	Jessica S.
Regression Tests 10	10/25/08	0	50	Rick S.
Regression Tests 11	12/05/08	0	10	Tom W.

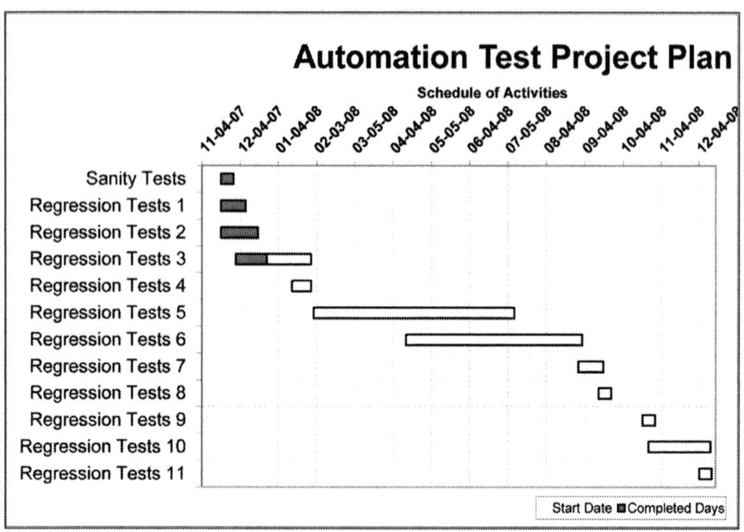

Network Diagram

List of Tasks of Automation Tests can be converted to network of activities which connects one to another to represent the complete automation tests in graphical representation

Example 1:

Assume the below table is the list of activities involved in the automation test project. Each activity has to be updated with the effort estimation, start date, end date and the resource allocated to the activity.

	Project Title	**Effort Estimate in XX**	**Planned Start Date**	**Planned End Date**	**Resource**
1	**Activity**				
1.1	**Task:Sanity Test**				
1.1.1	Sub Task: Environment Check				
1.1.2	Sub Task: Web Page Validation				

	Project Title	Effort Estimate in XX	Planned Start Date	Planned End Date	Resource
1.1.3	Sub Task: Operating System Compatibility Test			-	
2	**Activity**				
2.1	**Task**				
2.1.1	Sub Task:Regression Tests 1				
2.1.2	Sub Task:Regression Tests 2				
2.1.3	Sub Task:Regression Tests 3				
2.1.4	Sub Task:Regression Tests 4				
2.2	**Task**				
2.2.1	Sub Task:Regression Tests 5A				
2.2.2	Sub Task:Regression Tests 5B				
3	**Activity**				
3.1	**Task**				
3.1.1	Sub Task:Regression Tests 6				
3.1.2	Sub Task:Regression Tests 7				
3.1.3	Sub Task:Regression Tests 8				

Below Network Diagram represents the whole automation tests in single picture:

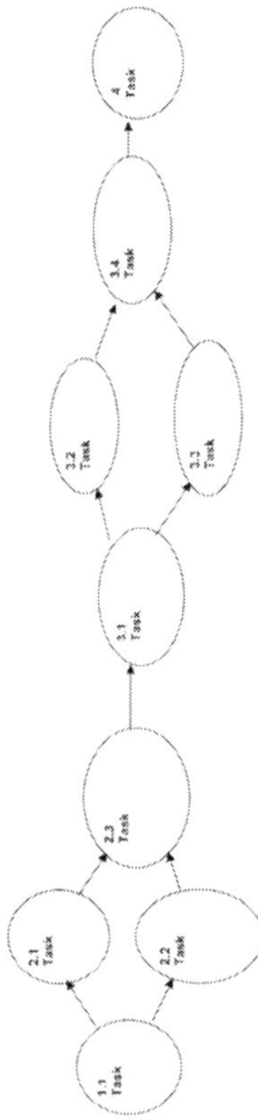

Once the network of automation tests designed, they can be listed further to calculate the time estimated for each tests in the table below.

		Unit of Time	**Unit of Time**	**Unit of Time**	**Unit of Time**	**Unit of Time**	**Unit of Time**	**Unit of Time**	**Unit of Time**
1	**Activity**								
1.1	Task:								
2	**Activity**								
2.1	Task								
2.2	Task								
2.3	Task								
3	**Activity**								
3.1	Task								
3.2	Task				horizontal bar				
3.3	Task								
3.4	Task								
4	**Activity**								

Selenium

Previous chapters give basics on how the automation projects work and what are the test estimation techniques and schedule techniques need to be implemented in various testing projects. This particular chapter starts directly with automation tools involved in the test automation projects.

Industry wide best practice in test automation is to look for the possibility of Selenium Implementation in web based testing projects. Selenium has been evolved over a period of time from 2004 and it is available in four different types at the moment in 2015: Selenium IDE, Selenium Core, Selenium RC and Selenium Grid. Selenium IDE (Integrated Development Environment) is available as an Add-in for Firefox. Selenium Grid is used for NFT (Non Functional Tests) like Performance Tests and Concurrent Tests. Selenium Web Driver is wide used across the platforms as a open source test automation tool and organizations build automation framework on top of selenium to make use of the tool for testing projects.

Selenium IDE

Firefox extension which allows record/play testing paradigm:

Selenium IDE act as a recording tool to capture the objects properties of the application under test and replay it back whenever required. The most important feature of automation is to build a framework around testing automation tool. This can be possible with selenium web driver as IDE work only for Firefox. So if the need is to test across browsers then test analyst has to choose right test automation tool.

Automates commands, but asserts must be entered by hand:

Selenium IDE has three types of commands called 'Actions', 'Assessors' and 'Assertions'. But these three types can only be entered manually into IDE and record option doesn't automatically add them into the script. So test analyst should be aware of various types of commands used under these three types

Creates the simplest possible Locator:

When recording the object properties, Selenium IDE picks any simplest object property as reference. This leads to failure of the script for the later cycles as the properties may change time to time. It is always advisable to change the property to any unique properties such as ID or xpath in such a way that the property which will not change across the test cycles.

Based on Selenese:

Selenium IDE commands are written in JAVASCRIPT and HTML. So these scripts are commonly known as Selenese.

How to Install Selenium IDE?

Install Firefox and click on Tools button and Add-ons button:

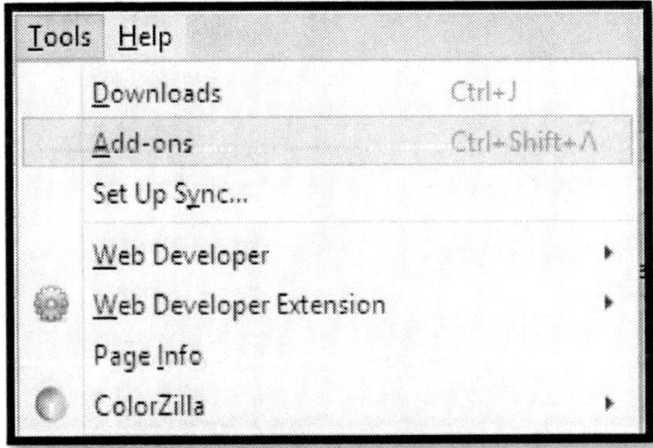

In the search box, search for Selenium IDE and download. Alternatively navigate to http://www.seleniumhq.org/download/ and download from the below link:

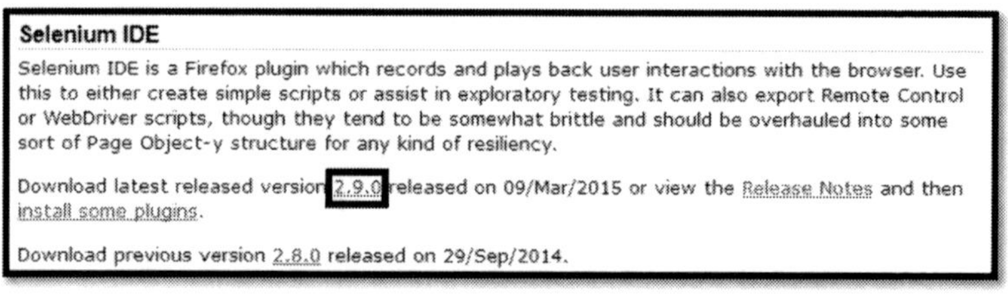

Selenium IDE

Selenium IDE is a Firefox plugin which records and plays back user interactions with the browser. Use this to either create simple scripts or assist in exploratory testing. It can also export Remote Control or WebDriver scripts, though they tend to be somewhat brittle and should be overhauled into some sort of Page Object-y structure for any kind of resiliency.

Download latest released version 2.9.0 released on 09/Mar/2015 or view the Release Notes and then install some plugins.

Download previous version 2.8.0 released on 29/Sep/2014.

Basic knowledge of Selenium IDE-Know How

Step1: Test Case Pane

Step2: Toolbar

Step3: Menu Bar

Step4: Log/Reference/UI-Element/Rollup Pane

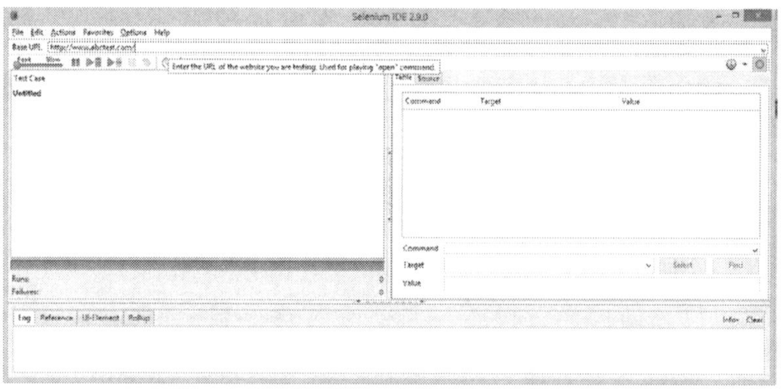

Test Case Pane:

The selenese script is displayed in the test case pane.

It has two tabs:

one for displaying the command in selenese (source) and their parameters in a readable "table" format-so it is easy to insert assessors and assertions as part of the script.

Toolbar: The toolbar of Selenium IDE contains buttons for controlling the test execution of your test cases, including step feature

Menu Bar:

File Menu: The File menu allows you to create, open and save test case and test suite files.

Edit Menu: The Edit menu allows copy, paste, delete, undo and select all operations for editing the commands in your test case.

Options Menu: The Options menu allows the changing of settings. You can set the timeout value for certain commands, add user-defined user extensions to the base set of Selenium commands, and specify the format (language) used when saving your test cases.

Help Menu:

Recording and Run settings

When Selenium-IDE is first opened, the record button is ON by default.

During recording, Selenium-IDE will automatically insert commands into your test case based on your actions.

Remember Base URL MODE - Using Base URL to Run Test Cases in Different Domains

Record Absolute recording mode – Run Test Cases in Particular Domain.

Running Test Cases

Run a Test Case Click the Run button to run the currently displayed test case.

Run a Test Suite Click the Run All button to run all the test cases in the currently loaded test suite.

Stop and Start The Pause button can be used to stop the test case while it is running. The icon of this button then changes to indicate the Resume button. To continue click Resume.

Stop in the Middle You can set a breakpoint in the test case to cause it to stop on a particular command. This is useful for debugging your test case. To set a breakpoint, select a command, right-click, and from the context menu select Toggle Breakpoint.

Start from the Middle You can tell the IDE to begin running from a specific command in the middle of the test case. This also is used for debugging. To set a startpoint, select a command, right-click, and from the context menu select Set/Clear Start Point.

Run Any Single Command Double-click any single command to run it by itself. This is useful when writing a single command. It lets you immediately test a command you are constructing, when you are not sure if it is correct. You can double-click it to see if it runs correctly. This is also available from the context menu.

Sample Script to use Wait, Assert and Assertion commands:

TC#1		
open	http://www.abctest.com	
click	id=abc-search	
type	id=abc-search	Tool efficient
click	//form[@id='abc-search-form']/div/span/i	
pause	3000	
assertTitle	abctest.com | imagination at work	
assertTextPresent	ABCTEST is translating the Industrial element	
verifyText	css=h2	Learn about ABCTEST's industry solutions that are powering the Industry

Sample Script to use Screenshot command:

Screenshottestcase		
open	/	
click	id=search	
type	id=search	SAP
clickAndWait	css=button.btn.btn-search	
captureEntirePageScreenshot	E:\Selenium IDE\ googlesearch.jpeg	

Selenium IDE Commands

allowNativeXpath(allow)
Arguments:
allow - boolean, true means we'll prefer to use native XPath
Syntax:
command: allowNativeXpath
Target: True
assertAlert – To Verify the Java Script Pop-Ups, similarly assertConfirmation.
answerOnNextPrompt(answer)
Arguments:

answer - the answer to give in response to the prompt pop-up
Instructs Selenium to return the specified answer string in response to the next JavaScript prompt [window.prompt()].

assertAlertPresent()
Generated from isAlertPresent()
Returns:
true if there is an alert
Has an alert occurred?

This function never throws an exception
assertAllButtons(pattern)
Generated from getAllButtons()
Returns:

the IDs of all buttons on the page
Returns the IDs of all buttons on the page.

assertAllFields(pattern)
Generated from getAllFields()
Returns:
the IDs of all field on the page
Returns the IDs of all input fields on the page.

assertAllLinks(pattern)
Generated from getAllLinks()
Returns:
the IDs of all links on the page
Returns the IDs of all links on the page.

Similarly some other commands:

assertAllWindowIds, assertAllWindowNames, assertAllWindowTitles, assertAttribute, assertAttributeFromAllWindows.

assertNotAllButtons, assertNotAllFields, assertNotAllWindowIds, assertNotAllWindowNames, assertNotAllWindowTitles, assertNotAttribute, assertNotAttributeFromAllWindows.

assertElementPresent(locator)
Generated from isElementPresent(locator)
Arguments:

locator - an element locator
Returns:
true if the element is present, false otherwise
Verifies that the specified element is somewhere on the page.

Similarly some other commands: assertElementNotPresent
assertEval(script, pattern)
Generated from getEval(script)
Arguments:

script - the JavaScript snippet to run
Returns:
the results of evaluating the snippet
Gets the result of evaluating the specified JavaScript snippet. The snippet may have multiple lines, but only the result of the last line will be returned.

Similarly: assertExpression,
assertHtmlSource(pattern)
Generated from getHtmlSource()
Returns:
the entire HTML source
Returns the entire HTML source between the opening and closing "html" tags.
assertLocation(pattern)
Generated from getLocation()
Returns:
the absolute URL of the current page
Gets the absolute URL of the current page.
assertNotXpathCount(xpath, pattern)
Generated from getXpathCount(xpath)
Arguments:

xpath - the xpath expression to evaluate. do NOT wrap this expression in a 'count()' function; we will do that for you.
Returns:
the number of nodes that match the specified xpath
Returns the number of nodes that match the specified xpath, eg. "// table" would give the number of tables.
Similarly: assertXpathcount

assertText(locator, pattern)
Generated from getText(locator)
Returns:
the text of the element

Gets the text of an element. This works for any element that contains text. This command uses either the textContent (Mozilla-like browsers) or the innerText (IE-like browsers) of the element, which is the rendered text shown to the user.

Similarly: assertTitle, assertTable, assertSpeed, assertPromt, assertVisible, aasertValue
assignId(locator, identifier)
Arguments:

locator - an element locator pointing to an element

identifier - a string to be used as the ID of the specified element
Temporarily sets the "id" attribute of the specified element, so you can locate it in the future using its ID rather than a slow/complicated XPath. This ID will disappear once the page is reloaded.

Similarly: assignIdAndWait
captureEntirePageScreenshot(filename, kwargs)
Arguments:

filename - the path to the file to persist the screenshot as. No filename extension will be appended by default. Directories will not be created if they do not exist, and an exception will be thrown, possibly by native code.

kwargs - a kwargs string that modifies the way the screenshot is captured. Example: "background=#CCFFDD". Currently valid options:
background
the background CSS for the HTML document. This may be useful to set for capturing screenshots of less-than-ideal layouts, for example where absolute positioning causes the calculation of the canvas dimension to fail and a black background is exposed (possibly obscuring black text).
Saves the entire contents of the current window canvas to a PNG file. Contrast this with the captureScreenshot command, which

captures the contents of the OS viewport (i.e. whatever is currently being displayed on the monitor), and is implemented in the RC only. Currently this only works in Firefox when running in chrome mode, and in IE non-HTA using the EXPERIMENTAL "Snapsie" utility. The Firefox implementation is mostly borrowed from the Screengrab! Firefox extension. Please see http://www.screengrab.org and http://snapsie.sourceforge.net/ for details.

Similarly: captureEntirePageScreenshotAndWait
check(locator)
Arguments:

locator - an element locator
Check a toggle-button (checkbox/radio)

Similarly: checkAndWait
chooseCancelOnNextConfirmation(),
chooseOkOnNextConfirmation(),
chooseOkOnNextConfirmationAndWait

Click, ClickAndWait, ClickAt, ClickAtAndWait, Close.

contextMenu, contextMenuAndWait, contextMenuAt, contextMenuAtAndWait.

createCookie, createCookieAndWait

deleteAllVisibleCookies()
Calls deleteCookie with recurse=true on all cookies visible to the current page. As noted on the documentation for deleteCookie, recurse=true can be much slower than simply deleting the cookies using a known domain/path.

Similarly: deleteAllVisibleCookiesAndWait, deleteCookie, deleteCookieAndWait,

doubleClick(locator)
Arguments:

locator - an element locator
Double clicks on a link, button, checkbox or radio button. If the double click action causes a new page to load (like a link usually does), call waitForPageToLoad.
Similarly: doubleClickAndWait, doubleClickAt, doubleClickAtAndWait.

echo(message)
Arguments:

message - the message to print
Prints the specified message into the third table cell in your Selenese tables. Useful for debugging.

fireEvent(locator, eventName)
Arguments:

locator - an element locator

eventName - the event name, e.g. "focus" or "blur"
Explicitly simulate an event, to trigger the corresponding "on*event*" handler.
Similarly: fireEventAndWait

focus(locator)
Arguments:

locator - an element locator
Move the focus to the specified element; for example, if the element is an input field, move the cursor to that field.
Similarly: focusAndWait

goBack()
Simulates the user clicking the "back" button on their browser.
Similarly: goBackAndWait

ignoreAttributesWithoutValue(ignore)
Arguments:

ignore - boolean, true means we'll ignore attributes without value at the expense of xpath "correctness"; false means we'll sacrifice speed for correctness.
Similarly: ignoreAttributesWithoutValueAndWait

open(url)
Arguments:

url - the URL to open; may be relative or absolute
Similarly: openWindow, openWindowAndWait

pause(waitTime)
Arguments:

waitTime - the amount of time to sleep (in milliseconds)
Wait for the specified amount of time (in milliseconds)
refresh()
Simulates the user clicking the "Refresh" button on their browser.
Similarly: refreshAndWait

removeAllSelections(locator)
Arguments:

locator - an element locator identifying a multi-select box
Unselects all of the selected options in a multi-select element.
Similarly: removeAllSelectionsAndWait, removeSelection, removeSelectionAndWait

removeScript(scriptTagId)
Arguments:

scriptTagId - the id of the script element to remove.
Removes a script tag from the Selenium document identified by the given id. Does nothing if the referenced tag doesn't exist.
Similarly: removeScriptAndWait
runScript(script)
Arguments:

script - the JavaScript snippet to run
Similarly: runScriptAndWait

select(selectLocator, optionLocator)
Arguments:

selectLocator - an element locator identifying a drop-down menu

optionLocator - an option locator (a label by default)
Select an option from a drop-down using an option locator.
Similarly: selectAndWait, selectFrame, selectPopUp, selectPopUpAndWait, selectWindow,

setTimeout(timeout)
Arguments:

timeout - a timeout in milliseconds, after which the action will return with an error
Specifies the amount of time that Selenium will wait for actions to complete.

Actions that require waiting include "open" and the "waitFor*" actions.
store(expression, variableName)
Arguments:

expression - the value to store

variableName - the name of a variable in which the result is to be stored.
This command is a synonym for storeExpression.

storeEval(script, variableName)
Generated from getEval(script)
Arguments:

script - the JavaScript snippet to run
Returns:
the results of evaluating the snippet

similarly: storeExpression etc......
storeXpathCount(xpath, variableName)
Generated from getXpathCount(xpath)
Arguments:

xpath - the xpath expression to evaluate. do NOT wrap this expression in a 'count()' function; we will do that for you.
Returns:
the number of nodes that match the specified xpath
Returns the number of nodes that match the specified xpath, eg. "//table" would give the number of tables.
submit(formLocator)
Arguments:

formLocator - an element locator for the form you want to submit
Submit the specified form. This is particularly useful for forms without submit buttons, e.g. single-input "Search" forms.

Similarly: submitAndWait
type(locator, value)
Arguments:

locator - an element locator

value - the value to type
Sets the value of an input field, as though you typed it in.

Similarly: typeAndWait
uncheck(locator)
Arguments:

locator - an element locator
Uncheck a toggle-button (checkbox/radio)

Similarly: uncheckAndWait
verifyAlert(pattern)
Generated from getAlert()
Returns:

The message of the most recent JavaScript alert

Similarly: verifyAlertNotPresent, verifyAlertPresent, verifyAllButtons, verifyAllFields, verifyAllLinks, verifyAllWindowNames, verifyAllWindowTitles etc....
verifyConfirmation(pattern)
Generated from getConfirmation()
Returns:
the message of the most recent JavaScript confirmation dialog
Retrieves the message of a JavaScript confirmation dialog generated during the previous action.

Similarly: verifyConfirmationNotPresent, verifyConfirmationPresent
verifyText(locator, pattern)
Generated from getText(locator)
Arguments:

locator - an element locator
Returns:
the text of the element

Similarly: verifyTitle, verifyTable etc....
waitForAlert(pattern)
Generated from getAlert()
Returns:
The message of the most recent JavaScript alert
Retrieves the message of a JavaScript alert generated during the previous action, or fail if there were no alerts.

Similarly: waitForAllButtons, waitForAllFields, waitForAllLinks, waitForAllWindowIds, waitForAllWindowNames, waitForAllWindowTitles,
waitForConfirmationPresent()
Generated from isConfirmationPresent()
Returns:
true if there is a pending confirmation

Has confirm() been called?

Similarly: waitForCondition
waitForTitle(pattern)
Generated from getTitle()
Returns:
the title of the current page
Gets the title of the current page.

Sample Selenium IDE Automation Scripts on Selenium Web Page

Download the projects at https://github.com/narayananpalani/testautomation and refer the samples here

Test Case using verifyTextPresent, assertTextNotPresent:

01_Selenium_tabs		
open	/projects/	
clickAndWait	link=Selenium Projects	
verifyText	link=Selenium WebDriver	Selenium WebDriver
assertText	link=Selenium IDE	Selenium IDE
clickAndWait	link=Download	
verifyTextPresent		Selenium Standalone Server
assertTitle	Downloads	
clickAndWait	link=Documentation	
verifyText	css=div.ads > h3	Donate to Selenium
assertTextNotPresent	mnfbmdfgmjfg	hndshsdfhdsfmjds
clickAndWait	link=Support	
verifyTitle	Getting Help	Getting Help
assertText	css=h2	User Group
clickAndWait	link=Support	
clickAndWait	link=Support	
clickAndWait	link=About	
verifyTitle	About Selenium	About Selenium

01_Selenium_tabs		
assertTitle	About Selenium	About Selenium

Test Case using assertText:

selenium_projects1		
open	/projects/	
clickAndWait	link=Selenium Projects	
verifyTextPresent		Selenium Projects
assertText	css=strong	Selenium is a suite of tools
clickAndWait	link=Selenium WebDriver	
verifyTitle	Selenium WebDriver	Selenium WebDriver
assertTitle	Selenium WebDriver	Selenium WebDriver

Test Case assertAlertNotPresent, verifyTextNotPresent, assertTitle

selenium_projects2		
open	/projects/webdriver/	
verifyTextPresent		Selenium is a suite of tools to automate web browsers across many platforms.
assertTextPresent		Donate to Selenium
clickAndWait	link=Selenium Projects	
verifyTextNotPresent	dmbmjbmSn	Djfgjhfkhfnks
assertAlertNotPresent	kdfkjdsb	Jhdfjhdb
clickAndWait	link=Selenium Grid	
verifyText	css=#mainContent > p	With the release of Selenium 2.0, the Selenium Server now has built-in Grid functionality. To see the how to configure this, please see the wiki.
assertTitle	Selenium Grid	Selenium Grid

Test Case using verifyTable, assertTable

selenium_projects3		
open	/projects/grid/	
clickAndWait	link=Selenium Projects	
clickAndWait	link=Selenium IDE	
verifyTable	css=table.0.0	Selenium IDE is an integrated development environment for Selenium scripts. It is implemented as a Firefox extension, and allows you to record, edit, and debug tests.
assertTable	css=table.0.0	Selenium IDE is an integrated development environment for Selenium scripts.

Test Case using verifyElementPresent

selenium_projects4		
open	/projects/	
clickAndWait	link=Selenium Projects	
clickAndWait	link=Selenium Remote Control	
verifyElementPresent	//img[@alt='rc arch diagram']	Internet Explorer
verifyElementPresent	//img[@alt='rc arch diagram']	Firefox
verifyElementPresent	//img[@alt='rc arch diagram']	safari

Test Case using verifyElementPresent,verifyText,assertElementPresent, assertText, verifyElementPresent, verifyTable:

selenium_projects5		
open	/projects/	
clickAndWait	link=Selenium Projects	
clickAndWait	link=Download	
verifyElementPresent	//div[@id='mainContent']/p	
verifyText	link=Latest Releases	Latest Releases
assertElementPresent	//div[@id='mainContent']/div[14]/div[2]/table/tbody/tr/td/a[3]	
assertText	//div[@id='mainContent']/table/tbody/tr[4]/td[4]/a	Download
verifyElementPresent	//div[@id='side']/div/div/a/img	
verifyTable	//div[@id='mainContent']/table[2].4.1	

Test Case using assertText, verifyText, assertValue, verifyValue:

selenium_projects6		
open	/projects/	
clickAndWait	link=Selenium Projects	
clickAndWait	link=Download	
clickAndWait	link=Documentation	
verifyText	css=a.reference.internal	Note to the Reader - Docs Being Revised for Selenium 2.0!
verifyElementPresent	link=Introduction	
verifyText	link=Test Automation for Web Applications	Test Automation for Web Applications
verifyText	link=exact:To Automate or Not to Automate?	exact:To Automate or Not to Automate?
assertText	link=Introducing Selenium	Introducing Selenium
verifyElementPresent	link=Brief History of The Selenium Project	
assertElementPresent	link=Selenium's Tool Suite	
verifyText	link=Choosing Your Selenium Tool	Choosing Your Selenium Tool

selenium_projects6		
assertText	link=Supported Browsers and Platforms	Supported Browsers and Platforms
verifyText	link=Flexibility and Extensibility	Flexibility and Extensibility
assertElementPresent	link=exact:What's in this Book?	
verifyText	link=The Documentation Team–Authors Past and Present	The Documentation Team–Authors Past and Present
assertElementPresent	link=Selenium-IDE	
verifyText	xpath=(//a[contains(text(),'Introduction')])[2]	Introduction
verifyTitle	Selenium Documentation — Selenium Documentation	
assertElementPresent	link=Installing the IDE	
verifyElementPresent	link=Installing the IDE	
assertElementPresent	link=Opening the IDE	
verifyText	link=IDE Features	IDE Features
verifyElementPresent	link=Building Test Cases	
assertText	link=Using Base URL to Run Test Cases in Different Domains	Using Base URL to Run Test Cases in Different Domains
verifyText	link=Using Base URL to Run Test Cases in Different Domains	Using Base URL to Run Test Cases in Different Domains
assertElementPresent	link=Selenium Commands – "Selenese"	
assertElementPresent	link=Script Syntax	
verifyText	link=Test Suites	Test Suites
assertText	link=Commonly Used Selenium Commands	Commonly Used Selenium Commands
verifyText	link=Verifying Page Elements	Verifying Page Elements
assertText	link=exact:Assertion or Verification?	exact:Assertion or Verification?
verifyElementPresent	link=Locating Elements	
verifyText	link=Matching Text Patterns	Matching Text Patterns
assertElementPresent	link=The "AndWait" Commands	

selenium_projects6		
verifyElementPresent	link=The waitFor Commands in AJAX applications	
verifyText	link=Sequence of Evaluation and Flow Control	Sequence of Evaluation and Flow Control
assertElementPresent	link=Store Commands and Selenium Variables	
verifyText	link=Store Commands and Selenium Variables	Store Commands and Selenium Variables
assertText	link=JavaScript and Selenese Parameters	JavaScript and Selenese Parameters
verifyText	link=echo - The Selenese Print Command	echo - The Selenese Print Command
assertText	link=Alerts, Popups, and Multiple Windows	Alerts, Popups, and Multiple Windows
verifyText	link=Debugging	Debugging
assertText	link=Writing a Test Suite	Writing a Test Suite
verifyText	link=User Extensions	User Extensions
assertText	link=Format	Format
verifyText	link=Executing Selenium-IDE Tests on Different Browsers	Executing Selenium-IDE Tests on Different Browsers
assertText	link=Troubleshooting	Troubleshooting
verifyTitle	Selenium Documentation — Selenium Documentation	
verifyElementPresent	link=Introducing WebDriver	
assertText	link=exact:How Does WebDriver 'Drive' the Browser Compared to Selenium-RC?	exact:How Does WebDriver 'Drive' the Browser Compared to Selenium-RC?
verifyText	link=WebDriver and the Selenium-Server	WebDriver and the Selenium-Server
assertElementPresent	link=Setting Up a Selenium-WebDriver Project	
verifyText	link=Migrating from Selenium 1.0	Migrating from Selenium 1.0

selenium_projects6		
assertElementPresent	link=Introducing the Selenium-WebDriver API by Example	
verifyElementPresent	link=Selenium-WebDriver API Commands and Operations	
assertElementPresent	link=Driver Specifics and Tradeoffs	
verifyText	link=Selenium-WebDriver's Drivers	Selenium-WebDriver's Drivers
assertText	link=Alternative Back-Ends: Mixing WebDriver and RC Technologies	Alternative Back-Ends: Mixing WebDriver and RC Technologies
verifyText	link=Running Standalone Selenium Server for use with RemoteDrivers	Running Standalone Selenium Server for use with RemoteDrivers
assertText	link=Additional Resources	Additional Resources
verifyText	link=Next Steps	Next Steps
verifyTitle	Selenium Documentation — Selenium Documentation	
verifyText	link=Explicit and Implicit Waits	Explicit and Implicit Waits
assertElementPresent	link=RemoteWebDriver	
verifyText	link=AdvancedUserInteractions	AdvancedUserInteractions
assertText	link=Browser Startup Manipulation	Browser Startup Manipulation
verifyText	link=HTML5	HTML5
assertText	link=Parallelizing Your Test Runs	Parallelizing Your Test Runs
verifyTitle	Selenium Documentation — Selenium Documentation	
verifyElementPresent	xpath=(//a[contains(text(),'Introduction')])[3]	
assertText	link=How Selenium RC Works	How Selenium RC Works
verifyText	link=Installation	Installation
assertText	link=From Selenese to a Program	From Selenese to a Program
verifyText	link=Programming Your Test	Programming Your Test

selenium_projects6		
assertText	link=Learning the API	Learning the API
verifyText	link=Reporting Results	Reporting Results
assertText	link=Adding Some Spice to Your Tests	Adding Some Spice to Your Tests
assertText	link=Server Options	Server Options
verifyText	link=Specifying the Path to a Specific Browser	Specifying the Path to a Specific Browser
assertText	link=Selenium RC Architecture	Selenium RC Architecture
verifyText	link=Handling HTTPS and Security Popups	Handling HTTPS and Security Popups
assertText	link=Supporting Additional Browsers and Browser Configurations	Supporting Additional Browsers and Browser Configurations
assertText	link=Troubleshooting Common Problems	Troubleshooting Common Problems
assertText	link=Test Design Considerations	Test Design Considerations
verifyText	link=Introducing Test Design	Introducing Test Design
assertText	link=Types of Tests	Types of Tests
assertText	link=Validating Results	Validating Results
verifyText	link=Location Strategies	Location Strategies
assertText	link=Wrapping Selenium Calls	Wrapping Selenium Calls
assertText	link=UI Mapping	UI Mapping
verifyText	link=Page Object Design Pattern	Page Object Design Pattern
verifyText	link=Data Driven Testing	Data Driven Testing
assertElementPresent	link=Database Validation	
verifyTitle	Selenium Documentation — Selenium Documentation	
verifyText	link=Quick Start	Quick Start
assertText	link=exact:What is Selenium-Grid?	exact:What is Selenium-Grid?

selenium_projects6		
assertElementPresent	link=When to Use It	
verifyText	link=Selenium-Grid 2.0	Selenium-Grid 2.0
assertText	link=Selenium-Grid 1.0	Selenium-Grid 1.0
verifyText	link=How Selenium-Grid Works–With a Hub and Nodes	How Selenium-Grid Works–With a Hub and Nodes
verifyTitle	Selenium Documentation — Selenium Documentation	
verifyText	link=Configuring Selenium-Grid	Configuring Selenium-Grid
assertText	link=Hub Configuration	Hub Configuration
verifyText	link=Node Configuration	Node Configuration
verifyText	link=Timing Parameters	Timing Parameters
verifyText	link=Customizing the Grid	Customizing the Grid
assertText	link=Getting Command-Line Help	Getting Command-Line Help
assertText	link=Common Errors	Common Errors
verifyTitle	Selenium Documentation — Selenium Documentation	
verifyText	link=Actions	Actions
verifyText	link=Accessors/Assertions	Accessors/Assertions
assertText	link=Locator Strategies	Locator Strategies
verifyElementPresent	link=Using User-Extensions With Selenium-IDE	
assertElementPresent	link=Using User-Extensions With Selenium RC	
verifyElementPresent	link=.NET client driver configuration	
assertText	link=Importing Sel2.0 Project into Eclipse using Maven	Importing Sel2.0 Project into Eclipse using Maven
verifyText	link=Importing Sel2.0 Project into IntelliJ Using Maven	Importing Sel2.0 Project into IntelliJ Using Maven
assertText	link=Migrating From Selenium RC to Selenium WebDriver	Migrating From Selenium RC to Selenium WebDriver

selenium_projects6		
verifyText	link=How to Migrate to Selenium WebDriver	How to Migrate to Selenium Web-Driver
assertText	link=Why Migrate to WebDriver	Why Migrate to WebDriver
verifyText	link=Before Starting	Before Starting
assertText	link=Getting Started	Getting Started
verifyElementPresent	xpath=(//a[contains(text(),'Next Steps')])[2]	
assertText	link=Common Problems	Common Prob-lems
verifyText	css=#mainContent > div.related > ul > li > a	Selenium Docu-mentation
assertText	css=#mainContent > div.related > ul > li.right > a[title="Note to the Reader - Docs Being Revised for Selenium 2.0!"]	Next
verifyElementPresent	id=footerLogo	
selectWindow	null	
verifyElementPresent	link=Selenium Documentation	
assertText	link=next	Next
verifyText	link=Note to the Reader - Docs Being Revised for Selenium 2.0!	Note to the Reader - Docs Being Re-vised for Selenium 2.0!
assertText	css=em	Docs Being Re-vised for Selenium 2.0
verifyElementPresent	name=submit	
verifyText	name=submit	
assertElementPresent	css=a > img	
assertValue	css=li > input[type="image"]	Java
verifyValue	//input[@value='csharp']	Csharp
assertText	//input[@value='python']	
verifyText	//input[@value='ruby']	
assertValue	//input[@value='php']	Php
verifyValue	//input[@value='perl']	Perl
assertValue	//input[@value='javascript']	Javascript

Selenium Test Automation Framework

This is one of the very important chapter in this entire book which explains about the entire selenium framework construction in step by step approach. Readers are requested to download the practice projects from the link provided at the end of the chapter and follow the instructions given in this chapter-so it will help in practical experience of how to construct or design or structure a framework of selenium from scratch!

Why Selenium is an important automation tool?

Until early 2006, there was no particular open source tool (free tool) in the market which prove to be a stable and trusted to implement in testing projects. When selenium occupied the market, it has expanded rapidly and it is one and only open source tool wide used for web based testing(comparing to any other paid tools/licensed tools)

Automation Framework is the combination of tools and their integration to benefit the test automation of particular application under test (AUT). Cost and time are two primary factors while considering tools for the framework design. Since Selenium Web Driver and tools like TestNG, Ant are freeware and stable releases from open source community, this attracts build an expert automation system that handles the software for multiple test releases.

This particular automation framework design needs additional expertise in understanding test automation and how the maintenance work can be minimized by developing an intelligent system around the automation tools available.

Automation Framework Using Selenium Web Driver:

Prerequisite:

Download Eclipse from http://eclipse.org/downloads/

Note: Eclipse is famous for Java Integrated Development Environment (IDE); Since Java is wide used for Selenium Test Automation, it is good to automate using Java Programming as a scripting language (not 'Java script language')

High Level Automation Design:

Selenium Web Driver for Hybrid TestNG framework

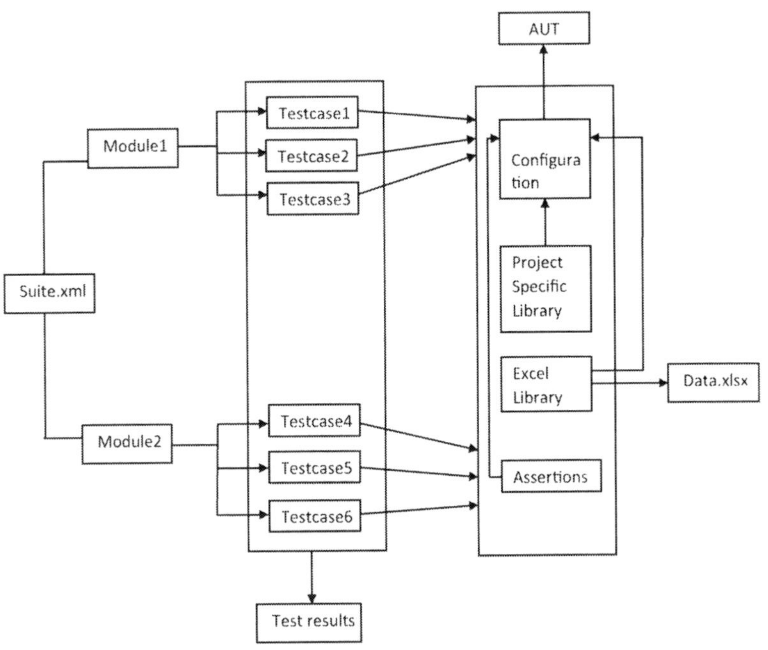

How to design the automation Framework from the ground?

Install JAVA

Java programming is a famous and important programming language in testing industry and testers with Java knowledge are paid high in the job markets!

Please download java from following link:

http://www.oracle.com/technetwork/java/javase/downloads/index.html

Product / File Description	File Size	Download
Linux x86	146.89 MB	jdk-8u45-linux-i586.rpm
Linux x86	166.88 MB	jdk-8u45-linux-i586.tar.gz
Linux x64	145.19 MB	jdk-8u45-linux-x64.rpm
Linux x64	165.24 MB	jdk-8u45-linux-x64.tar.gz
Mac OS X x64	221.98 MB	jdk-8u45-macosx-x64.dmg
Solaris SPARC 64-bit (SVR4 package)	131.73 MB	jdk-8u45-solaris-sparcv9.tar.Z
Solaris SPARC 64-bit	92.9 MB	jdk-8u45-solaris-sparcv9.tar.gz
Solaris x64 (SVR4 package)	139.51 MB	jdk-8u45-solaris-x64.tar.Z
Solaris x64	95.88 MB	jdk-8u45-solaris-x64.tar.gz
Windows x86	175.98 MB	jdk-8u45-windows-i586.exe
Windows x64	180.44 MB	jdk-8u45-windows-x64.exe

How to understand whether the Java is installed in the computer or not?

Once the exe file has been downloaded from the website, double click on the exe file and run the installation of the JAVA program in the computer. Once it is completed, kindly check the C:/ Drive's Program Files folder. This folder should have 'JAVA' folder with JDK and JRE sub folders. Once these folders are displayed in the computer, it means that the Java installation is completed but the configuration has to be done to make sure that the JAVA files are identified by the computer.

JAVA Configuration

Once Java has been installed successfully, JAVA_HOME and PATH has to be set up in the system as follows:

Right click on 'This PC' and select Properties:

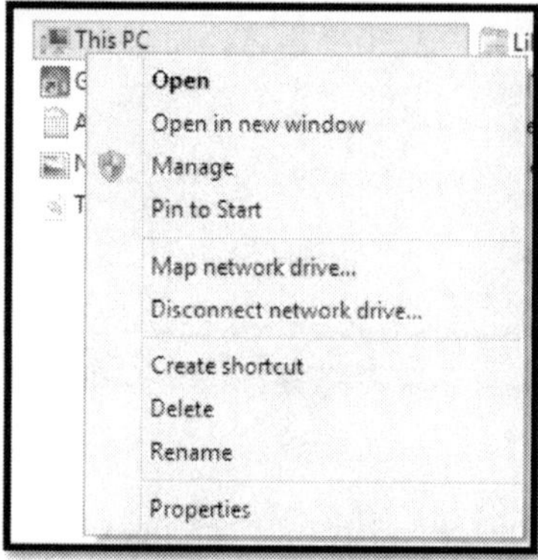

Alternatively Navigate to Control Panel and select Advanced System Settings. In Advanced Tab, click on Environment Variables:

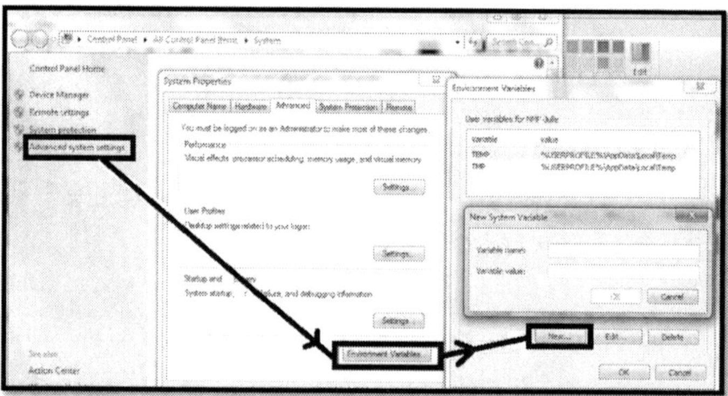

Click on New button and enter the location of JDK folder:

Note: Based on your Java version, the folder name differ. It is better to navigate to the location and copy the path as below:

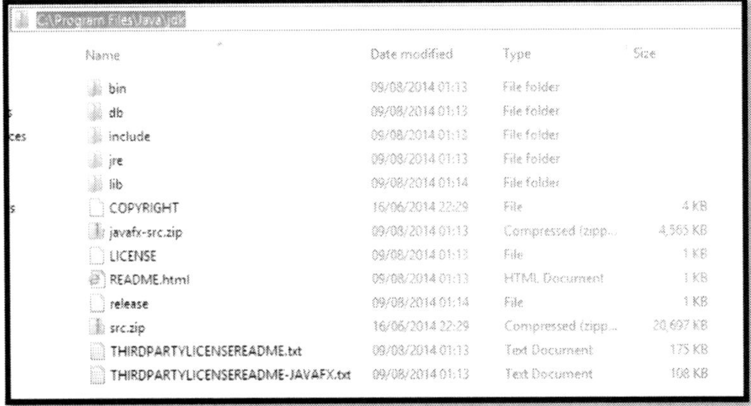

Similarly click on the New button again to enter path as follows:

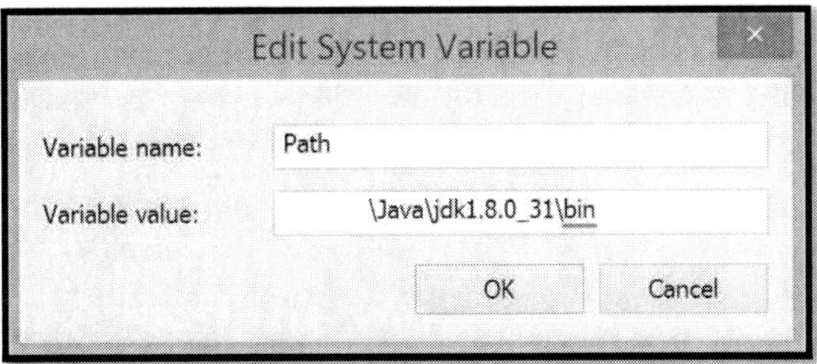

Note: Make sure that you have mentioned the path including bin folder as above. You can take a copy of this path just by clicking on the bin folder as below:

This PC › OS (C:) › Program Files › Java › jdk ›

Name	Date modified	Type	Size
bin	09/08/2014 01:13	File folder	
db	09/08/2014 01:13	File folder	
include	09/08/2014 01:13	File folder	
jre	09/08/2014 01:13	File folder	
lib	09/08/2014 01:14	File folder	
COPYRIGHT	16/06/2014 22:29	File	4 KB
javafx-src.zip	09/08/2014 01:13	Compressed (zipp...	4,565 KB
LICENSE	09/08/2014 01:13	File	1 KB
README.html	09/08/2014 01:13	HTML Document	1 KB
release	09/08/2014 01:14	File	1 KB
src.zip	16/06/2014 22:29	Compressed (zipp...	20,697 KB
THIRDPARTYLICENSEREADME.txt	09/08/2014 01:13	Text Document	175 KB
THIRDPARTYLICENSEREADME-JAVAFX.txt	09/08/2014 01:13	Text Document	108 KB

Why JAVA_HOME and PATH has been updated in Environment Variable

Whenever the java programs compiled and executed in computer, required JAVA files has to be referred during compilation and execution. So the computer need to know where the JAVA files located and what is the respective PATH of bin folder. So the file location is provided through JAVA_HOME and bin folder location is provided through PATH set up. Once it is completed, it is a good practice to restart computer and check the version of JAVA through Command Prompt. Simply running the command JAVA -VERSION will provide the java version in command prompt which proves that the JAVA installation has been completed successfully.

Alternative way to set up JAVA_HOME and PATH is through Command Prompt. This can be done by launching Command Prompt as follows.

Step1: Press Windows+R (to open RUN)
Step2: Type CMD, Press Enter
Step3: In Command Prompt, Type' SET JAVA_HOME = c:/ Program Files/Java'
Step4: Type 'SET PATH = %PATH%;%JAVA_HOME%\bin'

Once JAVA Installation and configuration has been completed, it is required to install Eclipse as it act as a tool to write JAVA codes!

Launch Eclipse

Download latest eclipse version from http://eclipse.org/downloads/

Once downloaded, please install it and open Eclipse from the location it is downloaded by clicking on eclipse.exe as follows:

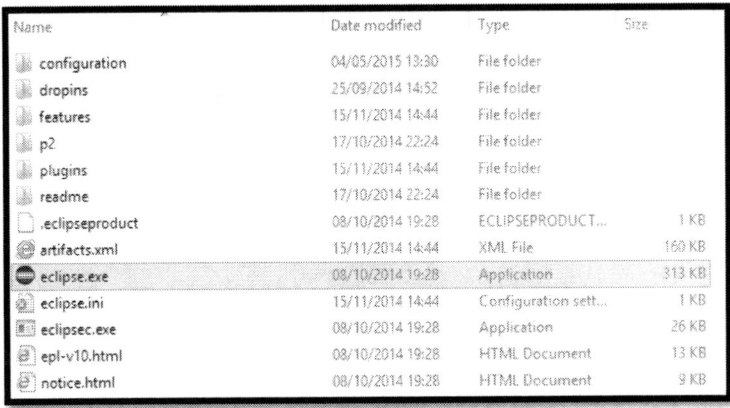

Name Date modified Type Size
configuration 04/05/2015 13:30 File folder
dropins 25/09/2014 14:52 File folder
features 15/11/2014 14:44 File folder
p2 17/10/2014 22:24 File folder
plugins 15/11/2014 14:44 File folder
readme 17/10/2014 22:24 File folder
.eclipseproduct 08/10/2014 19:28 ECLIPSEPRODUCT... 1 KB
artifacts.xml 15/11/2014 14:44 XML File 160 KB
eclipse.exe 08/10/2014 19:28 Application 313 KB
eclipse.ini 15/11/2014 14:44 Configuration sett... 1 KB
eclipsec.exe 08/10/2014 19:28 Application 26 KB
epl-v10.html 08/10/2014 19:28 HTML Document 13 KB
notice.html 08/10/2014 19:28 HTML Document 9 KB

Figure: Eclipse Exe file to launch eclipse

Verify that the eclipse is getting launched successfully:

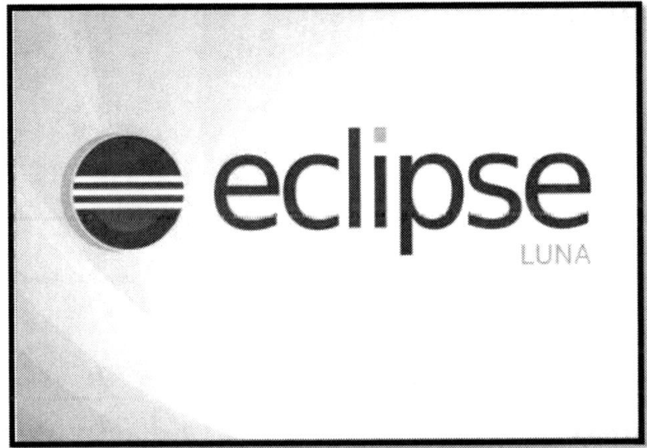

Set workspace for the Eclipse project as this location will be the primary location to save all the java files which are going to be used for the automation framework:

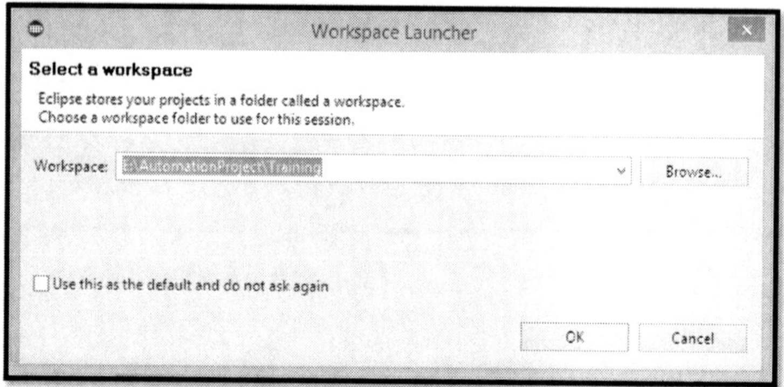

Once the workspace has been provided the welcome page appears as below and 'Workbench' button on the top right side of the window has to be clicked to view workbench and write the new programs:

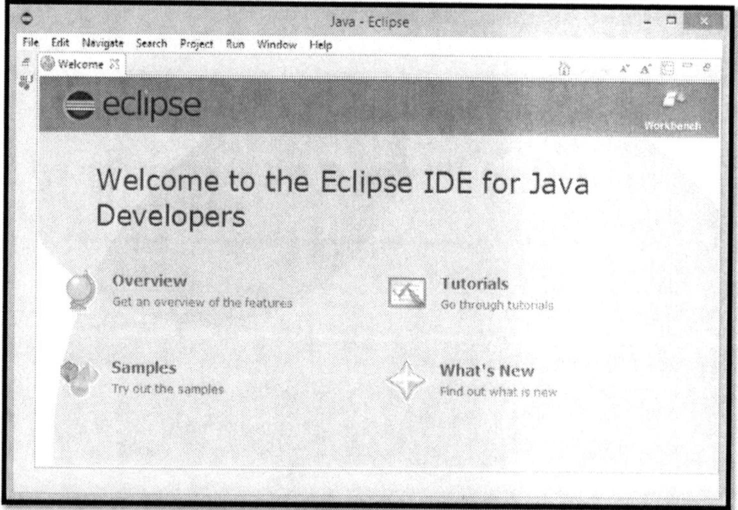

Package Explorer

This is the left panel where the projects are listed along with source code of the program required for the automation framework:

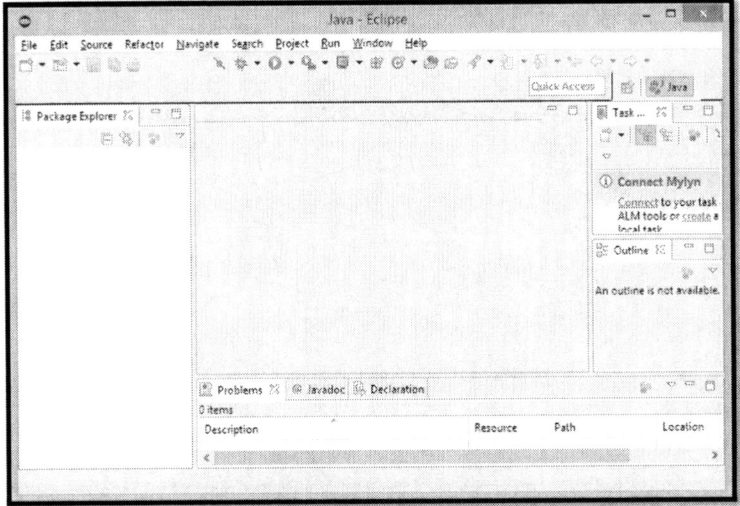

Create new project with the name SAF (Selenium Automation Framework):

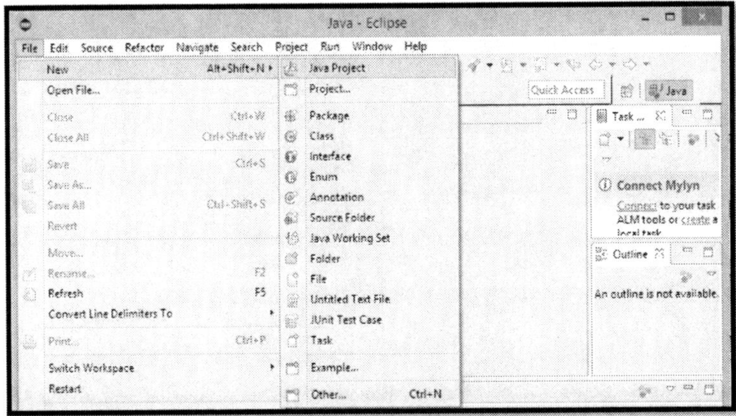

This SAF (Selenium Automation Framework) will act as a primary project for all the extensions and the test scripts used across the testing project0.

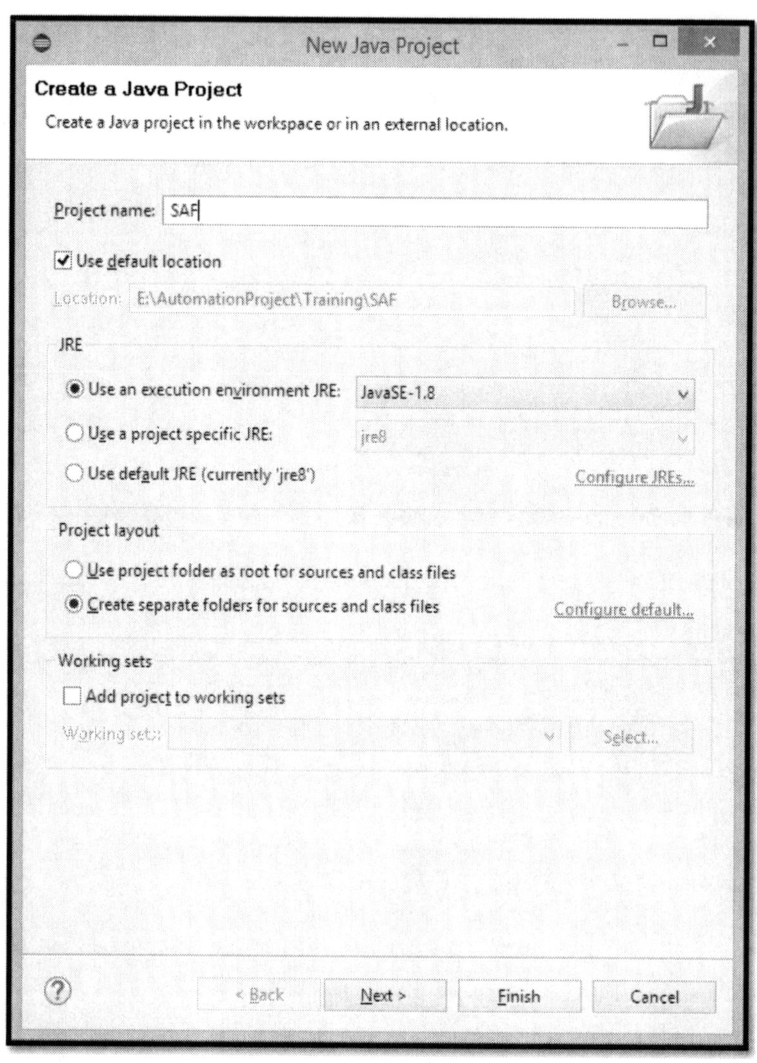

Once the folder is created, this can be viewed in eclipse as follows:

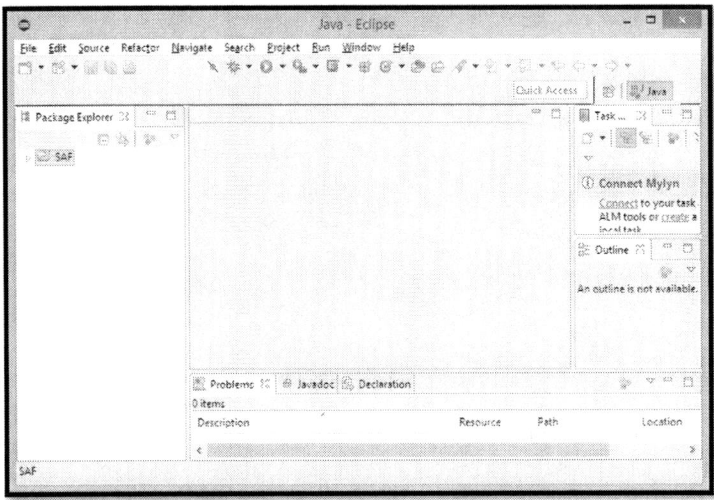

The new SAF project will be listed as follows in package explorer:

Note: JRE System Library is a custom folder created for the test project automatically. If it is not created for available in different folder, that means either eclipse would have been updated to the latest version or the folder creation is incorrect.

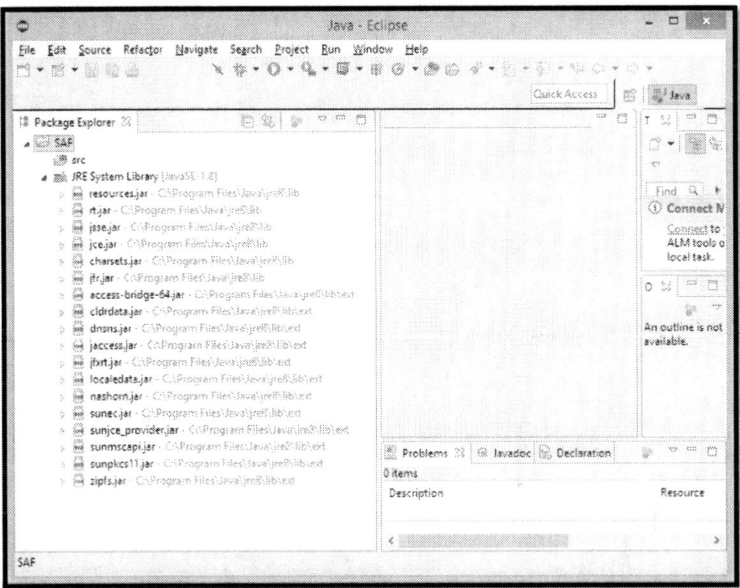

Create Selenium Automation Framework Packages

Right click on the SAF Project, click on New and click on Package to create new packages which are the most wanted facilities of the automation framework.

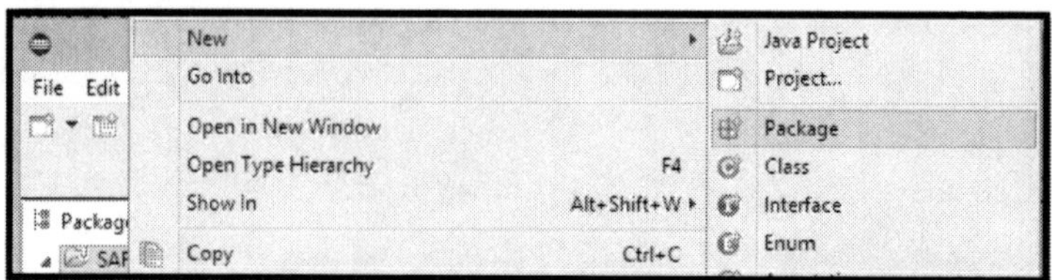

Create a Package named com.stta.property

This package is required to have reusable properties such as xpath property and parameters such as website urls, browser details at central location. So we can insist the automation framework to run from particular url in specific browser, just by updating the files in this package!

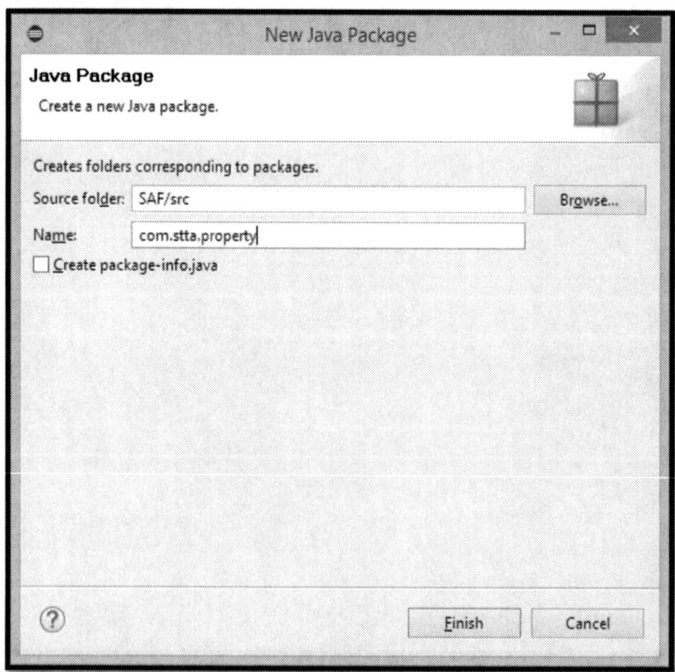

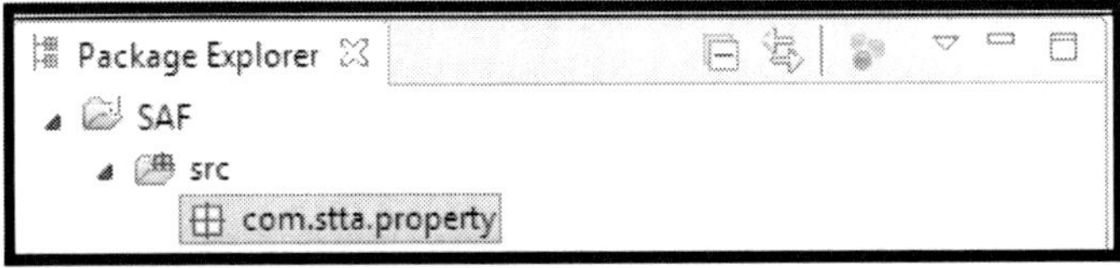

Create package com.stta.Logging

Similar to the package above, create another package and name it as com.stta.Logging

This package is a very important facility of any automation framework to capture the exceptions, failures and traces of test execution using logs.

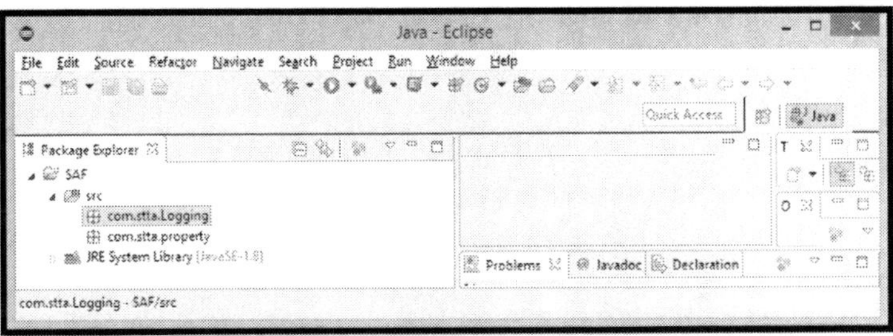

Create package com.stta.ExcelFiles

All the related data sheets can be downloaded and kept under this package. This can be possible by right click on the package and paste the required excel files to this package.

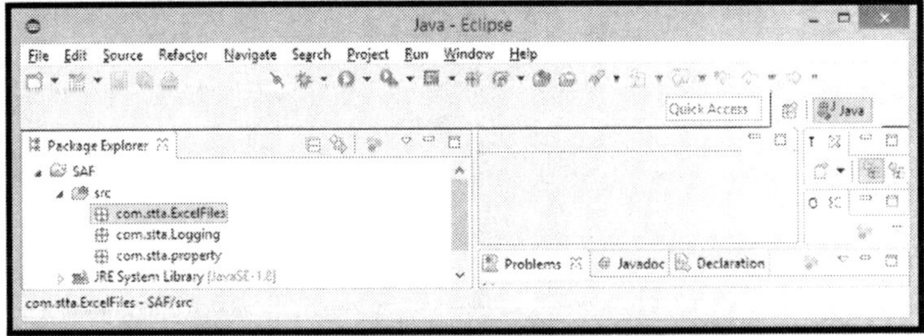

Create package com.stta.utility

Reusable java scripts, reusable functions and other centralized file properties can be managed from this folder.

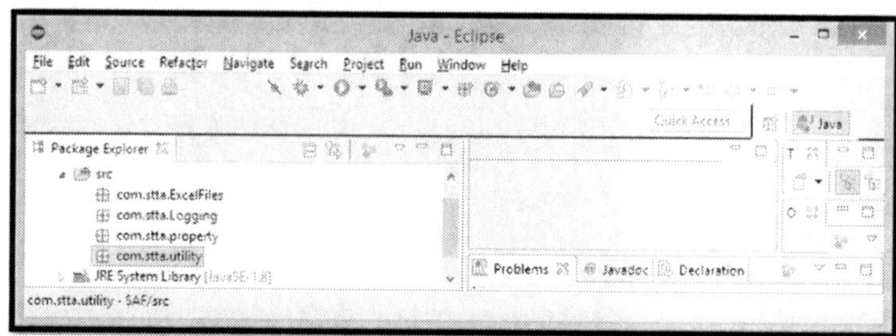

Create Test Script based package com.stta.SuiteOne, com.stta.SuiteTwo and com.stta.TestSuiteBase

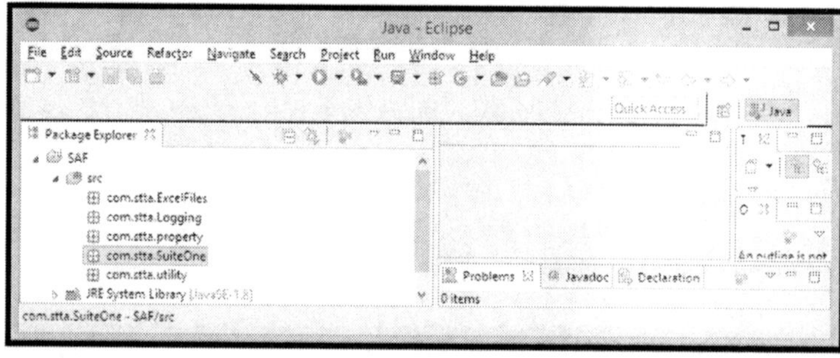

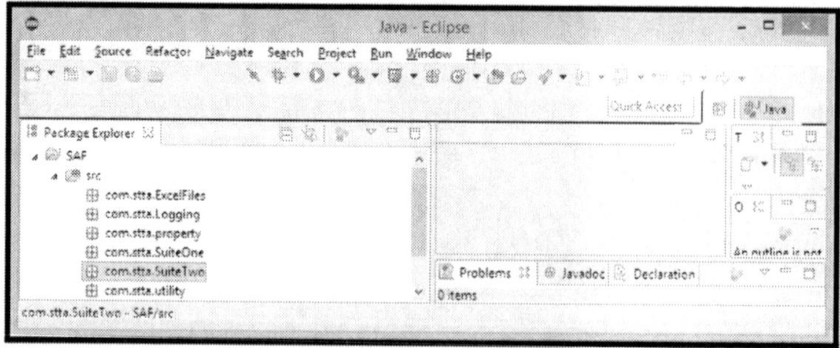

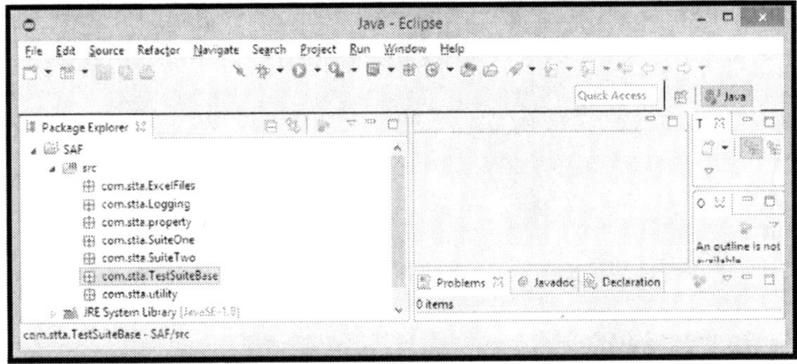

Create com.stta.xslt folder

All the test report-ability logics can be saved under this package so that the latest versions and maintenance of the test reports made simple.

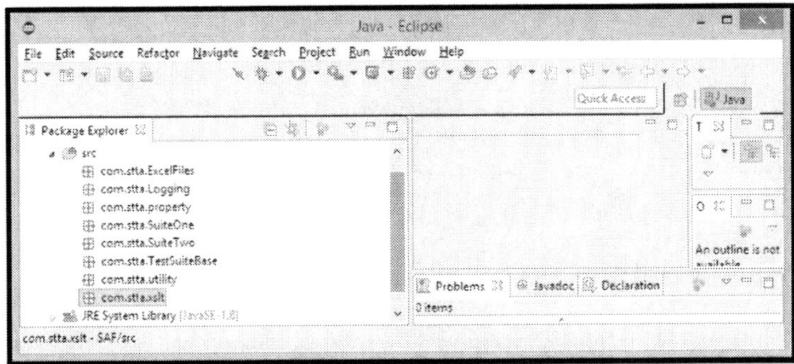

Create a Folder name JAR files to have all the relevant JAR files

When the automation framework is designed, it is a mixture of more than one extendable jar files downloaded from various source locations. Also each jar file differ from their old versions due to latest defect fixes. So it is important to keep all the installed jar files of the automation framework from this particular folder.

Right click on the project, click on New and click on Folder:

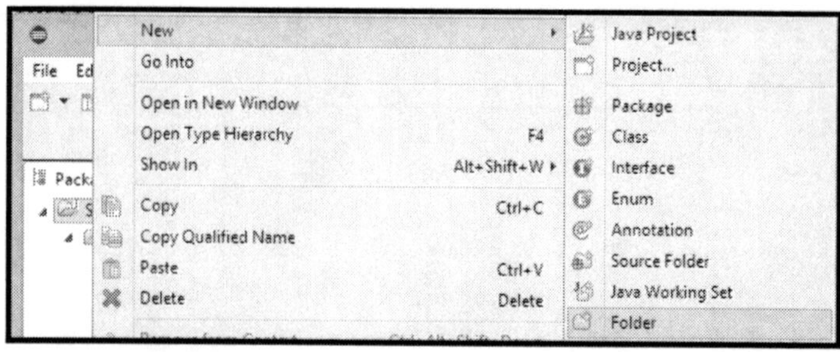

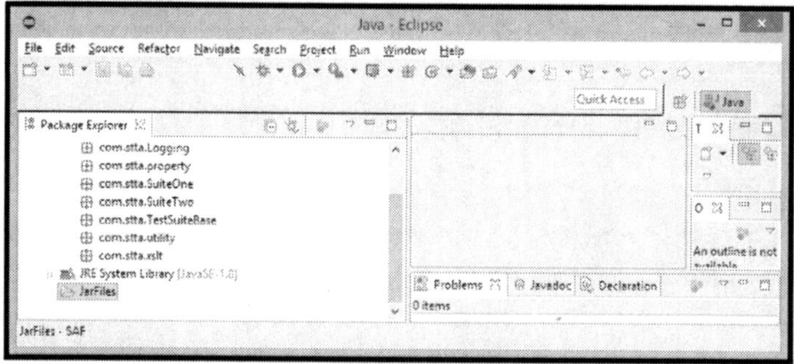

Required downloadable jar files from various locations:

Apache POI API for Excel Data Driven Framework:

Selenium doesn't support excel based files at the latest releases and it is possible to read and write in excel files using Apache POI API files!

Following are the files helpful in extending the excel read/write facility:

poi-3.12-beta1-20150228.jar

poi-ooxml-3.12-beta1-20150228.jar

poi-ooxml-schemas-3.12-beta1-20150228.jar

Inside ' ooxml-lib' folder:

xmlbeans-2.6.0.jar

dom4j-1.6.1.jar

Note on dom4j.jar file: if this file is not found inside ooxml-lib folder, it means that the file has not been provided for latest versions of Apache API. So it is available from poi-bin-3.10-FINAL-20140208.zip version. You can download this from http://archive.apache.org/dist/poi/release/bin/

Note: version of the files differ based on the time it has been downloaded

Download the file from http://poi.apache.org/download.html

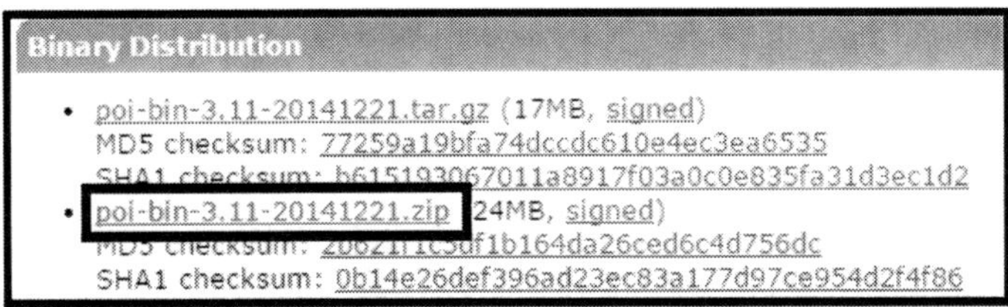

After downloading these files, place them into the JarFiles folder as follows:

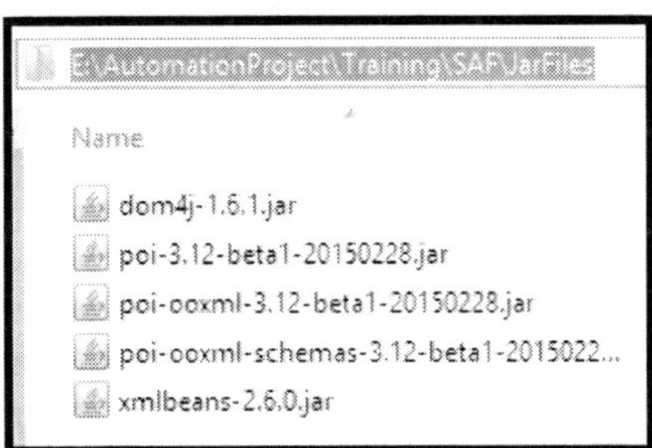

This means, you can view the JarFiles folder in Package Explorer after refreshing the folder:

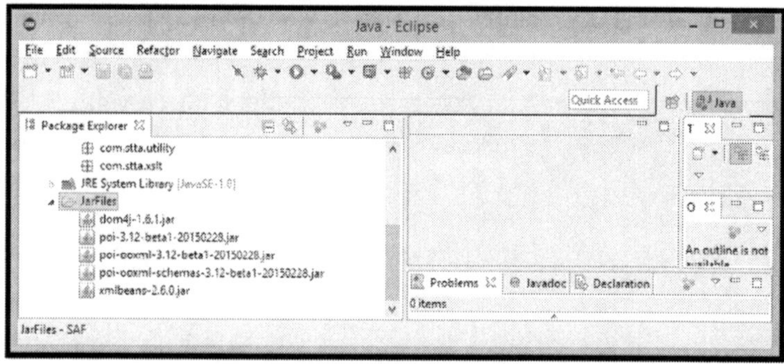

Download the Jar file for Logs extendibility:

Logging services such as execution time, test failure, success, exceptions are required to be captured during test execution. With the help of log4j file, it is possible to extend this facility in Selenium Automation Framework as the selenium web driver doesn't have log capturing technology in recent releases.

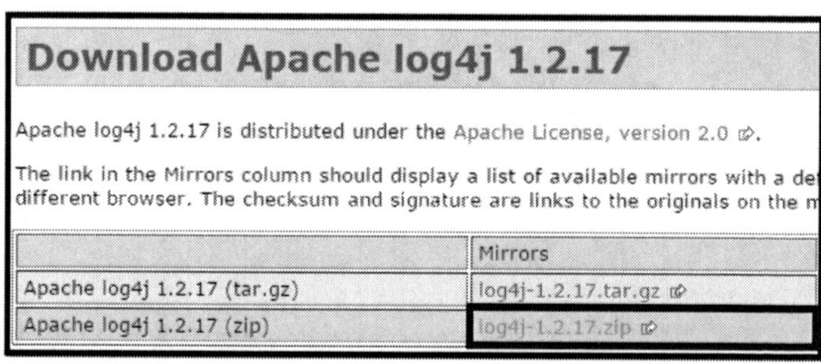

	Mirrors
Apache log4j 1.2.17 (tar.gz)	log4j-1.2.17.tar.gz
Apache log4j 1.2.17 (zip)	log4j-1.2.17.zip

Download the file from http://logging.apache.org/log4j/1.2/download.html

After extracting the file, please copy the file log4j from downloads:

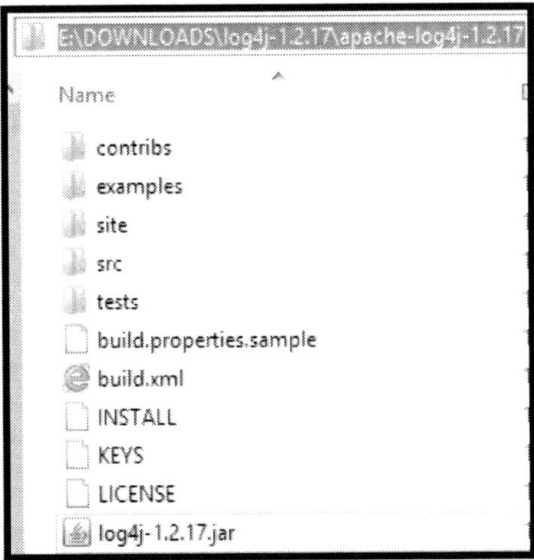

Paste this file into JarFiles folder which is created for the Selenium Automation Framework:

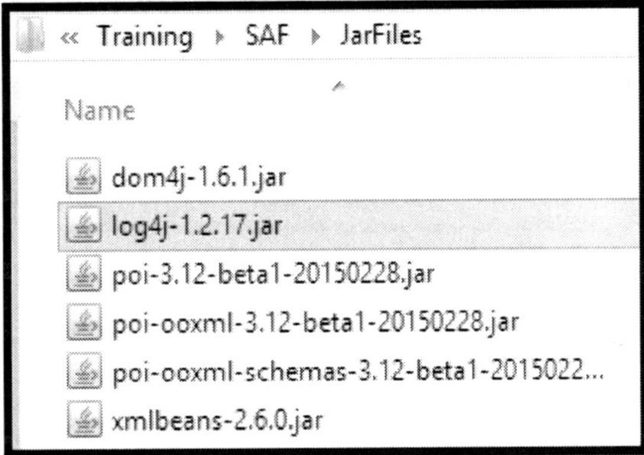

Main Selenium Web driver based Jar files for Selenium Automation Framework

The very important test engine of the automation framework is the testing tool. Especially Selenium is made up of JAR files which evolves over a period of time to upgraded versions. So make sure that the latest version of file has been downloaded from the link below.

Download the files from http://docs.seleniumhq.org/download/

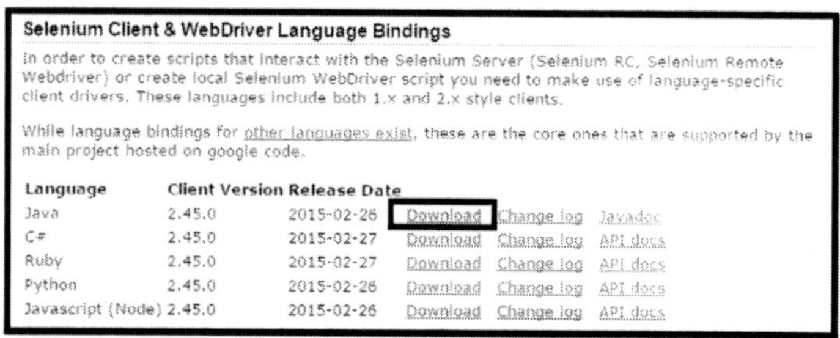

Once the files are downloaded, make sure that all the jar files from this file (including the jar files from sub folders of this file) are pasted into JarFiles folder which is created for the automation framework.

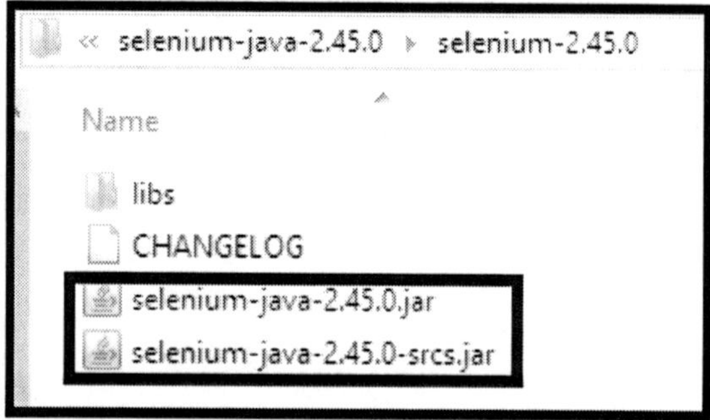

Make sure that the following files are included without missing any of them as each file play a major role in the automation framework:

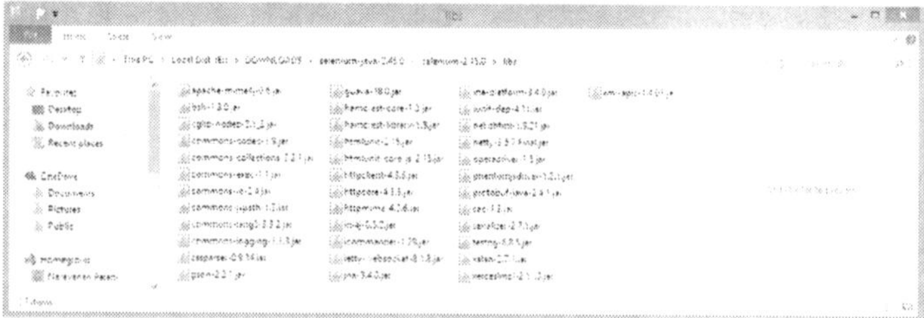

Once these files are pasted into JarFiles folder, this may look like the below structure:

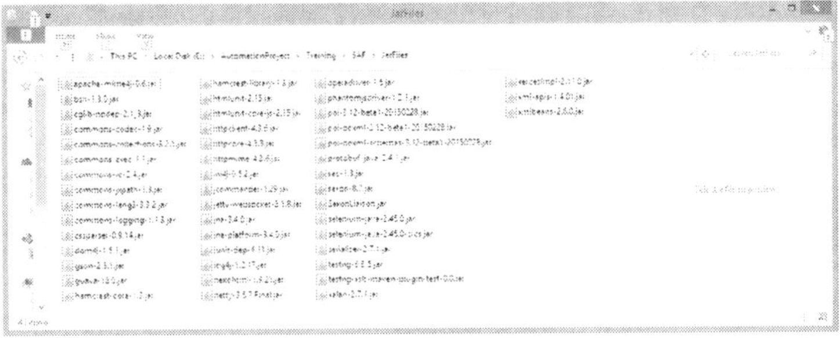

XSLT Report based Jar Files

Basic need of an automation framework is the test report! If the test reports are attractive, that gives positive impression on the automation framework from Project Managers and Test Managers. So XSLT report is one of the niche reporting method and extending XSLT to Selenium Automation Framework help in getting the test reports to share it across the stakeholders!

Download the saxon jar file from http://mvnrepository.com/artifact/net.sf.saxon/saxon/8.7

Alternatively both the files can be downloaded from the link given below:

https://github.com/prashanth-sams/testng-xslt-1.1.2/tree/master/lib

Once these two files are downloaded, place them into the JarFiles folder as follows:

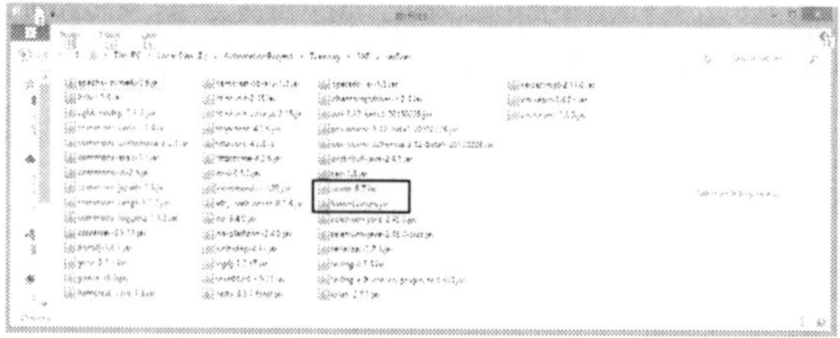

To combine the test results in XSL file, it is required to have TestNG compatible xsl file in the automation framework.

Download the zip file from https://github.com/prashanth-sams/testng-xslt-1.1.2

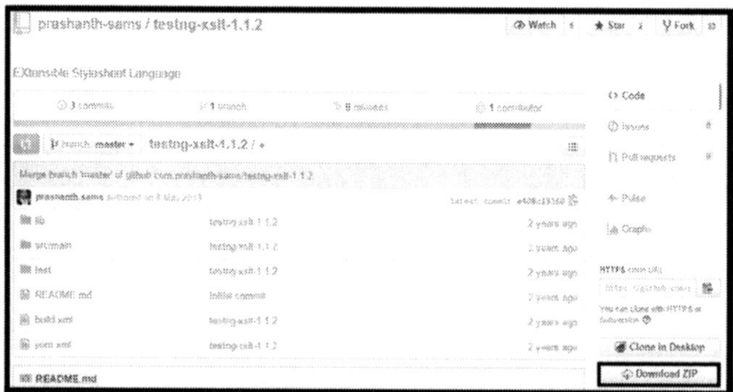

Once downloaded, navigate to the resources folder (testng-xslt-1.1.2-master\testng-xslt-1.1.2-master\src\main\resources)

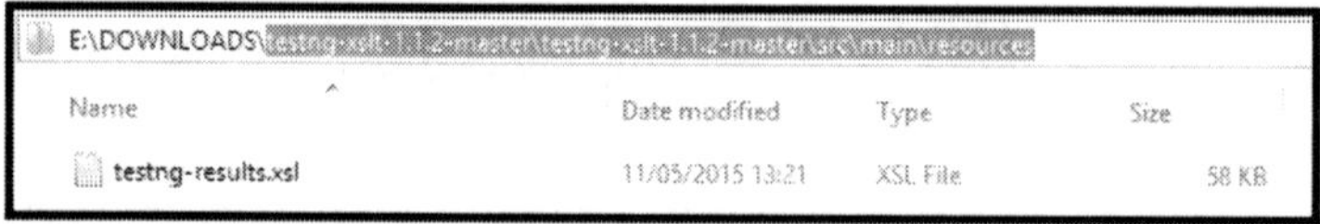

Copy the file testng-results.xsl and paste it to the Package created for the XSLT Reports as below:

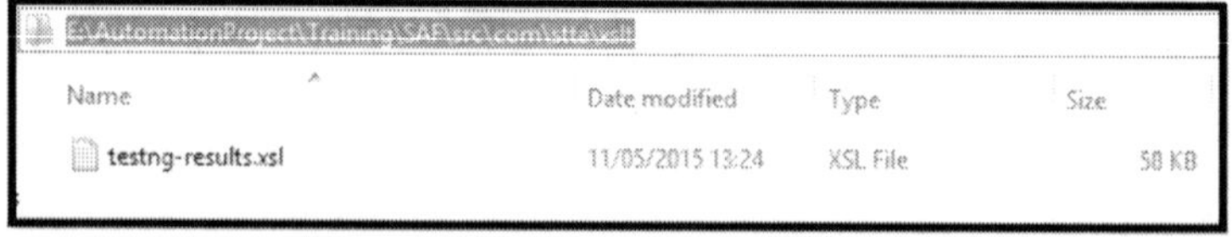

Once the file is located to this Package folder, this can be viewed in Package Explorer as follows:

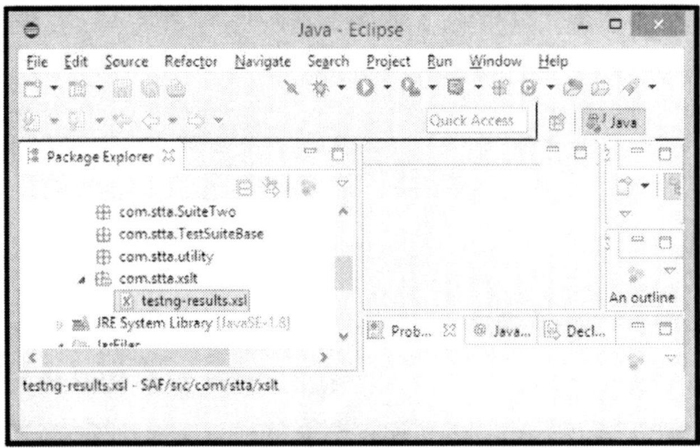

TestNG Plug-in to use the XSLT Reports

TestNG is used mainly to run the test scripts generated in Selenium. So this needs to be extended to XSLT reporting jar files using the plug-in. So the reports get the latest test execution status automatically. Download the plug-in from the below link and paste to the JarFiles folder as it is an important plug-in to capture the test results.

Link:

https://drive.google.com/file/d/0B6vnknygMB3IdzF4X2taWFRRMVE/edit

JarFiles Folder Structure after pasting the plug-in:

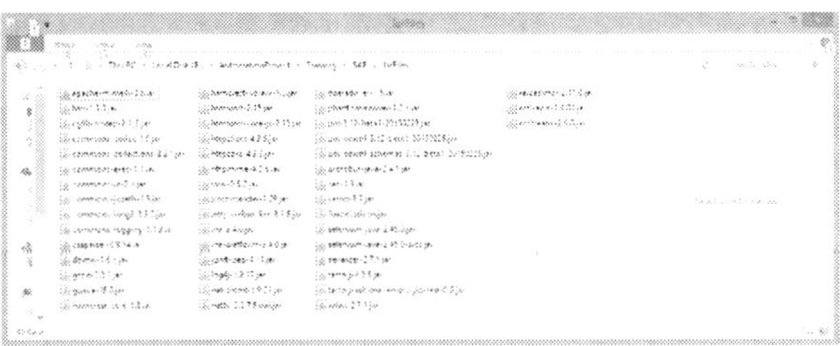

Project Build Path Configuration

The need of placing all the relevant JAR files into one central location in automation framework is to access them to configure the project SAF.

Right click on the folder SAF, click on Build Path and click on Configure Build Path as follows:

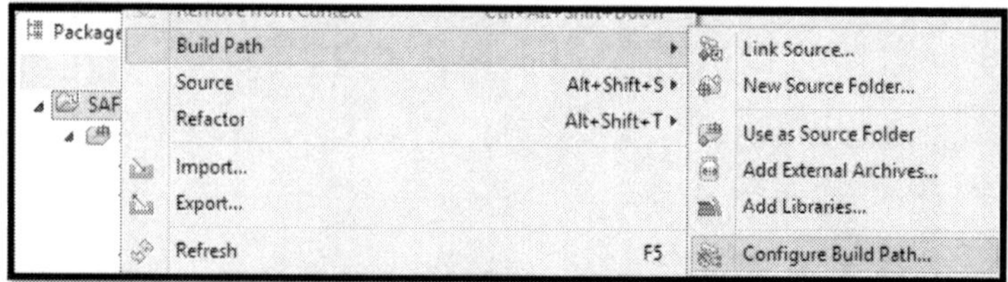

In Properties of SAF, click on the Libraries tab, click on Add External JARs button as follows:

Note: Make sure that the Libraries tab is clicked and then Add External JARs button is clicked from there.

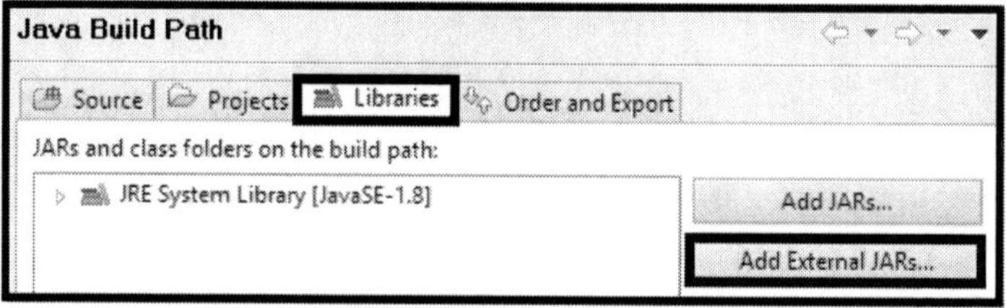

Select the path of the JarFiles folder and select all the JAR files in the folder and then click on Open button:

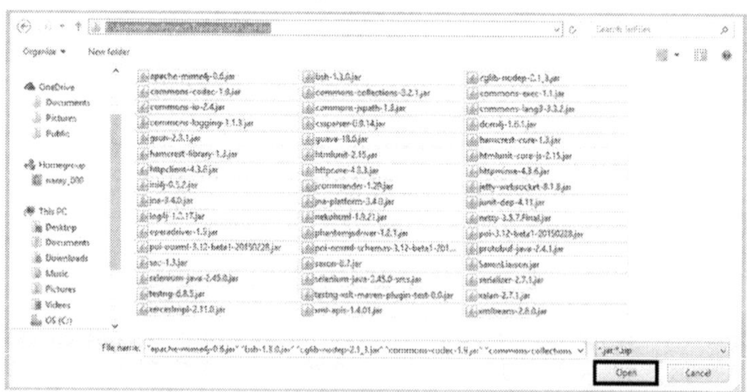

Once the files are selected, click on OK button and make sure that the files are added:

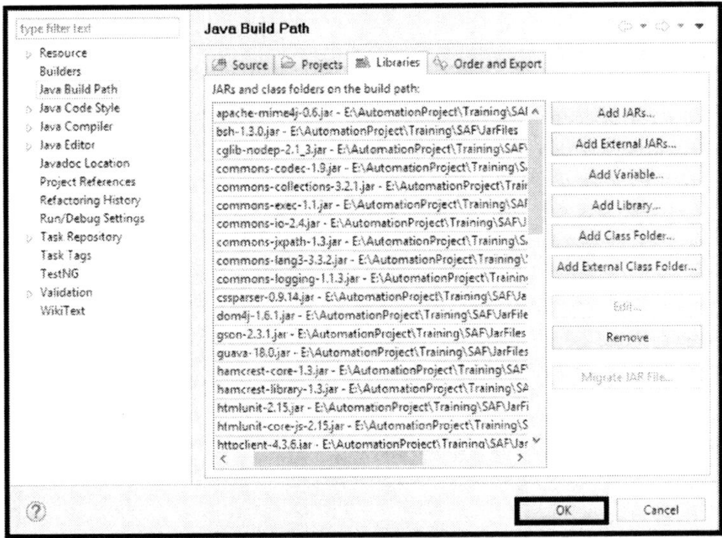

Once files are added, they can be found in the Referenced Libraries:

Note: Count the files from JarFiles Folder and this Reference Library to make sure that all the JARs have been selected to the build path.

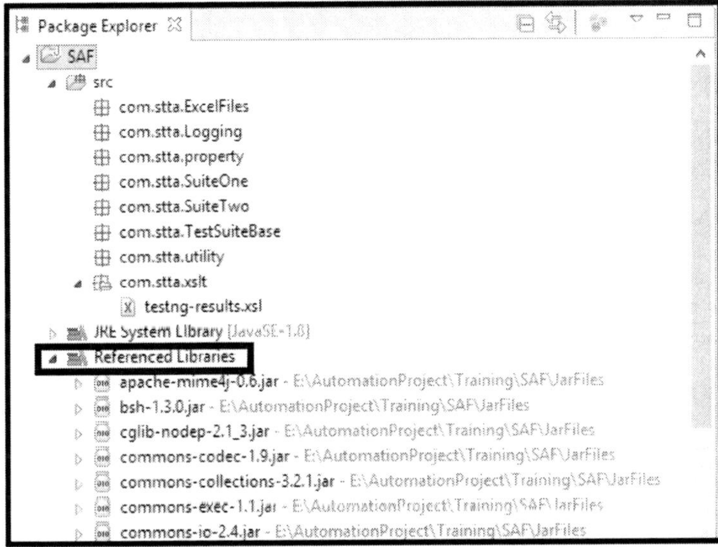

Excel Readability

Java program should be designed to interact to each column/row of test data to read and write the data as part of test execution. This can be done by using Read_XLS.java file.

Download the file from the below link and place it in the utility folder:

https://drive.google.com/file/d/0B6vnknygMB3INVFqYi03T2FrOXc/edit

Utility Folder:

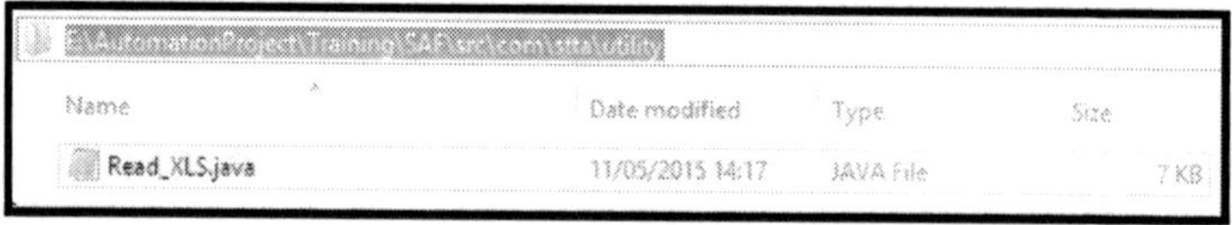

Once it is placed in Utility Folder this can be found at Package Explorer:

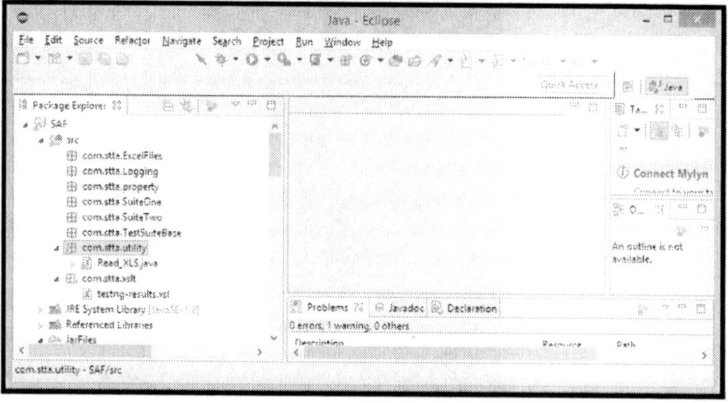

Suite Utility

It is a best practice to have the test scripts in different test cases and linked to respective test suites. So each test suite can be executed with the help of TestNG.

In order to have this flexibility, Suite Utility should be extended from a JAVA file as follows:

Download file from https://drive.google.com/file/d/0B6vnknygMB3ISGdURlYwU20xWms/edit

Paste the utility java file in Utility Folder:

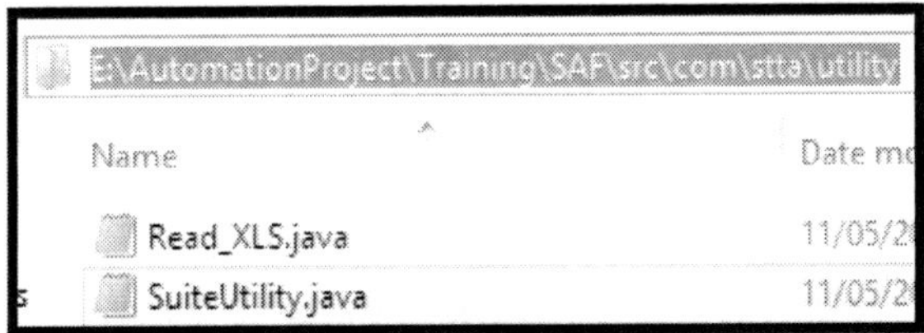

This can be found in Package Explorer as follows:

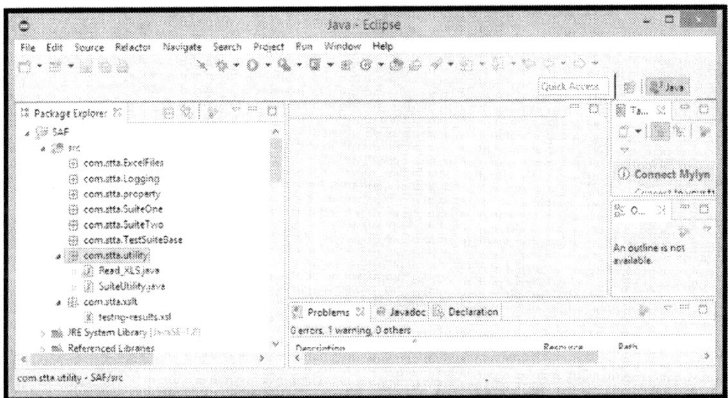

Test Execution through TestNG

Create exclusive test suites for each set of test cases and have the central testng.xml to execute required test scripts.

To facilitate this execution strategy, download the TestNG files and place them in test-output folder.

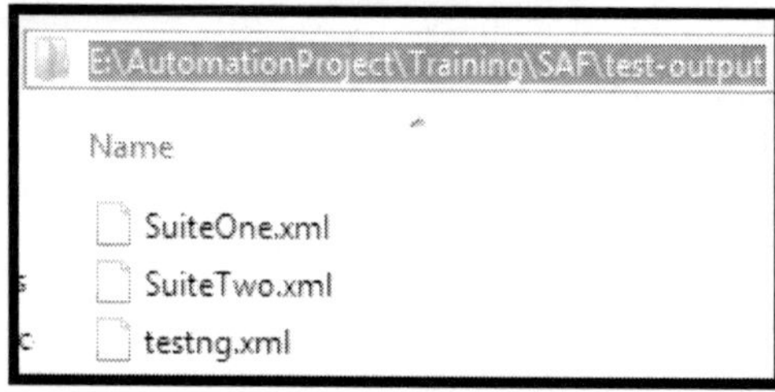

These TestNG files can be viewed from Package Explorer as follows:

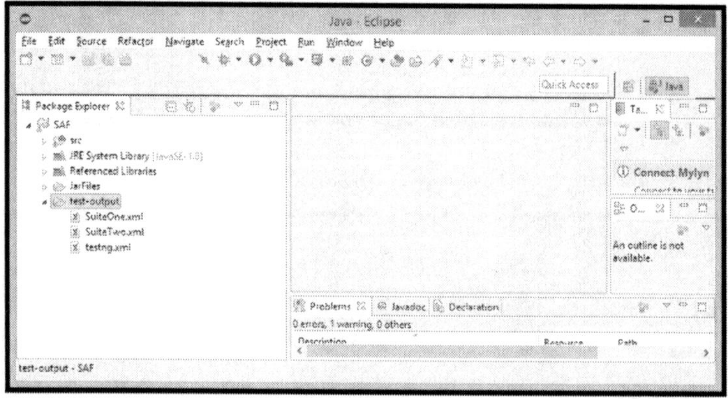

Place the files for logs and TestNG supported xsl files in xslt folder:

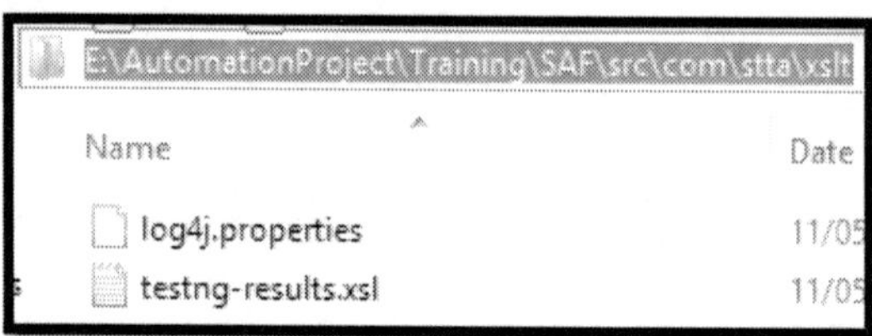

Create a file with name applog.log under com.stta.Logging

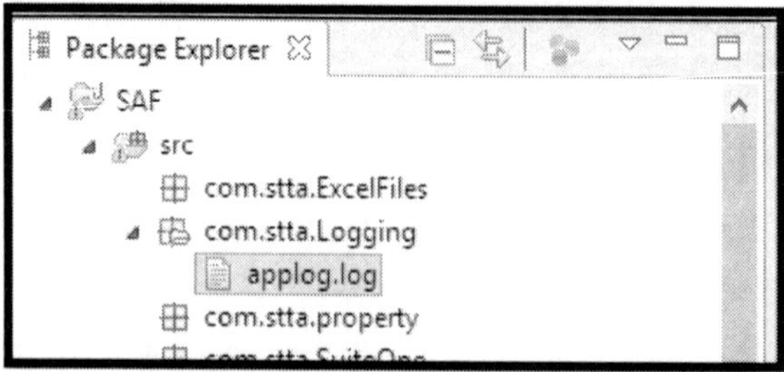

Log4J file basically capture the records which are executed currently by TestNG and update it to applog.log in the following format:

2015-05-17 10:27:07, 739 - rootLogger - INFO - All Excel Files Initialised successfully.

2015-05-17 10:27:07, 747 - rootLogger - INFO - Param. properties file loaded successfully.

2015-05-17 10:27:07, 747 - rootLogger - INFO - Objects. properties file loaded successfully.

2015-05-17 10:27:07, 747 - rootLogger - INFO - Execution started for SuiteOneBase.

Once the execution is completed, these logs can be captured from the following folder alternatively:

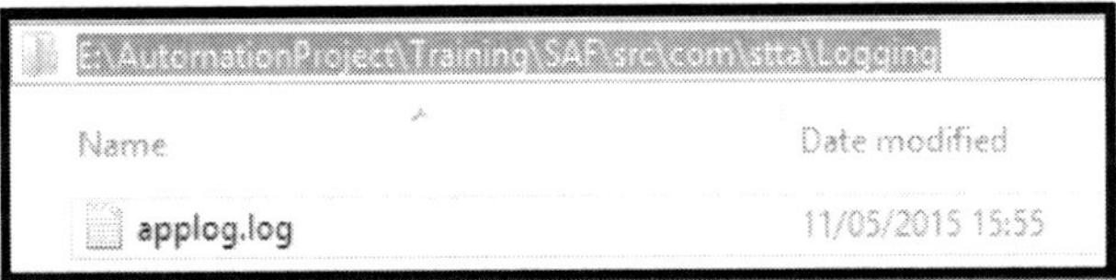

Once the log4j and tesng results files are saved in xslt folder, it can be viewed in eclipse as follows:

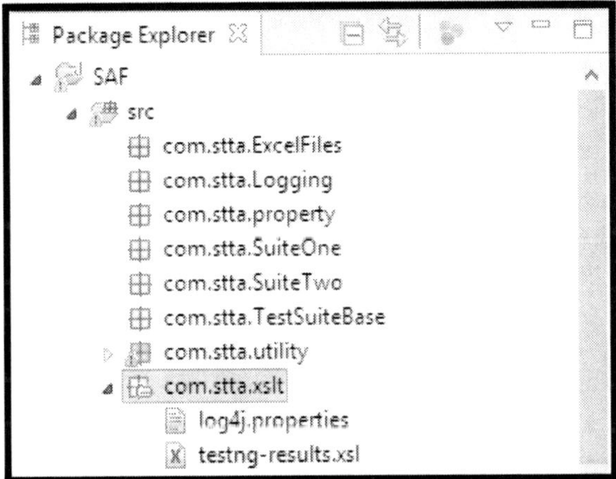

Place the executable TestNG xml files in new folder 'test-output' under SAF:

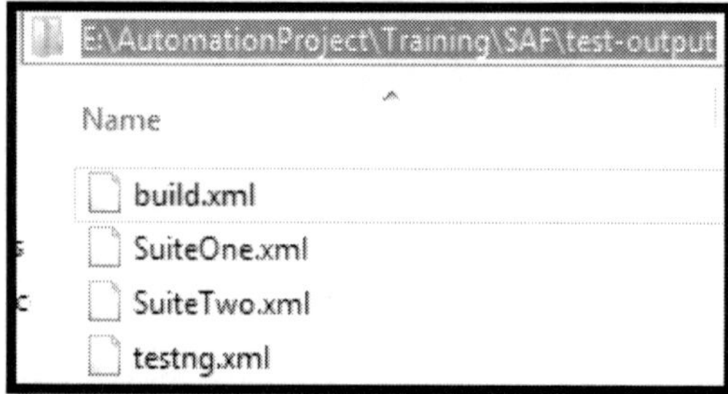

Once the TestNG files are added to the folder this can be viewed as follows:

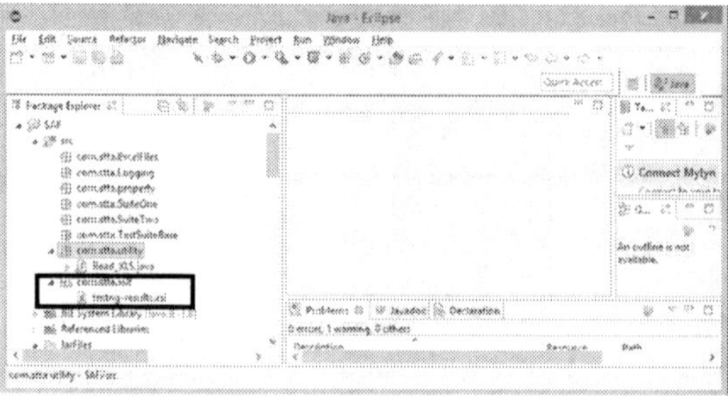

Run Test.bat for Ant Build

Once the tests are built in the automation framework, they can be combined using ant and run it from command prompt. So this build (ant) can be used in Jenkings.

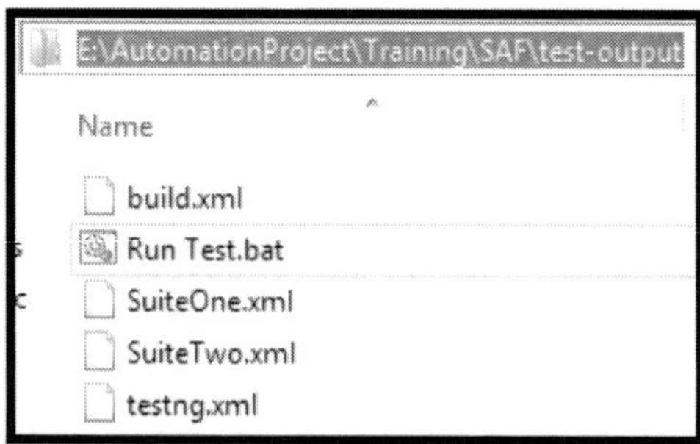

Run Test Bat File

To have such compatibility with test execution, it has to be controlled by servers or the central locations like Jenkins where the below bat file can be located and timed to have a build at particular test execution time:

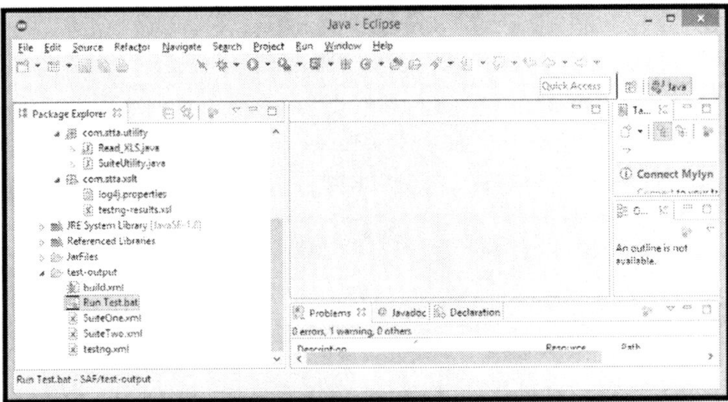

Property File

This file has to be updated with Parameters which are required for the test automation project

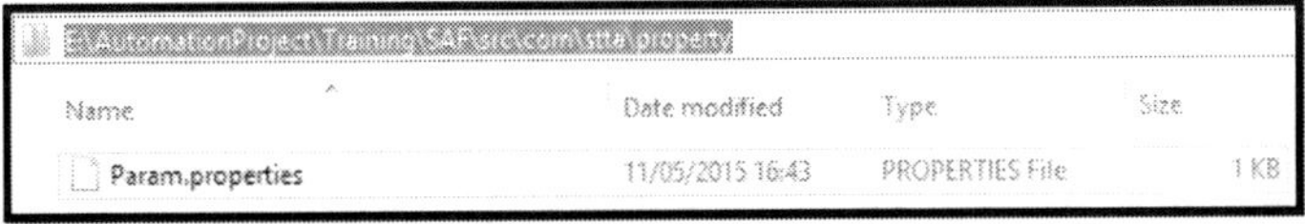

Each browser required for Selenium Framework has to be downloaded and listed here for the reference(except Firefox as it is an inbuilt feature):

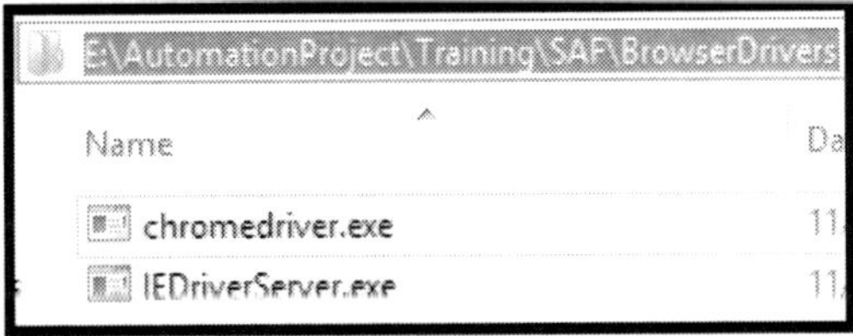

Each object (xpaths preferably) can be listed by object.properties file for ease of use. This is followed just to have multiple object files and replace them based on the test environment where the test execution is planned:

Customized screenshot utilities can be added to the projected and extended through TestNG in order to capture the test evidences:

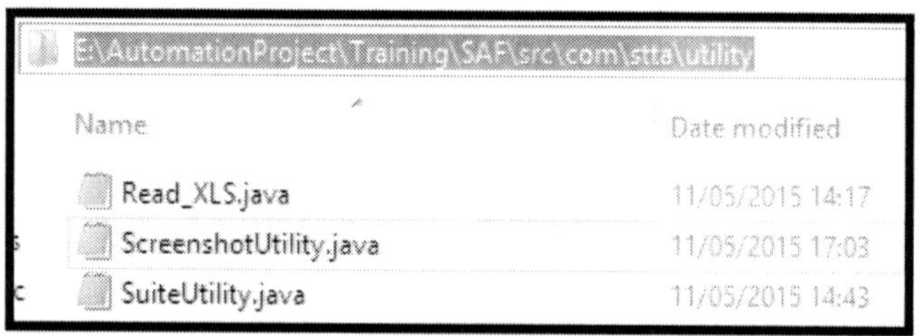

Excel Files for the Test Data of each iteration

TestSuiteList.xls centrally controls the sub set of the tests like SuiteOne, SuiteTwo etc

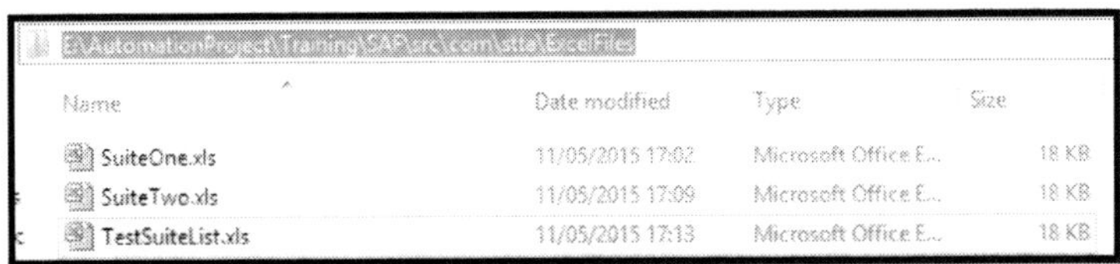

Running the Project from Ant

Navigate to the project folder in command prompt as follows and enter ant as command to know whether the ant is installed in the system or not:

If Ant is not installed, simply type 'Install Ant' in Google to find the steps as follows:

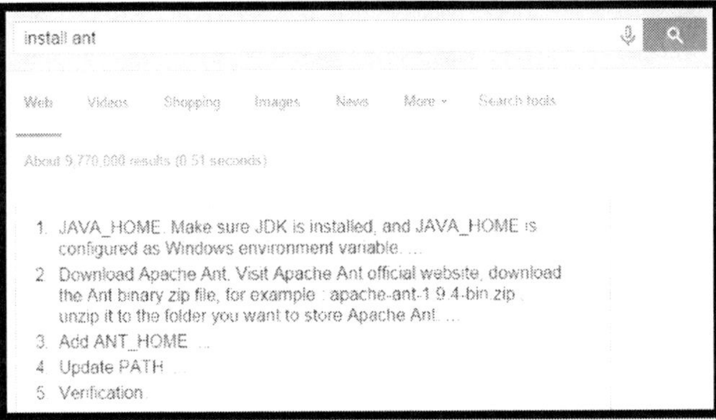

Once file has been downloaded from http://ant.apache.org/antlibs/bindownload.cgi this can be extracted to c:/ drive in the system. Once the file extracted to C:/ Drive, update the ANT_HOME and PATH in Environment Variables (Similar to JAVA_HOME and PATH which are explained earlier)

Ant Home

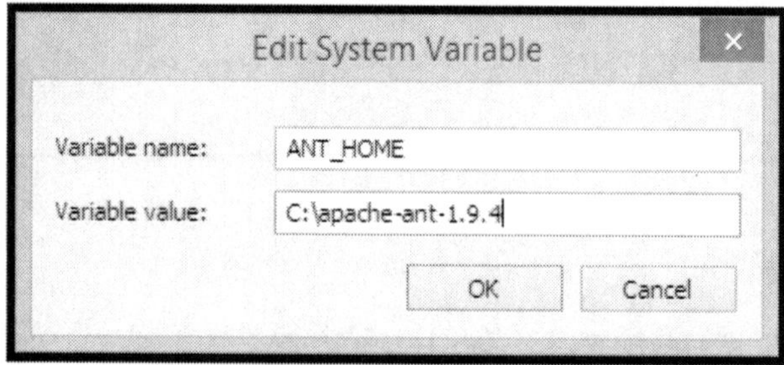

Path

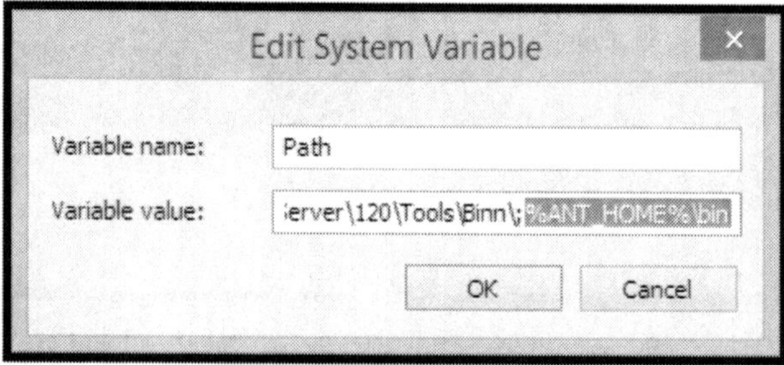

Once ANT_HOME, PATH has been set, this can be verified by entering the command 'ant -version':

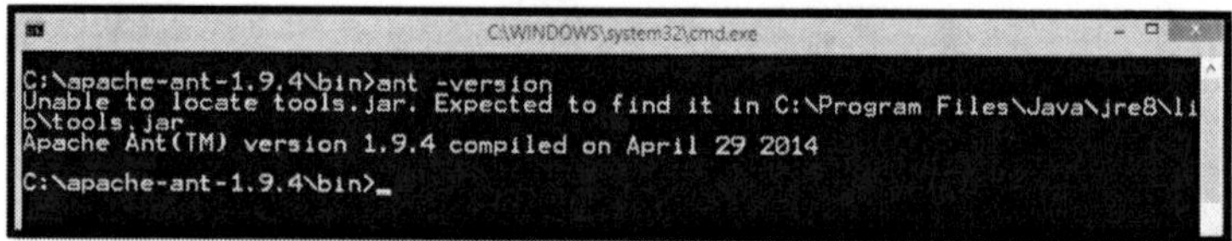

It the system displays ant versions and compilation date, it means that the installation is completed and just that the configuration needs to be updated for the automation framework.

Navigate to test-output folder of automation framework and check for the build using the query 'ant':

```
E:\AutomationProject\Training\SAF\test-output>ant
Unable to locate tools.jar. Expected to find it in C:\Program Files\Java\jre8\li
b\tools.jar
Buildfile: E:\AutomationProject\Training\SAF\test-output\build.xml

usage:
     [echo]
     [echo]            ant run will execute the test
     [echo]

BUILD SUCCESSFUL
Total time: 0 seconds
```

If the BUILD SUCCESSFUL message displayed, then the build is ready for the deployment!

Similar to the query above, ant clear query should result in BUILD SUCCESSFUL as the build has been placed in this folder for compilation:

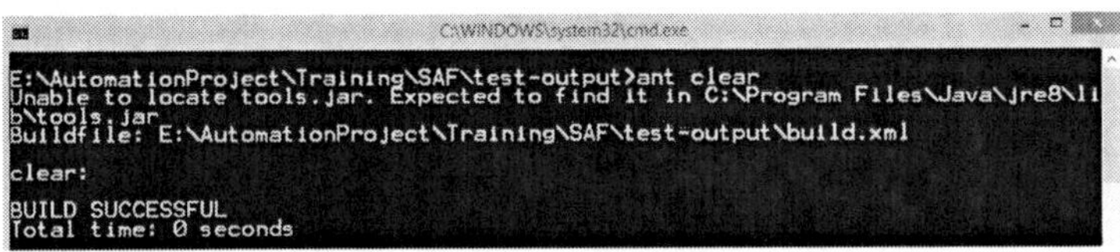

AutoIT

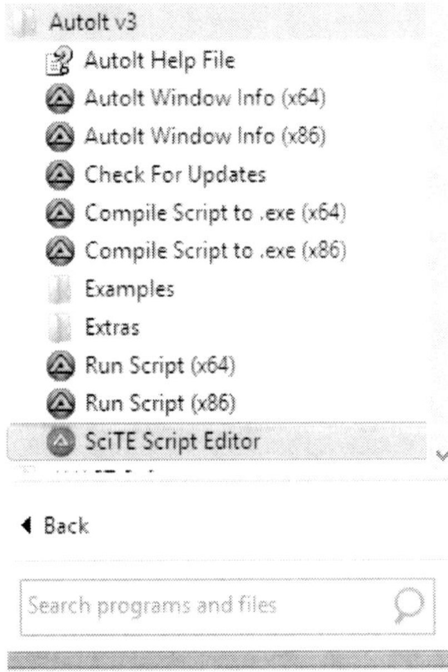

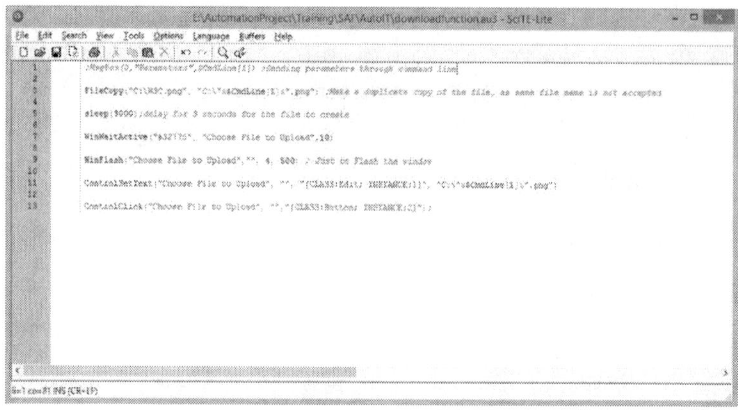

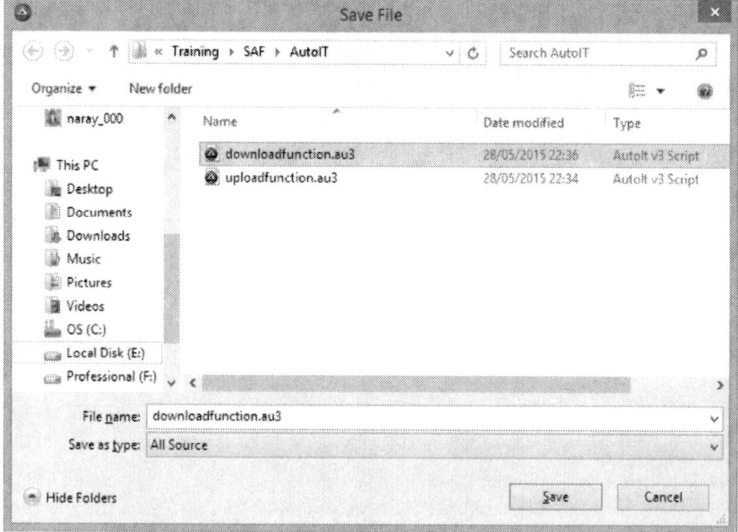

Related Videos to understand on Selenium Automation Framework:

https://www.youtube.com/user/seleniumcoaching

https://www.youtube.com/watch?v=yRHyCgy6fnM

https://www.youtube.com/watch?v=-eJ2cZXyJ0E

https://www.youtube.com/watch?v=O_9lThgxBEI

The entire project discussed on this section can be downloaded simply by this link:

https://drive.google.com/open?id=0B70x0BZZV5lzUXprYVZyVFRpaDg

Alternative Link for the same file:

https://drive.google.com/file/d/0B70x0BZZV5lzUXprYVZyVFRpaDg/view?usp=sharing

Instructions to download: Click on the link-->Open in Chrome-->Click Download button ('click download anyway button' if asked)-->Extract after download-->Place the AutomationProject Folder in C Drive or D Drive-->Once Placed, Install Eclipse as per the instructions in this section and follow below steps to access project.

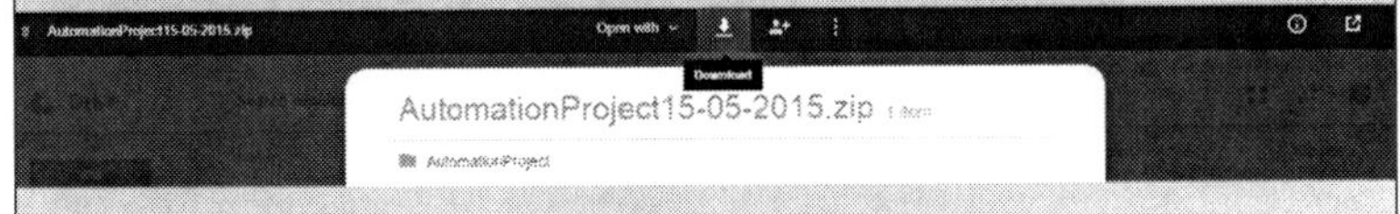

Steps to use the existing or ongoing Selenium Automation Project in Eclipse

Step1:

Place the AutomationFramework folder in C: Drive like this:

Step2:

Launch Eclipse from the folder where it has been installed (Unlike other software applications, eclipse needed to be launched by exe every time to open and access where as other softwares available in shortcuts or different links to access while launching them)

Open eclipse.exe (preferable Eclipse Luna):

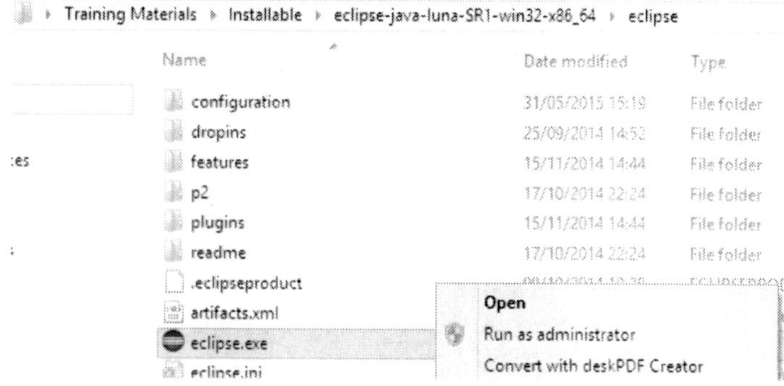

Step3:

Choose the folder of the automation framework folder and click on OK button:

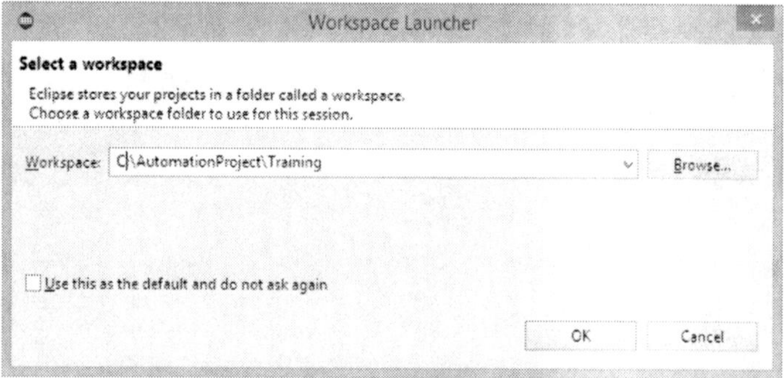

Eclipse Luna launches the screen:

Once opened Click on Workbench button and navigate to the workbench, Right click on the package explorer and choose Import:

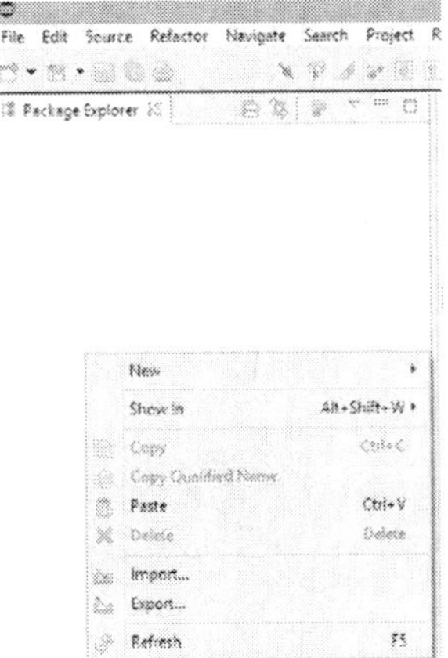

Choose Existing Project:

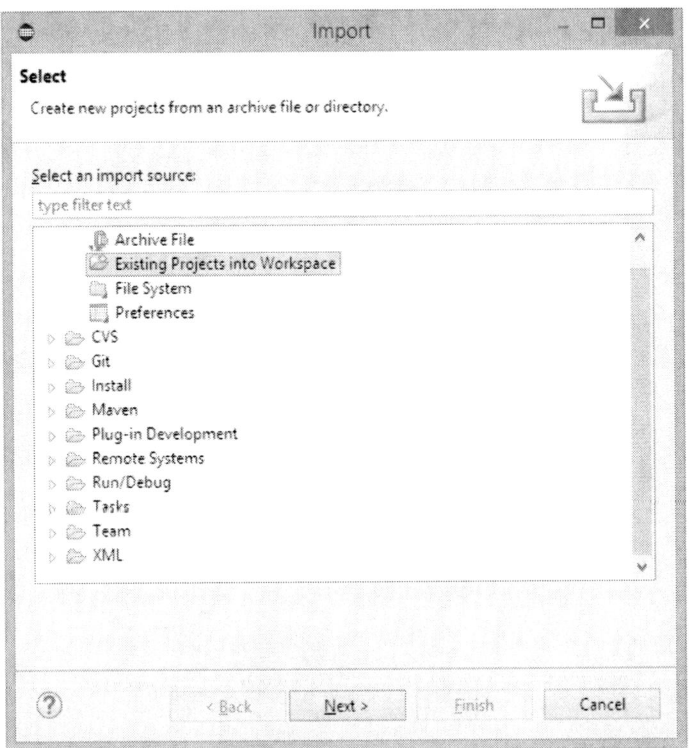

Click on the Browse button to choose the project and select both the checkboxes to search and copy the existing projects. Choose SAF project in the list and click on OK Button:

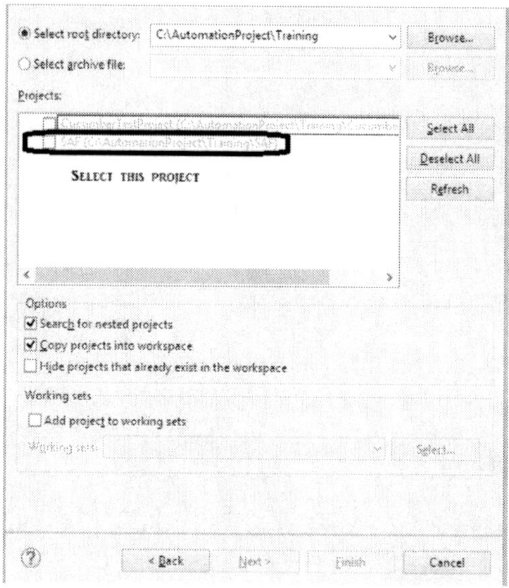

Once the SAF project is visible in Package Explorer, navigate to Configure Build Path as below:

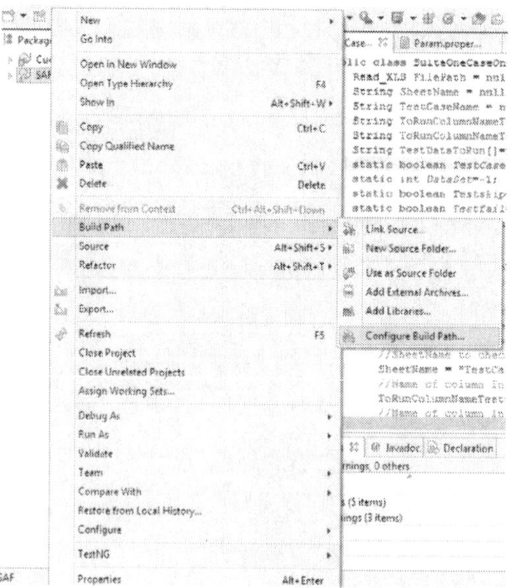

Right click on the folder SAF, click on Build Path and click on Configure Build Path as follows:

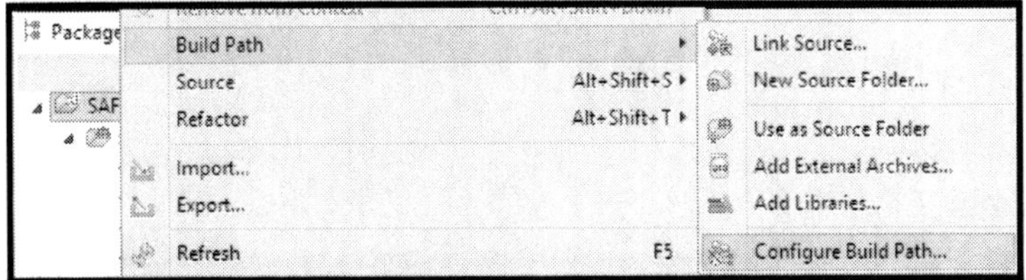

In Properties of SAF, click on the Libraries tab, click on Add External JARs button as follows:

Note: Make sure that the Libraries tab is clicked and then Add External JARs button is clicked from there.

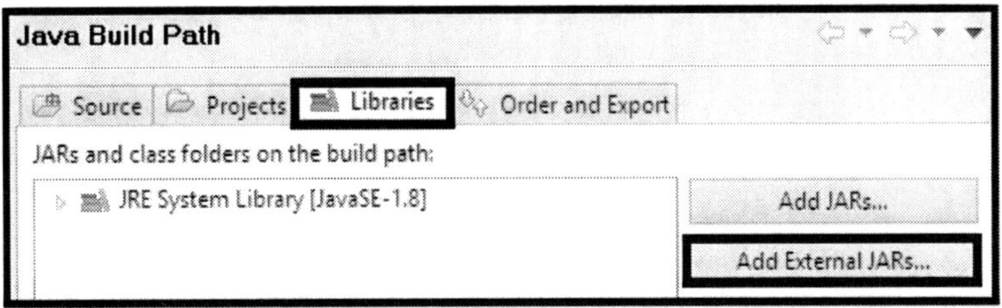

(Follow the same steps which are mentioned in this section to add all the external JARs)

Final Steps:

Click on Project--> Clean

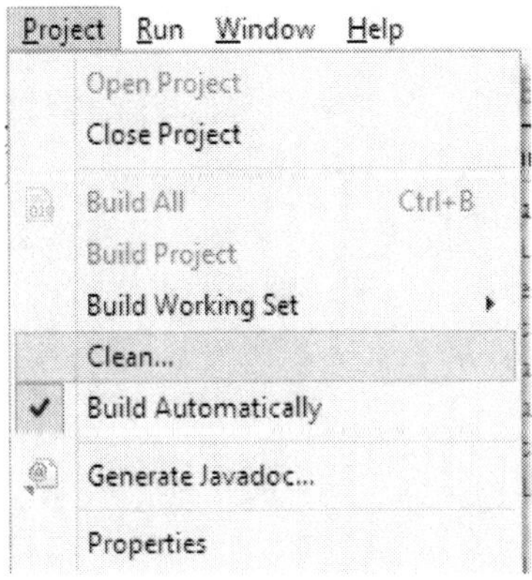

Click on Build Automatically or Build All (If it is enabled)

Now the project should be ready to execute.

Note:

Where to start the execution?: Step ' Test Execution through TestNG' in this chapter

SAF-->testoutput folder-->testng.xml file-->Right click-->Run As-->TestNG Suite

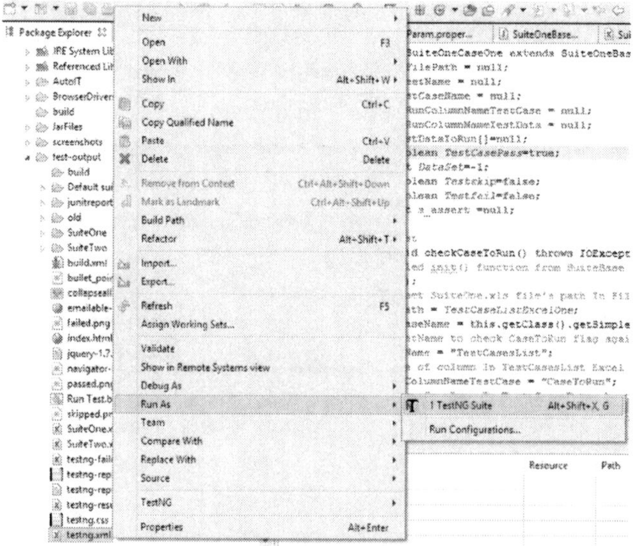

Where to start editing the scripts?

Navigate to SAF-->src-->com.stta.SuiteOne-->The Java Files where the scripts needed to be updated.

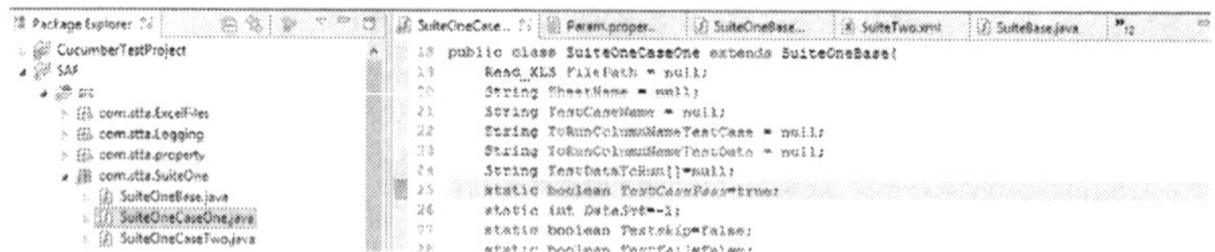

What should be the first step to review the code?

Start looking at param.properties for the URL and SuiteOneCaseOne for the navigation of the webpage while testing.

References:

What if there is an error while installing and configuring the selenium project in Eclipse?

http://stackoverflow.com/questions/2638016/why-no-projects-found-to-import

How to setup?

http://www.assertselenium.com/eclipse-2/how-to-setup-a-webdriver-project-in-eclipse/

http://stackoverflow.com/questions/18492668/how-to-execute-a-selenium-test-in-java

Need Certifications in Selenium?

Useful Links:

http://www.vskills.in/certification/Testing/Certified-Selenium-Professional

Selenium Web Driver Test Script Design Basics in JAVA

Basic Java programming knowledge is required in terms of coding the test scripts and maintaining the automation framework. As a first step, how to initiate a web based application inside a class of java file is described as follows:

```
1  package com.stta.SuiteOne;
2  import java.io.IOException;
3  import org.openqa.selenium.By;
4  import org.testng.SkipException;
5  import org.testng.annotations.AfterMethod;
6  import org.testng.annotations.AfterTest;
7  import org.testng.annotations.BeforeTest;
8  import org.testng.annotations.DataProvider;
9  import org.testng.annotations.Test;
10 import org.testng.asserts.SoftAssert;
11 import com.stta.utility.Read_XLS;
12 import com.stta.utility.SuiteUtility;
13
14 public class SuiteOneCaseOne extends SuiteOneBase{
15     @Test(dataProvider="SuiteOneCaseOneData")
16     public void SuiteOneCaseOneTest(){
17 // Enter Test Scripts Here
18     }
19
```

Every test script has to be started with package name (row 1) followed by set of imports required for the particular class in the program. For example, Selenium is required to perform automation test, so org.openqa.selenium.By is required to be mapped in import.

This is to navigate to org\openqa\selenium\ to refer relevant files required for the automation. Similar to selenium, TestNG (Automation Framework Tool) related imports has to be mentioned as part of imports.

As a generic nature of Java Program, class has to be defined by the class name (note that the file name and the class name has to be same)

Refer the section (Row 17) where the test scripts has to be written in order to invoke the application.

Launch Web Driver

```
Step1: Sample Scripts on web driver initiation

//To Initialize Firefox web browser.

WebDriver driver = new FirefoxDriver();

//To set time out 10 seconds.

driver.manage().timeouts().implicitlyWait(10, TimeUnit.
SECONDS);

//To maximize the browser.

driver.manage().window().maximize();

//To navigate to URL.

driver.get("http://www.abctest.com");

//To close the browser.

driver.close();
```

The above script will launch the respective web page and the close immediately. This script is sufficient if the browser requirement to test is only Mozilla Firefox. But most of the test projects are in need of cross browser testing. It means that the script written in

Selenium has to run in either Internet Explorer or Firefox or any given browser as per the requirement of the application.

Selenium supports Firefox, Chrome and Internet Explorer widely and it is easy to run the scripts using cross browsers in selenium framework.

As an initial implementation, browser drivers has to be places in BrowserDrivers folder in order to use the respective driver based on browser selection:

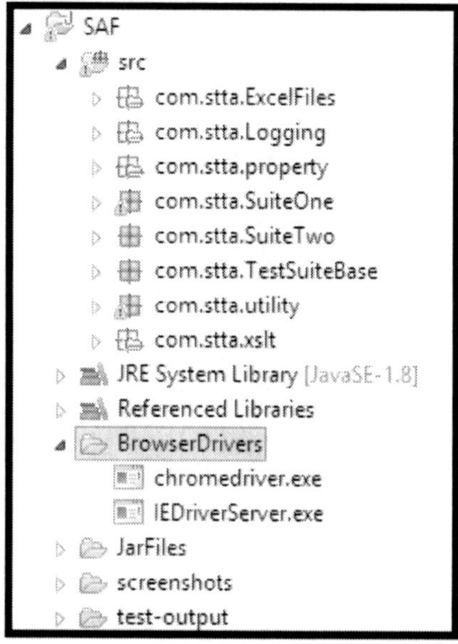

Firefox based driver is not required to provide as an external driver (similar to chrome and IE) as Firefox is supported by Selenium web driver by default.

Pre-requisite1 for Step2:

Create a Param.properties file and update the web url in the properties file. This will facilitate the script to launch the URL whenever required and it is one time activity to change the URL when there is a URL change and amendment.

```
SAF
  src
    com.stta.ExcelFiles
    com.stta.Logging
    com.stta.property
      Objects.properties
      Param.properties
    com.stta.SuiteOne
```

```
#Web Application URL
siteURL=http://www.abctest.com


#set Mozilla or Chrome or IE
testBrowser=Mozilla
```

Whenever the URL is getting changed for the project needs, it is not required to change in every part of the scripts generated. Just the param.properties has to be updated with right URL and the script is ready!

Similarly testBrowser represents the browser centrally from param. properties. If the entire script has to run Mozilla, this testBrowser has to be updated before the test Run.

Next step is to create reusable functions (classes) to handle the browsers as below

Pre-requisite1 for Step2 (Refer SuiteBase.Java file) :

When the browser is already opened in the system, the script has to pick it up automatically for the test execution. This has to be facilitated with the help of the scripts below

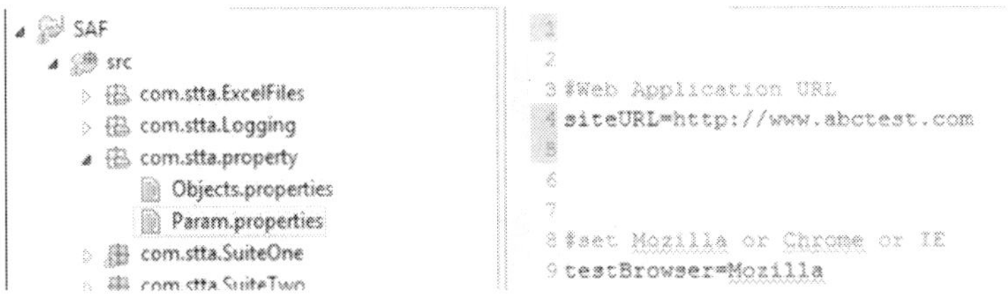

Similarly if no other driver exist in the system, automation framework should launch the browser based on the selection at param.properties as below

```
public void loadWebBrowser(){
    //Check If any previous webdriver browser Instance is exist then run new test In that existing webdriver browser Instance.
        if(Param.getProperty("testBrowser").equalsIgnoreCase("Mozilla") && ExistingmozillaBrowser!=null){
            driver = ExistingmozillaBrowser;
            return;
        }else if(Param.getProperty("testBrowser").equalsIgnoreCase("chrome") && ExistingchromeBrowser!=null){
            driver = ExistingchromeBrowser;
            return;
        }else if(Param.getProperty("testBrowser").equalsIgnoreCase("IE") && ExistingIEBrowser!=null){
            driver = ExistingIEBrowser;
            return;
        }
```

Step2(Reference: SuiteOneCaseOne.java file):

Same driver initation can be simplified by using reusable components such as loadbrowser

Now the scripts required to execute the web driver launch at any automation script (like SuiteOneCaseOne.java) is just containing two lines of code:

```
loadWebBrowser();

driver.get(Param.getProperty("siteURL"));
```

Close the webdriver

When there is no existing webdriver exist before launching the automation framework, then the script should launch a new browser, test the application and finally close the browser. If there is an existing browser, simply it has to be reused and it should not get closed at the end.

```
public void closeWebBrowser(){
    driver.close();
    //null browser Instance when close.
    ExistingchromeBrowser=null;
    ExistingmozillaBrowser=null;
    ExistingIEBrowser=null;
}
```

Read the data from excel sheets for data driven framework by locating the path of excel files as below.

```
public void init() throws IOException{
    //To initialise logger service.
    Add_Log = Logger.getLogger([illegible]);

    //Please change file's path strings below if you have stored them at location other than below.
    //Initializing Test Suite List(TestSuiteList.xls) File Path Using Constructor Of Read_XLS Utility Class.
    TestSuiteListExcel = new Read_XLS(System.getProperty([illegible])+[illegible]);
    //Initializing Test Suite One(SuiteOne.xls) File Path Using Constructor Of Read_XLS Utility Class.
    TestCaseListExcelOne = new Read_XLS(System.getProperty([illegible])+[illegible]);
    //Initializing Test Suite Two(SuiteTwo.xls) File Path Using Constructor Of Read_XLS Utility Class.
    TestCaseListExcelTwo = new Read_XLS(System.getProperty([illegible])+[illegible]);
```

The main instruction for any selenium based automation test is that the excel sheets should be closed completely before running the tests. As the excel which are opened at run time lead to errors in writing the data back to excel sheets.

> *For further reading and practice, download the projects at https://github.com/narayananpalani/testautomation*

Jason Phantom Ghost Driver Test Automation

PhantomJS is not a test framework but it facilitate the best test runner to run our tests! Headless testing of web applications (which means not using any web browser for testing!) is possible through Jason Phantom Ghost Driver.

Headless Browser Testing

This is the latest technology and fastest among the test automation where as this is not performed by any GUI based web browsers; Since the tests are running in background, they run in rapid speed with Selenium. This headless browser is a pure java solution designed based on Rhino Automation Engine and it is not dependent to any browser or operating system! Tests run in the background and provide results to tester faster than IE/Firefox/Chrome based tests.

Install PhantomJS

Download Jason Phantom through http://phantomjs.org/download.html

Once Installed, clicking on exe file inside bin folder displays this command prompt:

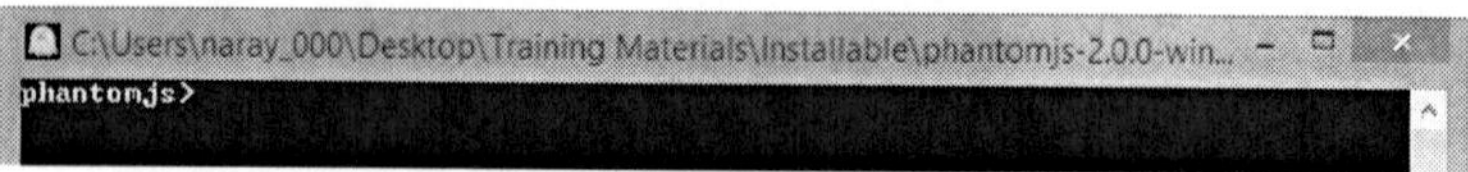

Download the JAR (phantomjsdriver-1.2.1.jar) to use in Eclipse based projects at

https://drive.google.com/a/raghava.co.uk/file/d/0B6vnknygMB3IczZQVGQzNTloZ2c/view

Alternatively this JAR file can be downloaded from Installable folder of https://github.com/narayananpalani/testautomation

Once the JAR file is downloaded, add it to the build path of the project.

How to add in the build path?

Right click on the project and Build Path>Configure Build Path>

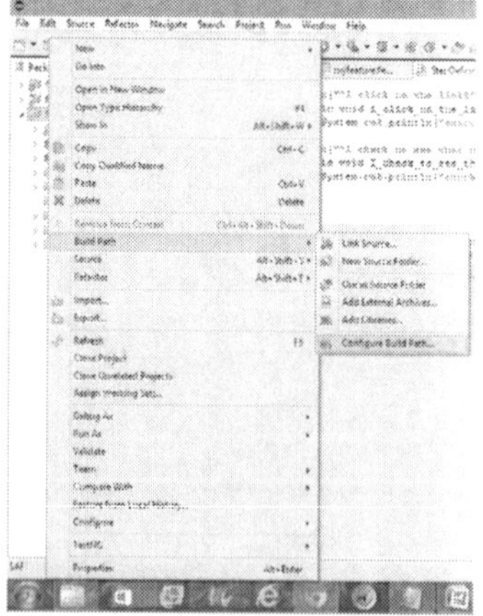

Select Libraries>Add External Jars>Select phantomjsdriver-1.2.1.jar. Once added, it looks like the below screenshot:

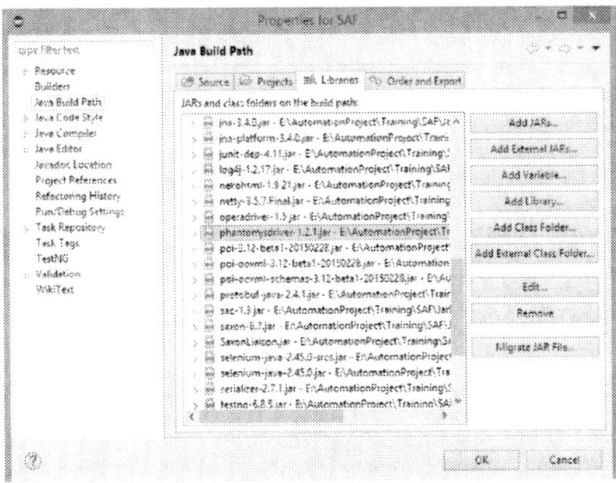

Once the phantomJs has been configured, go to your project java files and create a java file phantomjs.java and paste the below script (and make sure that the package name is edited in first line based on the package name in your project)

```
package com.stta.SuiteOne;

import java.io.File;
import java.io.IOException;
import java.util.concurrent.TimeUnit;

import org.apache.commons.io.FileUtils;
import org.openqa.selenium.By;
import org.openqa.selenium.JavascriptExecutor;
import org.openqa.selenium.OutputType;
import org.openqa.selenium.TakesScreenshot;
import org.openqa.selenium.WebDriver;
import org.openqa.selenium.phantomjs.PhantomJSDriver;
import org.openqa.selenium.phantomjs.PhantomJSDriverService;
import org.openqa.selenium.remote.DesiredCapabilities;
import org.testng.annotations.BeforeTest;
import org.testng.annotations.Test;

public class phantomjs {

 WebDriver driver;
```

@BeforeTest

public void setup() **throws** Exception {

//Set phantomjs.exe executable file path using DesiredCapabilities.

DesiredCapabilities capability = **new** DesiredCapabilities();

//Make sure that the path of exe file has been provided here with / for //every folder like the below:

capability.setCapability(PhantomJSDriverService.PHANTOMJS_EXECUTABLE_PATH_PROPERTY, "C:/Users/naray_000/Desktop/Training Materials/Installable/phantomjs-2.0.0-windows/phantomjs-2.0.0-windows/bin/phantomjs.exe");

driver = **new** PhantomJSDriver(capability);driver.manage().timeouts().implicitlyWait(15, TimeUnit.SECONDS);

}

@Test

public void phantomTest() **throws** IOException{

driver.get("http://www.reed.co.uk/");

driver.findElement(By.*xpath*("id('topSignInLink')")).click();

//Update your registered user name driver.findElement(By.*xpath*("id('topSignInEmail')")).sendKeys("test@test.com");

//Update your registered password

driver.findElement(By.*xpath*("id('topSignInPassword')")).sendKeys("abcd1234");

```
driver.findElement(By.xpath("id('topSignInPanel')/div[4]/div/span/input")).click();

driver.findElement(By.xpath("id('keywords')")).sendKeys("Software Tester");

driver.findElement(By.xpath("id('location')")).sendKeys("cv313qd");

driver.findElement(By.xpath("id('homepageSearchButton')")).click();

JavascriptExecutor js = (JavascriptExecutor) driver;

js.executeScript("javascript:window.scrollBy(250, 350)");

driver.findElement(By.xpath("id('jobSection27977887')/div/header/div/h3/a")).click();


driver.findElement(By.xpath("id('applyBtn')")).click();

driver.findElement(By.xpath("id('submitBtn')")).click();

 //To capture page screenshot and save In D: drive.

File scrFile = ((TakesScreenshot)driver).getScreenshotAs(OutputType.FILE);

FileUtils.copyFile(scrFile, new File("C:\\Test.jpeg"), true);

 }

}
```

Once the JAVA file is added to the project, right click on the java file and Run As, TestNG suite. Since it is headless browser test, it runs in the background and provide the results once completed!

Maven Test Automation

Apache Maven is helpful to build the projects and manage the java based projects as Process Object Model (POM) of Maven is wide used across IT industry for test automation. Primarily it is an excellent build automation tool!

How to Install Maven from Eclipse IDE?

It can be installed in Eclipse IDE through Help tab>Install New Software>

Enter URL as http://download.eclipse.org/technology/m2e/releases

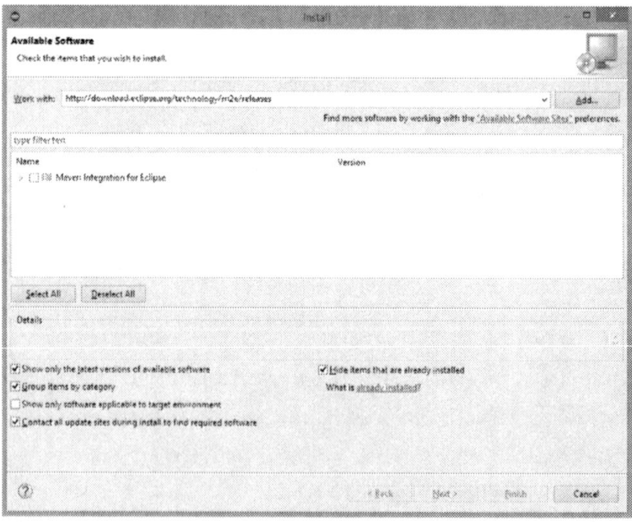

Once it has been installed at Eclipse it can be verified by Window tab>Preferences>

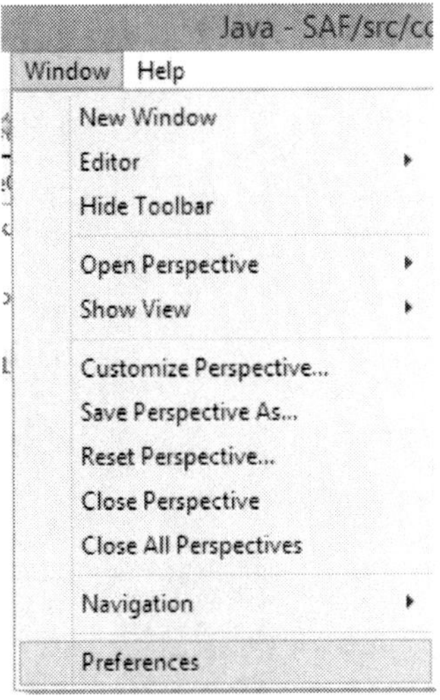

Display Maven in the list as follows:

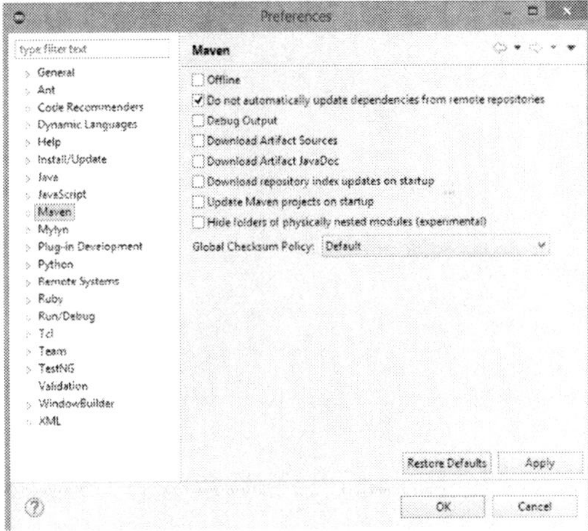

Press OK and then go ahead to create a new maven project for your automation project!

Create Maven Project

New project can be created by File>New>Other

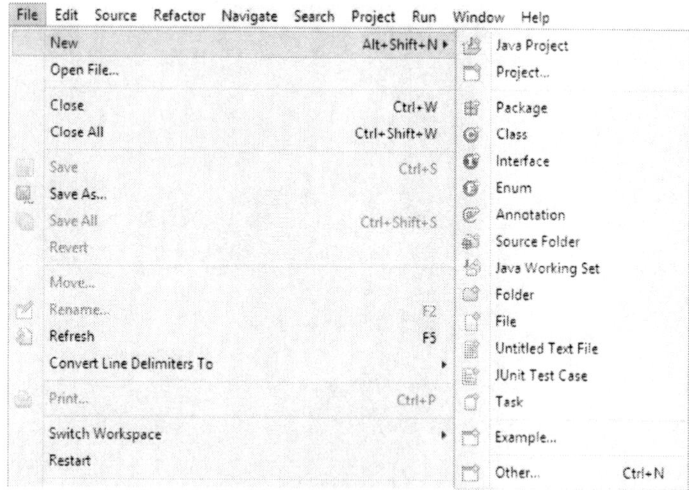

Select a Maven Folder>Maven Project as follows:

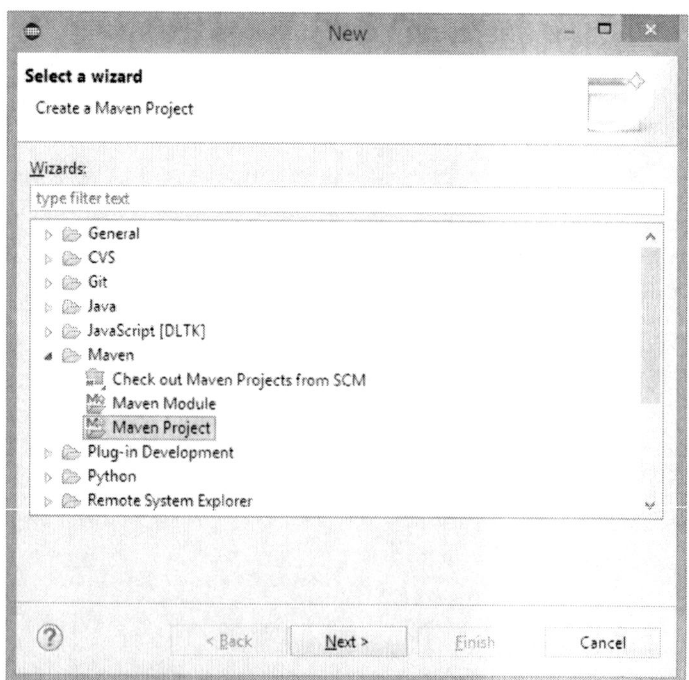

Click Next in the box below:

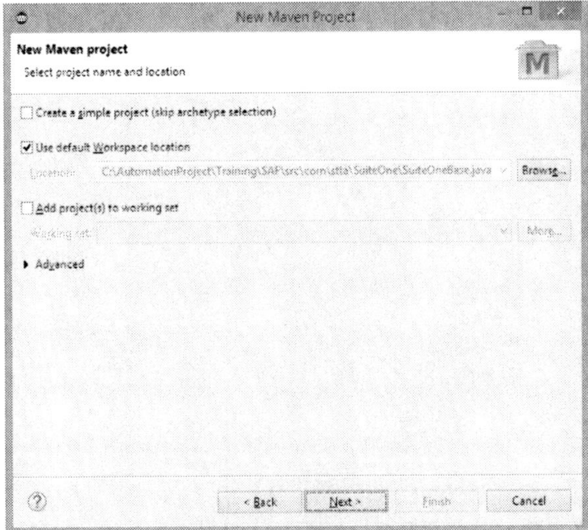

Select QuickStart Artificact ID as below and click on Next:

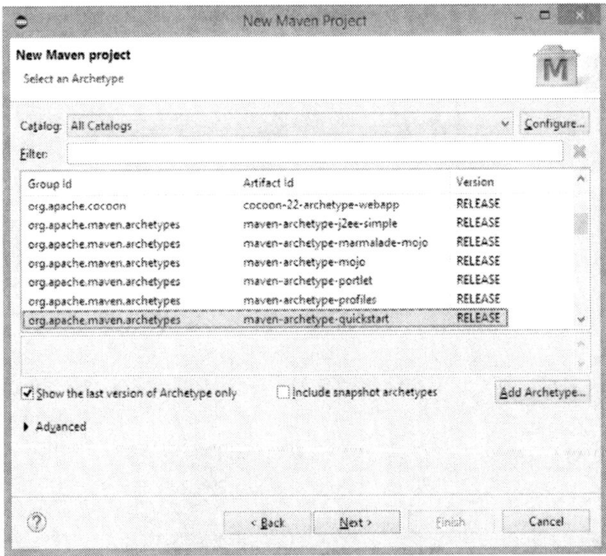

Enter the project details as below:

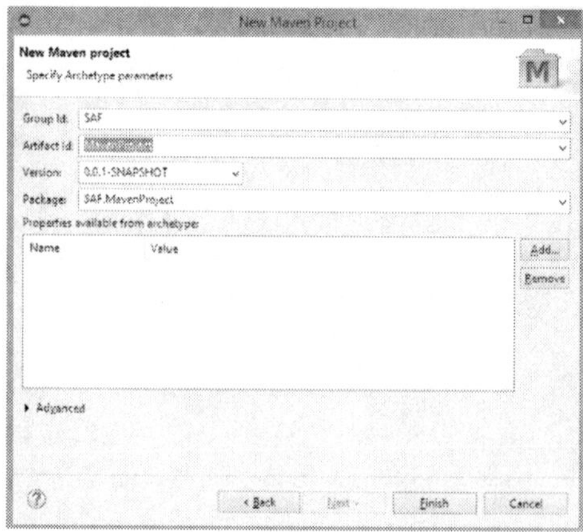

Select POM.xml and then navigate to the script to update the selenium and TestNG versions which are needed to the project:

```
CucumberTestProject
MavenProject
  src/main/java
  src/test/java
  JRE System Library [J2SE-1.5]
  Maven Dependencies
  Referenced Libraries
  src
  target
  pom.xml
SAF
```

```
<project xmlns="http://maven.apache.org/POM/4.0.0" xmlns:
  xsi:schemaLocation="http://maven.apache.org/POM/4.0.0
  <modelVersion>4.0.0</modelVersion>

  <groupId>SAF</groupId>
  <artifactId>MavenProject</artifactId>
  <version>0.0.1-SNAPSHOT</version>
  <packaging>jar</packaging>

  <name>MavenProject</name>
  <url>http://maven.apache.org</url>

  <properties>
    <project.build.sourceEncoding>UTF-8</project.build.
  </properties>
  <dependencies>
    <dependency>
      <groupId>org.seleniumhq.selenium</groupId>
      <artifactId>selenium-java</artifactId>
      <version>2.45.0</version>
    </dependency>
    <dependency>
    <groupId>org.testng</groupId>
    <artifactId>testng</artifactId>
    <version>6.8.5</version>
    <scope>test</scope>
  </dependency>
  </dependencies>
</project>
```

Sample POM File

<project xmlns=*"http://maven.apache.org/POM/4.0.0"*
xmlns:xsi=*"http://www.w3.org/2001/XMLSchema-instance"*
xsi:schemaLocation=*"http://maven.apache.org/POM/4.0.0 http://maven.apache.org/xsd/maven-4.0.0.xsd"*>
<modelVersion>4.0.0</modelVersion>

<groupId>SAF</groupId>
<artifactId>MavenProject</artifactId>

```
<version>0.0.1-SNAPSHOT</version>
<packaging>jar</packaging>

<name>MavenProject</name>
<url>http://maven.apache.org</url>

<properties>
<project.build.sourceEncoding>UTF-8</project.build.
sourceEncoding>
</properties>
<dependencies>
  <dependency>
   <groupId>org.seleniumhq.selenium</groupId>
   <artifactId>selenium-java</artifactId>
   <version>2.45.0</version>
  </dependency>
  <dependency>
  <groupId>org.testng</groupId>
  <artifactId>testng</artifactId>
  <version>6.8.5</version>
  <scope>test</scope>
</dependency>
 </dependencies>
</project>
```

Add External Jars of Selenium and TestNG

Main Selenium Webdriver based Jar files for Selenium Automation Framework:

The very important test engine of the automation framework is the testing tool. Especially Selenium is made up of JAR files which evolves over a period of time to upgraded versions. So make sure that the latest version of file has been downloaded from the link below.

Download the files from http://docs.seleniumhq.org/download/

Selenium Client & WebDriver Language Bindings

In order to create scripts that interact with the Selenium Server (Selenium RC, Selenium Remote Webdriver) or create local Selenium WebDriver script you need to make use of language-specific client drivers. These languages include both 1.x and 2.x style clients.

While language bindings for other languages exist, these are the core ones that are supported by the main project hosted on google code.

Language	Client Version	Release Date			
Java	2.45.0	2015-02-26	Download	Change log	Javadoc
C#	2.45.0	2015-02-27	Download	Change log	API docs
Ruby	2.45.0	2015-02-27	Download	Change log	API docs
Python	2.45.0	2015-02-26	Download	Change log	API docs
Javascript (Node)	2.45.0	2015-02-26	Download	Change log	API docs

Once the files are downloaded, make sure that all the jar files from this file (including the jar files from sub folders of this file) are pasted into JarFiles folder which is created for the automation framework.

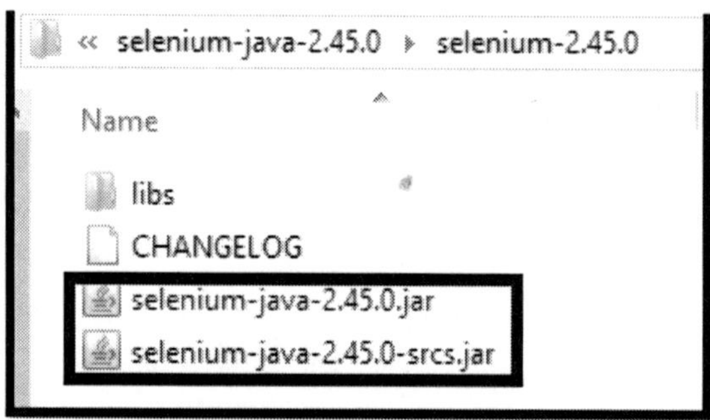

TestNG Plug-in to use the XSLT Reports:

TestNG is used mainly to run the test scripts generated in Selenium. So this needs to be extended to XSLT reporting jar files using the plugin. So the reports get the latest test execution status automatically. Download the plugin from the below link and paste to the JarFiles folder as it is an important plug-in to capture the test results.

Link:

https://drive.google.com/file/d/0B6vnknygMB3IdzF4X2taWFRRMVE/edit

JarFiles Folder Structure after pasting the plugin:

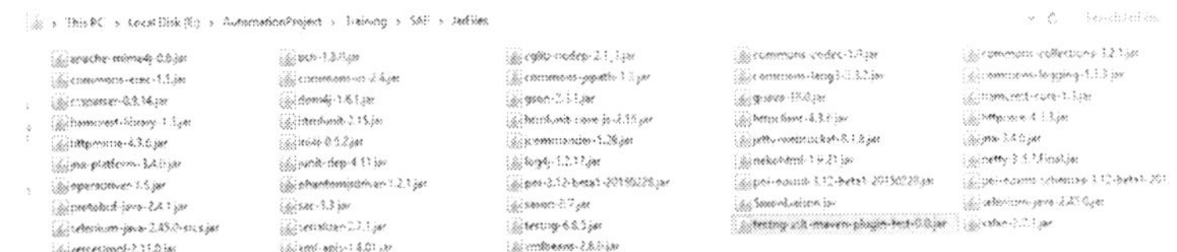

Project Build Path Configuration for Maven

The need of placing all the relevant JAR files into one central location in automation framework is to access them to configure the project MavenProject.

Right click on the folder MavenProject, click on Build Path and click on Configure Build Path as follows:

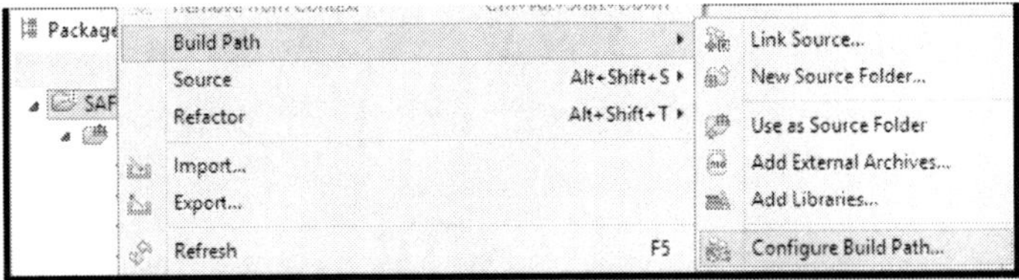

In Properties of Maven Project, click on the Libraries tab, click on Add External JARs button as follows:

Note: Make sure that the Libraries tab is clicked and then Add External JARs button is clicked from there.

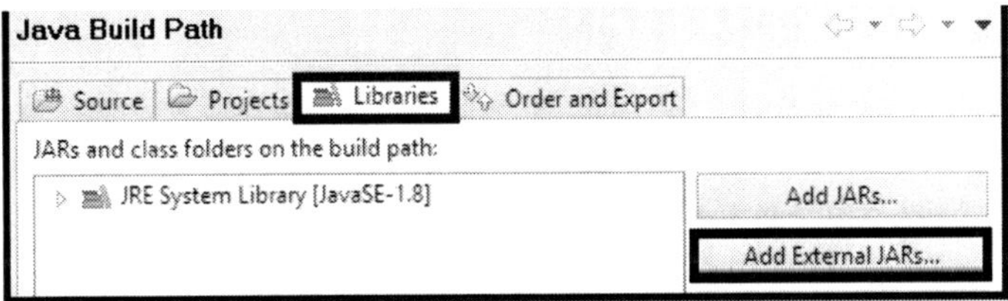

Select the path of the JarFiles (relevant to Selenium and TestNG) folder and select all the JAR files in the folder and then click on Open button:

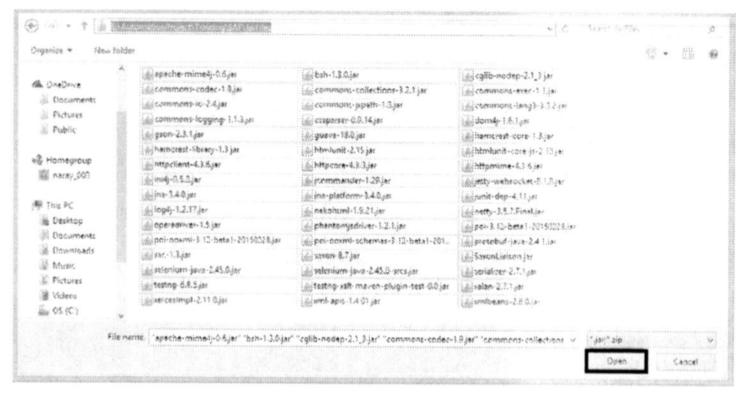

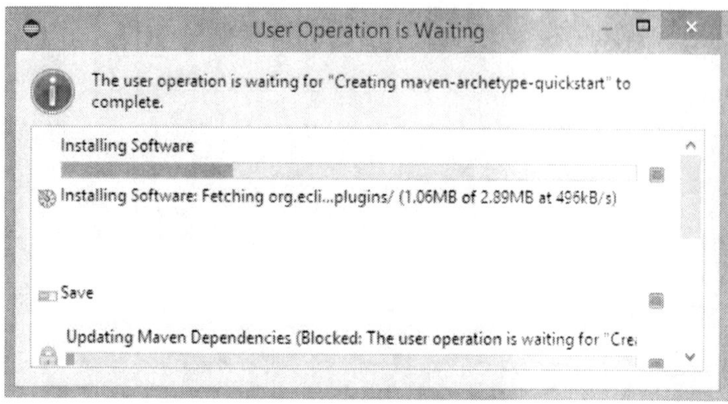

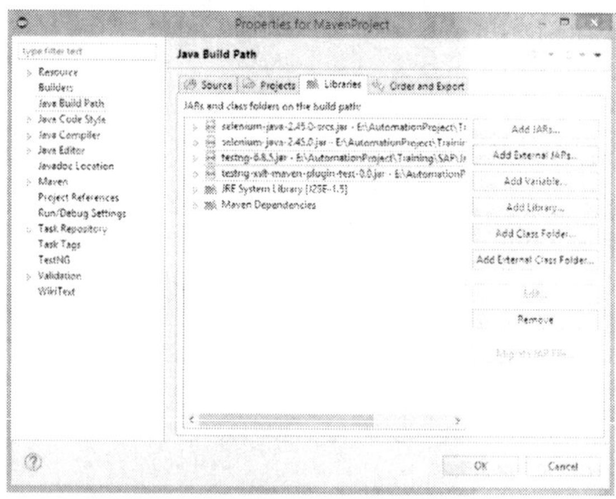

Make sure that the added external jar's version and the pom.xml's version of selenium & TestNG resemble same as per the script below:

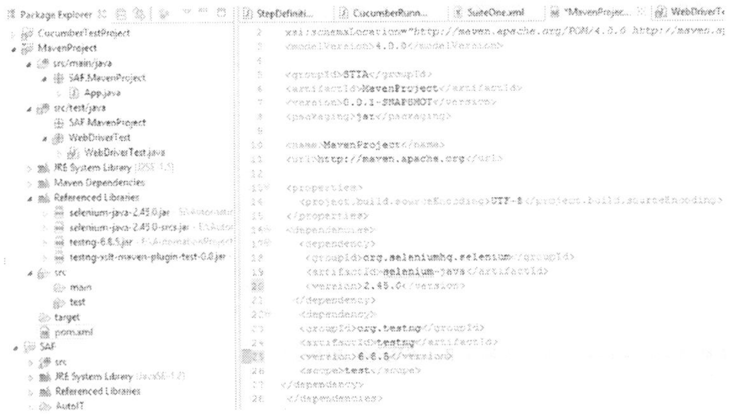

Delete the existing app.java project within src/test/java

Add the below script as a WebDriverTest.java:

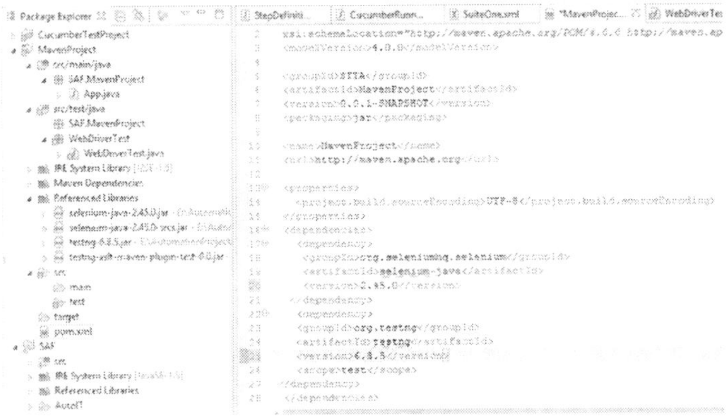

Script for Maven based Selenium Web Driver Project

/*This is a sample project on a job portal to login and apply for a job-make sure that you register for a valid account and update email id and password in the below script: */

package SAF.MavenProject;

import org.openqa.selenium.By;
import org.openqa.selenium.JavascriptExecutor;

```
import org.openqa.selenium.WebDriver;
import org.openqa.selenium.firefox.FirefoxDriver;
import org.testng.annotations.Test;

public class WebDriverTest {
 WebDriver driver;
  @Test
  public void verifySearch() {
   driver = new FirefoxDriver();
   driver.get("http://www.reed.co.uk/");

   driver.findElement(By.xpath("id('topSignInLink')")).click();
              driver.findElement(By.xpath("id('topSignInEmail')")).
sendKeys("test@gmail.com");
           driver.findElement(By.xpath("id('topSignInPassword')")).
sendKeys("abcd1234");
      driver.findElement(By.xpath("id('topSignInPanel')/div[4]/div/
span/input")).click();
                    driver.findElement(By.xpath("id('keywords')")).
sendKeys("Software Tester");
                     driver.findElement(By.xpath("id('location')")).
sendKeys("cv313qd");
      driver.findElement(By.xpath("id('homepageSearchButton')")).
click();
     JavascriptExecutor js = (JavascriptExecutor) driver;
      js.executeScript("javascript:window.scrollBy(250, 350)");
        driver.findElement(By.xpath("id('jobSection27977887')/div/
header/div/h3/a")).click();
    driver.findElement(By.xpath("id('applyBtn')")).click();
    driver.findElement(By.xpath("id('submitBtn')")).click();
   driver.quit();
  }
}
```

Run Maven Test

Once the script is added and the amendments are made, Run the test by right clicking on the pom.xml and select Maven Test:

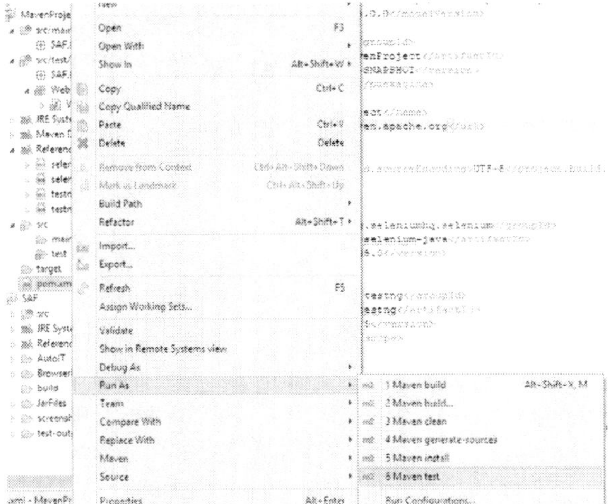

How to run the Maven Project from Command Prompt?

Download Maven from the link below:

http://maven.apache.org/download.cgi

Set Environment Variables:

Navigate to Control Panel and select Advanced System Settings. In Advanced Tab, click on Environment Variables:

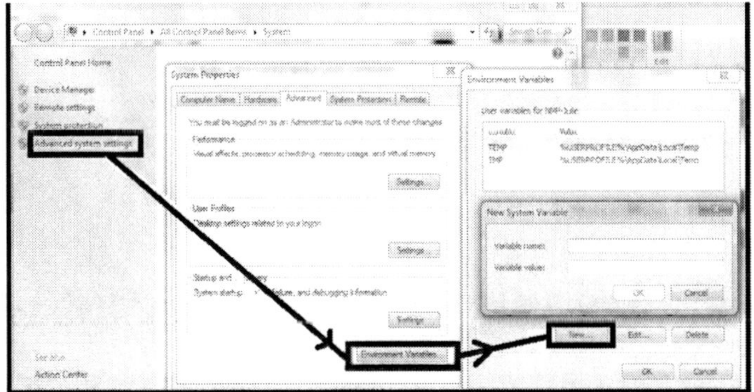

Click on New button and enter the location of JDK folder:

Update the M2_HOME in Environment Variables:

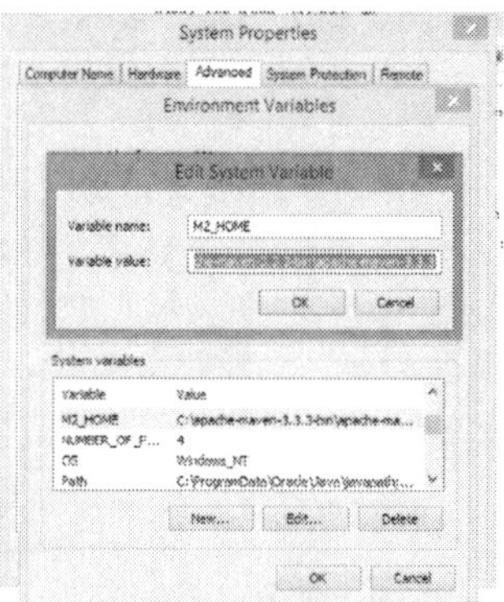

Set the path as the bin file location of the Maven folder:

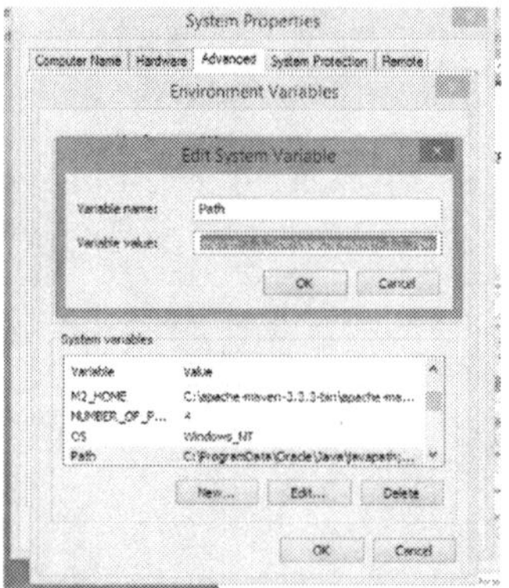

How to check the Maven Project has been installed?

Type mvn -version from command prompt as below:

```
Microsoft Windows [Version 6.3.9600]
(c) 2013 Microsoft Corporation. All rights reserved.

C:\Users\naray_000>mvn -version
Apache Maven 3.3.3 (7994120775791599e205a5524ec3e0dfe41d4a06; 2015-04-22T12:57:37+01:00)
Maven home: C:\apache-maven-3.3.3-bin\apache-maven-3.3.3
Java version: 1.8.0_45, vendor: Oracle Corporation
Java home: C:\Program Files\Java\jdk1.8.0_45\jre
Default locale: en_GB, platform encoding: Cp1252
OS name: "windows 8.1", version: "6.3", arch: "amd64", family: "dos"
```

Create a folder within C: Drive or any valid Drive:

Navigate to the folder and type mvn archetype:generate

```
C:\WINDOWS\system32\cmd.e
Microsoft Windows [Version 6.3.9600]
(c) 2013 Microsoft Corporation. All rights reserved.

C:\Users\naray_000>mvn -version
Apache Maven 3.3.3 (7994120775791599e205a5524ec3e0dfe41d4a06; 2015-04-22T12:57:37+01:00)
Maven home: C:\apache-maven-3.3.3-bin\apache-maven-3.3.3
Java version: 1.8.0_45, vendor: Oracle Corporation
Java home: C:\Program Files\Java\jdk1.8.0_45\jre
Default locale: en_GB, platform encoding: Cp1252
OS name: "windows 8.1", version: "6.3", arch: "amd64", family: "dos"

C:\Users\naray_000>cd\

C:\>d:
The device is not ready.

C:\>cd Maven
The system cannot find the path specified.

C:\>cd Maven

C:\Maven>mvn archetype:generate
```

Press Enter for all the numbers asked:

```
C:\WINDOWS\system32\cmd.exe - mvn archetype:generate
...
number or apply filter (format: [groupId:]artifactId, case sensitive contains): 653:
...
value for property 'groupId': :
```

Enter com.demopack as group id:

Artifact ID:

```
property 'groupId': : com.demopack
property 'artifactId': : MavenProject
```

Build Success:

```
Choose a number or apply filter (format: [groupId:]artifactId, case sensitive con
Choose org.apache.maven.archetypes:maven-archetype-quickstart version:
1: 1.0-alpha-1
2: 1.0-alpha-2
3: 1.0-alpha-3
4: 1.0-alpha-4
5: 1.0
6: 1.1
Choose a number: 6:
Define value for property 'groupId': : com.demopack
Define value for property 'artifactId': : MavenProject
Define value for property 'version':  1.0-SNAPSHOT: :
Define value for property 'package':  com.demopack: :
Confirm properties configuration:
groupId: com.demopack
artifactId: MavenProject
version: 1.0-SNAPSHOT
package: com.demopack
 Y: :
[INFO] ----------------------------------------------------------------------------
[INFO] Using following parameters for creating project from Old (1.x) Archetype:
[INFO] ----------------------------------------------------------------------------
[INFO] Parameter: basedir, Value: C:\Maven
[INFO] Parameter: package, Value: com.demopack
[INFO] Parameter: groupId, Value: com.demopack
[INFO] Parameter: artifactId, Value: MavenProject
[INFO] Parameter: packageName, Value: com.demopack
[INFO] Parameter: version, Value: 1.0-SNAPSHOT
[INFO] project created from Old (1.x) Archetype in dir: C:\Maven\MavenProject
[INFO] ----------------------------------------------------------------------------
[INFO] BUILD SUCCESS
[INFO] ----------------------------------------------------------------------------
[INFO] Total time: 06:18 min
[INFO] Finished at: 2015-10-03T16:07:24+01:00
[INFO] Final Memory: 13M/68M
[INFO] ----------------------------------------------------------------------------

C:\Maven>
```

Once the build is success, verify that the src folder and pom.xml getting created within MavenProject and go ahead and edit the script as described earlier in eclipse steps.

How to add the project into scheduled tasks of Jenkins and why?

When the automation tests are long running by itself and provide test results, it is always feasible to time it in most possible ways. Many projects target on evening test executions as the test goes on overnight and provide test results by morning.

How to set up the Eclipse executable project in Jenkins?

Steps:

1) Install Jenkins and open the url localhost:8080

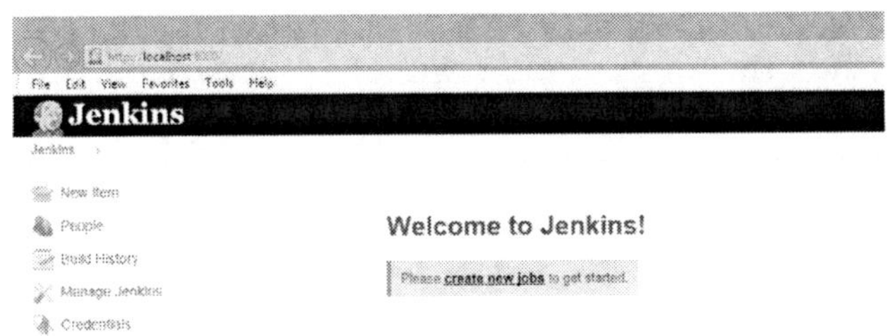

2. Once Jenkins is opened, click on Add New Item (new project)

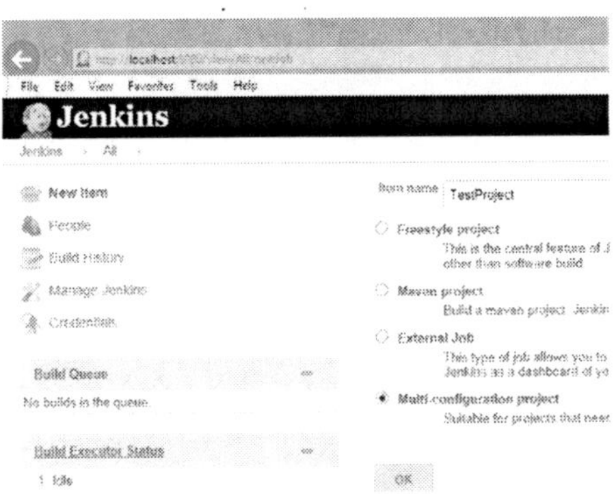

3. Click Configure>Build>Add a build step>Execute Windows batch command

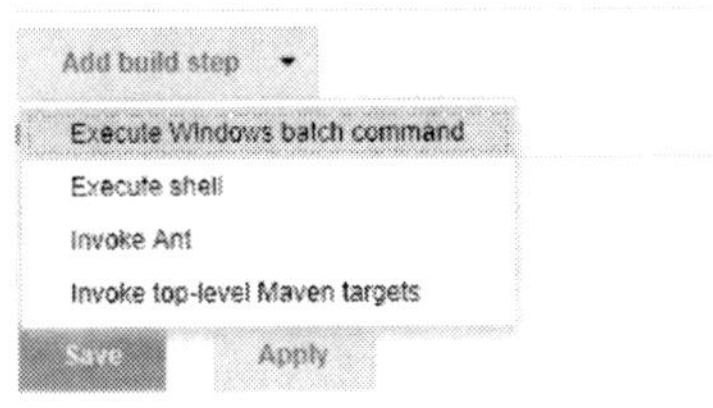

You can run the Eclipse project from command line as follows:

C: \eclipse\eclipsec -nosplash -application org.eclipse.jdt.apt.core.aptBuild -data %WORKSPACE%

So add the respective command line to run the eclipse project command line instructions from Jenkin itself.

4. Post Build Actions section> Add your email id

Schedule the projects in Jenkins

Automation projects can be scheduled in Jenkins with specific timings! This can be done by adding Crone Expression to the build.

Crone Expression:

String comprised of five fields with whitespace

For Eg: H 16 04 10 * which means 16:4PM; 04: 04th Day;10:October

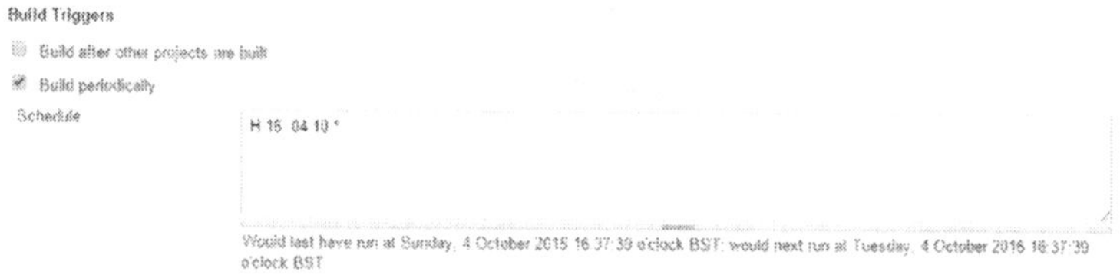

Build Triggers

Build after other projects are built

Build periodically

Schedule H 16 04 10 *

Would last have run at Sunday, 4 October 2015 16:37:39 o'clock BST; would next run at Tuesday, 4 October 2016 16:37:39 o'clock BST

Automation Framework using Selenium Web driver with DotNet

DotNet based Selenium Web driver projects using C++ Programming is a most wanted skillset in IT Testing Domain! Especially Integrating the project from Feature file (as Scenarios), Step Definitions, Selenium Objects and Functions and then build the project to deploy and run in tools such NUnit/Gallio/MSTest or alternatively schedule it through Jenkins is something end to end automation Implementation possibility at the moment in the industry!

Step by Step Approach!

Step1: Install Visual Studio

Navigate to any best solution of visual studio (free version preferably for training) at:

https://www.visualstudio.com/products/free-developer-offers-vs.aspx

Step2:Install and Configure Specflow

Select Tools and then 'Extensions and Updates' in Visual Studio and search online for SpecFlow (whatever the relevant latest version); Select the SpecFlow for Visual Studio 2013 (any latest version) extension to download and install. Restart Visual Studio to enable the extension. (Perform all necessary configurations required for BDD projects as per the Specflow chapter)

Step3: Selenium Web Driver for DotNet

Install Selenium Web driver through Package Manager Console as follows:

Select Tools and then Package Manager Console

PM>

Command: PM> Install-Package Selenium.WebDriver

Make sure that the following references are updated in the project

Selenium WebDriver API .NET Bindings and Selenium WebDriver .NET Bindings support classes:

- References
  - Microsoft.VisualStudio.QualityTools.UnitTestFramework
  - nunit.framework
  - SpecRun.SpecFlowPlugin
  - System
  - System.Drawing
  - TechTalk.SpecFlow
  - TechTalk.SpecRun
  - WebDriver
  - WebDriver.Support

Reference: https://www.nuget.org/packages/Selenium.WebDriver

Step4: Feature File

Right click on the project, select Add Item and choose Specflow Feature File and Add to open the new feature file:

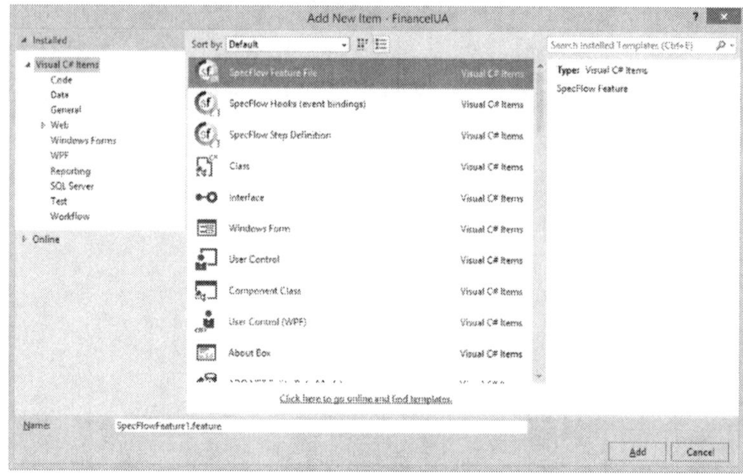

It would have been added and .cs file would have been associated by itself:

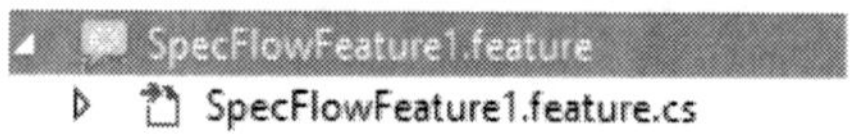

Write a scenario like this Example:

Feature: Currency Exchange Rate in ABC Bank

In order to avoid silly mistakes

As a anonymous user

I want to check average INR exchange rate of banks in London

@RegressionTests

Scenario: average INR exchange rate of banks in London

Given I have opened the ABC Accounts page

And I have grabbed average "INR" rate in Exchange Rate section

Then I set "INR" currency in ABC Banks Today Exchange rates section

When I compare calculated and rate along with fee values the result should be correct

Click on Generate Step Definitions:

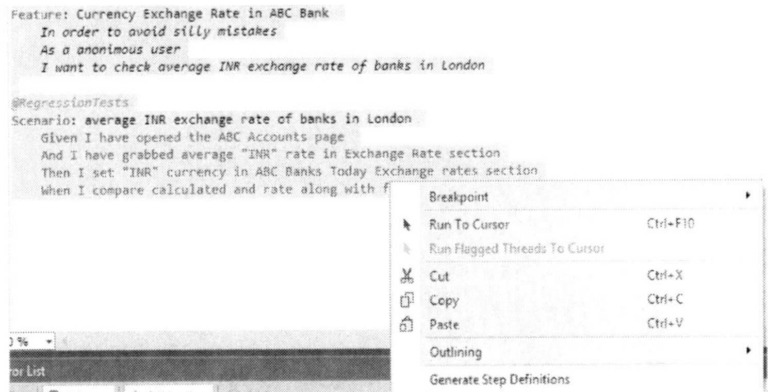

Copy to clipboard and paste them to different .cs file to edit further:

```
[Given(@"I have opened the ABC Accounts page")]
public void GivenIHaveOpenedTheABCAccountsPage()
{
    ScenarioContext.Current.Pending();
}

[Given(@"I have grabbed average ""(.*)"" rate in Exchange Rate section")]
public void GivenIHaveGrabbedAverageRateInExchangeRateSection(string p0)
{
    ScenarioContext.Current.Pending();
}
```

[Then(@"I set ""(.*)""" currency in ABC Banks Today Exchange rates section")]

public void ThenISetCurrencyInABCBanksTodayExchangeRatesSection(string p0)

{

ScenarioContext.Current.Pending();

}

[When(@"I compare calculated and rate along with fee values the result should be correct")]

public void WhenICompareCalculated AndRateAlongWithFeeValuesTheResultShouldBeCorrect()

{

ScenarioContext.Current.Pending();

}

Another Example:

Develop the feature file with scenarios in Gherkin format and save it as a .feature file

*Refer Gherkin/Specflow sections

Example:

Feature: Currency Exchange Rate in ABC Bank

In order to avoid silly mistakes
As a anonymous user
I want to check average USD exchange rate of banks in London

@RegressionTests
Scenario: average USD exchange rate of banks in London

Given I have opened the ABC Finance page
And I have grabbed average "*USD*" rate in Average Rate section
Then I set "*USD*" currency in ABC Banks rates section
When I compare calculated and grabbed values the result should be equal to "*4*" decimal

Step5: Step Definitions

In the .cs file associated to your feature file, write the line based script.

Right click on the Feature file and select Generate Step Definitions' and copy that to clipboard and paste to this .cs file and then edit the .cs files with valid Selenium Functions.

Example:

```
using System;
using System.Collections;
using FinanceIUA.PageObjects;
using NUnit.Framework;
using OpenQA.Selenium;
//using OpenQA.Selenium.Firefox;
using OpenQA.Selenium.Chrome;
using TechTalk.SpecFlow;

----

----

[BeforeScenario()]
public void Setup()
{
//driver = new FirefoxDriver();
//This is the initiation of a chrome browser and the location where
the driver is:
driver = new ChromeDriver(@"E:\driver");
```

```
//driver = new ChromeDriver();
}

---

---

[Given(@"I have opened the ABC Finance page")]
public void GivenIHaveOpenedTheABCFinancePage()
{
financePage = ABCFinancePage.NavigateTo(driver);
driver.Manage().Timeouts().ImplicitlyWait(TimeSpan.
FromSeconds(10));
driver.Navigate().GoToUrl("http://www.abcbank.org/");
}
```

For further reading and practice, download the projects at https://github.com/narayananpalani/testautomation

How to run the Visual Studio based Selenium Project in NUnit?

NUnit gives the flexibility to run the visual studio based projects with minor settings update as follows,

1. Install NUnit
2. In Tools>Settings> Select checkbox for Enable Visual Studio Support and Use solution configs when opening VS solutions

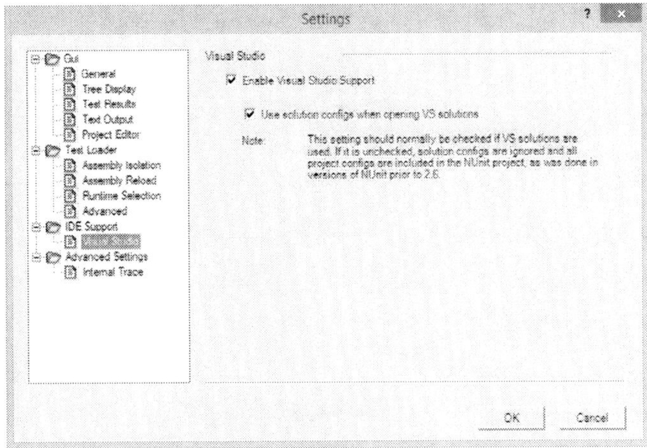

3. In Tree Display, select the checkbox for 'Show checkboxes' which will allow user to select the respective tests to run during test execution:

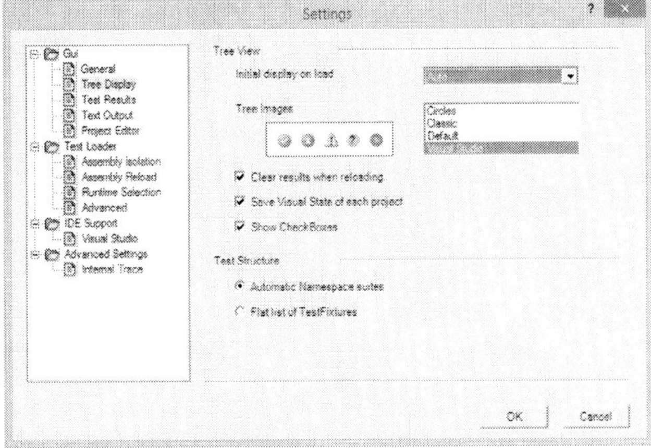

Once the tests are executed, click on Tools>Save Results as XML to save the test results

ReportUnit

This tool helps in developing an html based report out of xml report of NUnit.

Download URL: http://reportunit.relevantcodes.com/

Once the tool has been downloaded, run the tool from command line with following syntax:

reportunit [input-folder-path] [output-folder-path]

Assume that the xml files of test results are stored at C drive's Result folder and you need the ReportUnit Reports at Reports folder, this can be done using following steps:

1. Install Reportunit
2. Go to command line where Reportunit is placed
3. Enter the commands below:
reportunit "C:\Results" "C:\Reports"

These steps enable to get the html based reports within the folder Reports-which can be shared to stakeholders in html format.

How to set up the NUnit executable project in Jenkins?

Steps:

1. Install Jenkins and open the url localhost:8080
2. Once Jenkins is opened, click on Add New Item (new project)
3. Click Configure>Build>Add a build step>Execute Windows batch command
   You can run the Eclipse project from command line as follows:
   [PATH]\bin\nunit-console.exe [Path]\Selenium.Tests.dll /xml=nunit-result.xml

   If the project is Visual Studio/TFS based Sln project:
   [PATH]\bin\nunit-console.exe [Path]\SeleniumTests.sln /xml=nunit-result.xml

So add the respective command line to run the nunit project command line instructions from Jenkin itself.

4. Post Build Actions section> Test Report XMLs >Type 'nunit-result.xml'

5. Post Build Actions section> Add your email id

Unified Functional Testing- Test Automation Basics

Tools	Quick Test Professional (Unified Functional Testing)
Vendor	HP
Description	Quick Test Professional (QTP) is an automated functional Graphical User Interface (GUI) testing tool that allows the automation of user actions on a web or client based computer application. It is primarily used for functional regression test automation. QTP uses a scripting language built on top of VBScript to specify the test procedure, and to manipulate the objects and controls of the application under test.
Testing Process	The QuickTest testing process consists of 7 main phases: 1. Create your test plan 2. Recording a session on your application 3. Enhancing your test 4. Debugging your test 5. Running your test on a new version of your application 6. Analyzing the test results 7. Reporting defects
Features & Benefits	1. Key word driven testing 2. Suitable for both client server and web based application 3. VB script as the script language 4. Better error handling mechanism 5. Excellent data driven testing features

HP Unified Functional Testing (formerly Quick Test Professional) is a wide accepted tool for web based testing and standalone applications testing. Though the web browser based testing has huge competitions with open source tools such as Selenium Web Driver,

JMeter and other tools, UFT has high value over the automation stability and maintainability.

Selenium Web Driver is famous open source tool used by the industry and the only challenge with Selenium is that the test automation for Standalone applications are not possible (Until 2014). The future versions may extend the facilities from time to time. But HP UFT provide support to number of applications in the latest version.

Astra QuickTest is the primary tool developed which lead to develop Mercury QTP. Mercury introduced QTP during Nov 2002 and this has been changed as HP QTP in the year 2007. QTP is an object based testing tool used for functional and regression testing. Since it follows keyword driven approach, it is flexible to build automation framework around the test engine.

GUI and web applications are supported by QTP and multi-lingual support also available as one of the key feature of the tool!

Activex, Visual basic and Web are the default Add-ins to HP UFT where as the application specific add-ins are available along with license of the tool based on the need.

VB Script is the programming language used in HP UFT and the it is very important to understand how to script for UFT using VB Script-so this will reduce the amount of repeated scripts and increase the reusability over the period of time during test cycles.

Five Phase of Test Automation using HP UFT

Prepare: Design the test approach and collect the details of testable items, data, requirements and test environment

Create: Design test scripts

Verify: Unit testing on the test scripts prepared

Integrate: Connect to the test management, framework, defect tracking system

Maintain: Update/Amend/Facilitate the changes to the test scripts for new test cycles.

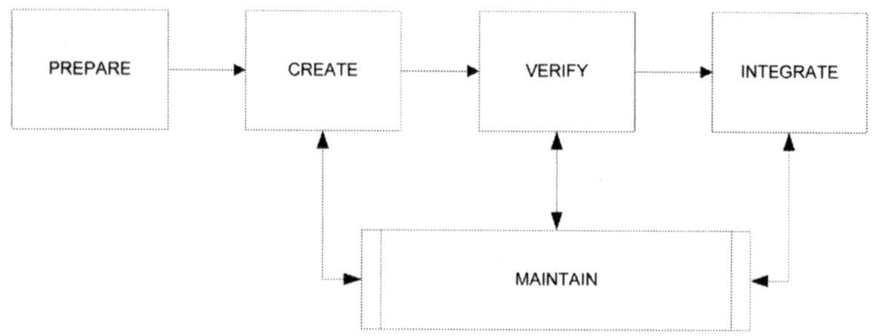

User Interface of HP UFT

Earlier versions of HP QTP 10

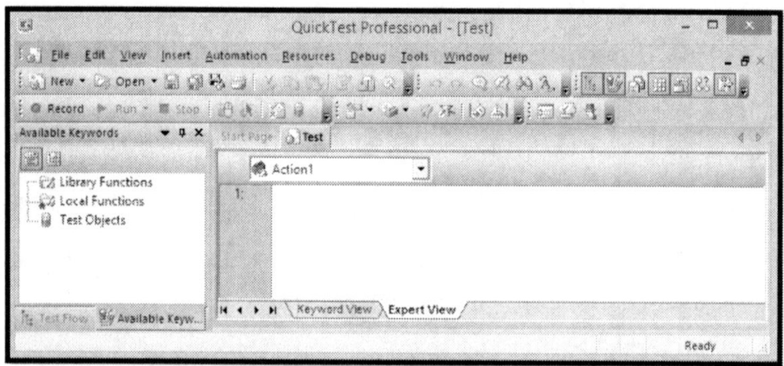

User Interface in the latest version of HP UFT 11.0

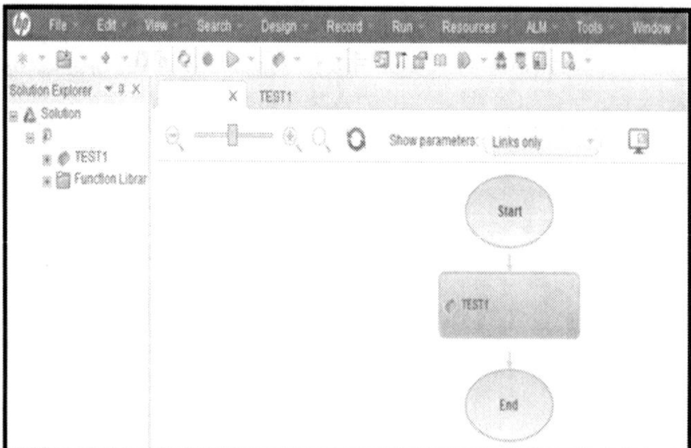

Capture the level at Run Mode

Navigate to Tools>Options to set the object properties capturing level based on the tests performed in the application under test. If the tool capture most of the objects, it is easy to have a condensed object repository with possible objects from the application. At the same time, this leads due delay in test execution when the objects are huge in size.

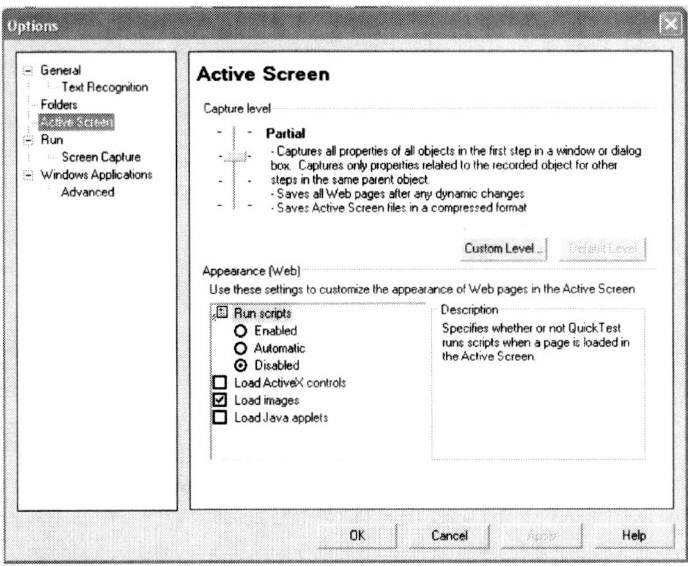

With HP UFT, it is possible to set up the delay between the steps by adding the delay time in the screen below. When the responsiveness of the application is slow, it is recommended to have slow running tool to test and capture the evidence where as the test will fail when it run fast during the slow page navigations of certain web based tests without any reason. So it is always recommended to design the test and perform unit tests to make sure that the speed of the test has been controlled.

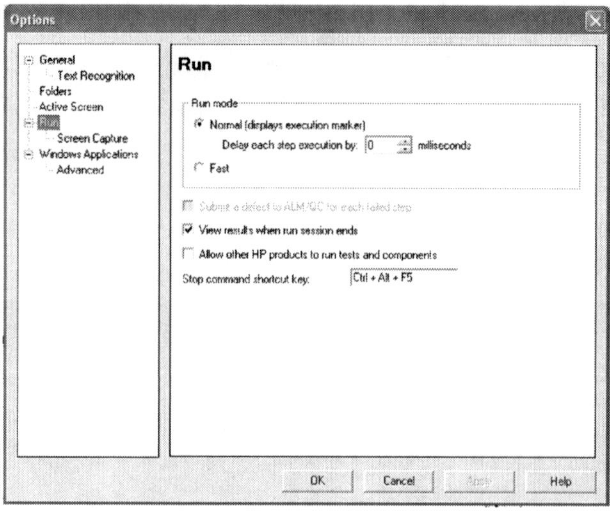

Perform a basic test using Record and Playback

Click on Record and then select 'Record and run test on any open Windows based application', click OK button:

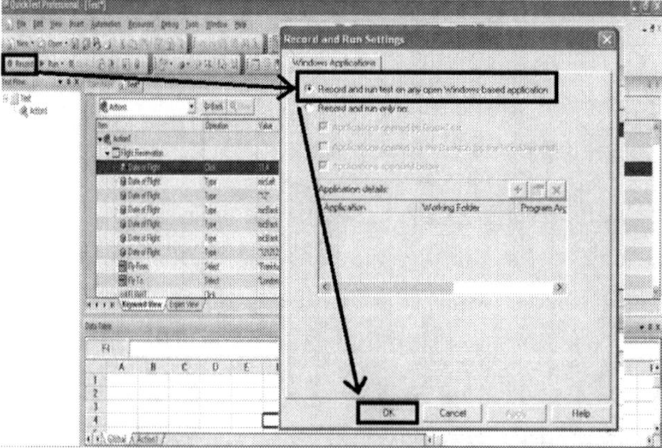

Record and Playback is not an efficient way to automating the tests where as this feature is provided to understand how the automation tool has been designed and how it captures the test application properties by itself. The efficient way of performing automation test is to design the test scripts which are automatically captured during Record in this feature.

Perform a basic test using this feature by,

1. Click on Record button
2. Navigate to the page where the automation is required and perform the actions like click, edit, enter etc.
3. Once the test is completed, click on Stop button and save the test with valid name.

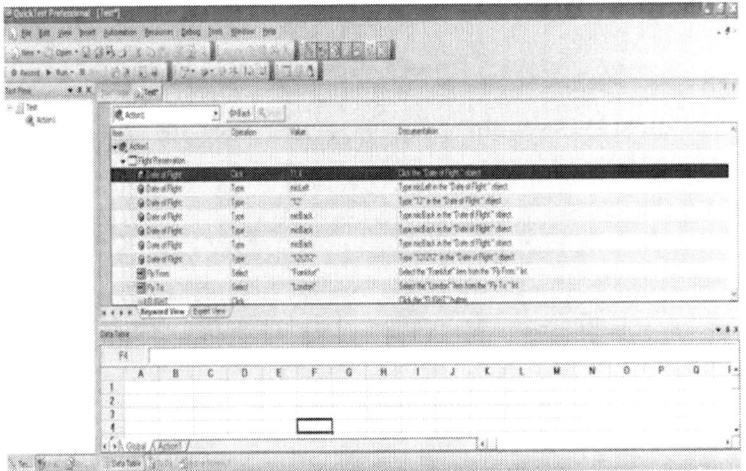

Playback:After Recording the scripts, if Run button is pressed, the entire test repeated by the automation tool to see the test results.

How to launch the browser in HP UFT

System Utility command is wide used to launch the applications using HP UFT as below:

SystemUtil.Run (FileName, Parameters, Path, Operation)

Example:

Open Internet Explorer by providing path of the exe file:
SystemUtil.Run "C://Program Files/Internet Explorer/IEXPLORE.EXE"
Alternative way to open Internet Explorer:

SystemUtil.Run "iexplore.exe", "", "C:\Program Files\Internet Explorer\"

Open a web page along with Internet Explorer:

SystemUtil.Run "iexplore.exe", "http://www.abctest.com"

Open a notepad from HP UFT:

SystemUtil.Run "notepad.exe"

Open notepad file which is already created in the system:

SystemUtil.Run "notepad.exe", "D:\SampleFile.txt"

How to write a reusable Launch Browser Script:

```
Public Function Web_LaunchURL (strAppURL, strBrowserType)
'Input value(s) are:
'String strAppURL
'Output Value(s) are:
SystemUtil.Run "iexplore", strAppURL, "", ""
Call Web_Execution_log (1, strAppURL&" is launched", "PASS")
End Function
```

Following are the regularly used QTP functions as part of the script:

Input Box Function

Syntax:

InputBox(prompt, title, default, xpos, ypos, helpfile, context)

Example:

sName= InputBox("Enter Your Name", "Type Here", "help.hlp", 321321)

Sample script for the input box command:

```
Option Explicit
Dim sPrompt, sTitle, sHelpFile, sRes
Dim vDef
Dim nYPos, nXPos, nContext
sPrompt = "What is your name: sTitle = "Employee Data"
```

```
vDef = "Enter Here"
nXPos = 100: nYPos = 100: nContext = 1001
sHelpFile = "C:\WINDOWS\system32\winhelp.hlp"
sRes = InputBox(sPrompt, sTitle, vDef, nXPos, nYPos, sHelpFile, nContext)
```

Message Box Function

Syntax:
MsgBox(prompt, buttons, title, helpfile, context)
MsgBox "message"

Example:
MsgBox "Hello World"

IF Loop:

Sample Test Script in IF loop for HP UFT:

This if loops checks the length of the sChars. If is it more than 0 then it checks the value if it belong to the category between 97 and 122. If yes, it displays message box to enter upper case as first letter. Else it displays the words in ascending order as output.

```
Dim sChars
Dim nCharCode
sChars = "UnifiedFunctionalTesting"
If Len(sChars) > 0 Then
nCharCode = Asc(sChars)
If nCharCode >= 97 And nCharCode <= 122 Then
MsgBox "The first char must be uppercase"
Else
MsgBox nCharCode
End If
End If
```

Program to validate the test data in a VB Script Function:

sText="Welcome"

```
Function CheckText (sText)
Dim nChar
If Len(sText) > 0 Then
nChar = Asc(sText)
If nChar >= 65 And nChar <= 90 Then
CheckText = “The first character in the word is uppercase”
ElseIf iChar >= 97 And nChar <= 122 Then
CheckText = “The first character in the word is lowercase”
Else
CheckText = “The first character isn’t alphabetical”
End If
Else
CheckText = “Please enter something for the sText”
End If
End Function
```

For further reading and practice, download the projects at https://github.com/narayananpalani/testautomation

UFT Test Automation Framework using Excel VBA

Since HP UFT is technically coded with the help of VB Script programming language, it is possible only through Automation Experts to design and maintain the scripts for testing projects. To enhance the automation tool with handy test data based excel sheets and run the test from excel based documents, certain types of Excel VBA based UFT Automation Frameworks are designed in order to run the tests from Excel sheets. So the changes, amendments to the scripts can be controlled from excel files and any business user can handle this by getting minimum instructions on how to handle the Excel VBA based tool to run the automation tests in HP UFT.

Types of popular Excel VBA based Test Automation Frameworks

- Keyword Driven Framework
- Data Driven Framework
- Table Driven Framework

How Keyword Driven Frameworks are designed?

HP UFT has to be called from Excel file using Driver Script in order to execute the required test scripts for the testing projects. Press Alt+F11 to open Visual Basic Editor of Excel sheet and create the following Sub-Routine:

```
Private Sub ExecuteExcel_Click()
Dim Aut 'As Application
   On Error Resume Next
'This is the main script to call HP UFT from Excel sheet:
      Set Aut = GetObject(, "QuickTest.Application")
      If Err.Number <> 0 Then
         Err.Clear
      End If
      Set Aut = CreateObject("QuickTest.Application")
      If Err.Number <> 0 Then
'If HP UFT is not installed in the test system, this message
should be displayed:
         MsgBox "HP Unified Functional Test must be installed
to run this Framework!"
         Exit Sub
      End If
   On Error GoTo 0
   Aut.Launch
   Aut.Visible = True
   Aut.Options.Run.RunMode = "Normal"
'Location of the test scripts are provided here:
   Aut.Open "<Location of the UFT test script folder> ", True
   Aut.Test.Run
   Set Aut = Nothing ' Release the Application object
End Sub
```

Sample Excel VBA based Keyword Driven Framework:

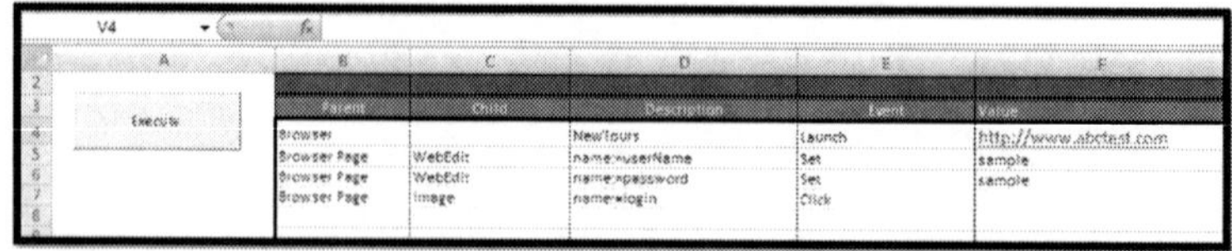

Parent	Child	Description	Event	Value
Browser		NewTours	Launch	http://www.abctest.com
Browser Page	WebEdit	name:=userName	Set	sample
Browser Page	WebEdit	name:=password	Set	sample
Browser Page	Image	name:=login	Click	

Execute button has been assigned to macro: ExecuteExcel_Click and test scripts are converted to each column from Column B to F. Any changes in the objects in near future, simple change over the excel sheet will be suffice in order to maintain this keyword driven framework. Since the test scripts are listed from Excel sheet and converted as a test executable script (.vbs) during test execution, HP UFT should be installed to run these tests.

Sample Table Driven Framework using HP UFT and Selenium Web Driver

Test projects which need multiple test engines such as UFT and Selenium, it is possible to develop the code to test from Excel based Automation Framework.

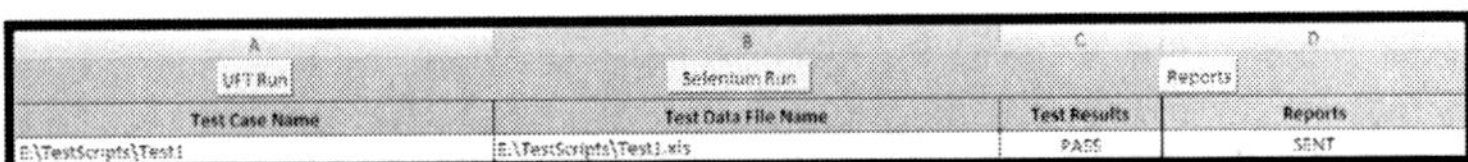

A	B	C	D
UFT Run	Selenium Run		Reports
Test Case Name	Test Data File Name	Test Results	Reports
E:\TestScripts\Test1	E:\TestScripts\Test1.xls	PASS	SENT

'Script to Run HP UFT from Excel VBA:

```
Function UftRun()
Dim xl, bk, s, RowNo, qtpTest, qtpResults, qtp, qtpTestResults
Set qtp = CreateObject("QuickTest.Application")
qtp.Launch
qtp.Visible = True
'qtp.WindowState = "Maximized"
'qtp.Activateview = "ExpertView"
'app.Open "new text document", True
'app.test.Run, True
'Set xl = CreateObject("Excel.Application")
'Set bk = xl.Workbooks.Open("E:\AutomationFramework.xls")
Set s = ActiveWorkbook.Worksheets("Sheet1")
RowNo = 3
s.Cells(RowNo, 3).Value = ""
While Trim(LCase(s.Cells(RowNo, 1))) <> "end"
qtp.Open (s.Cells(RowNo, 1))
'Set s = Nothing
'qtp.Test.Settings.Resources.DataTablePath = s.Cells(RowNo, 2)
```

```
SetqtpResults=CreateObject("QuickTest.RunResultsOptions")
qtp.Test.Run qtpResults, True
qtpResults.ResultsLocation = "E:\Results\"
s.Cells(RowNo, 3).Value = "PASS"
RowNo = RowNo + 1
Wend
qtp.Quit
Set qtp = Nothing
'bk.Close
Set s = Nothing
Set bk = Nothing
Set xl = Nothing
'qtp.Test.Close
OpenFile "E:\TestScripts\Reports\TestReport.html"
AddNewCase 1, "Load Homepage", "Homepage Rendered
OK", "Homepage Rendered OK", "Pass"
AddNewCase 2, "Customer Search", "Customer Record Found",
"Record Not Found", "Fail"
AddNewCase 3, "Close Browser", "Browser Closed OK",
"Browser Closed OK", "Pass"
CloseFile
End Function
```

'Script to Run Selenium from Excel VBA

```
Sub Selenium_Run()
Dim selenium As New SeleniumWrapper.WebDriver
selenium.Start "firefox", "http://www.google.com/"
selenium.Open "http://www.google.com"
selenium.Type "name=q", "Paris"
selenium.Click "name=btnG"
selenium.stop
End Sub
```

Ranorex

Perform the below actions to start the new test:

File>Click New Solution

New>Test Case

New>Recording solution

Click Record>Global Recording>Start

Note:Click on the web page and after all the actions, click on stop button.

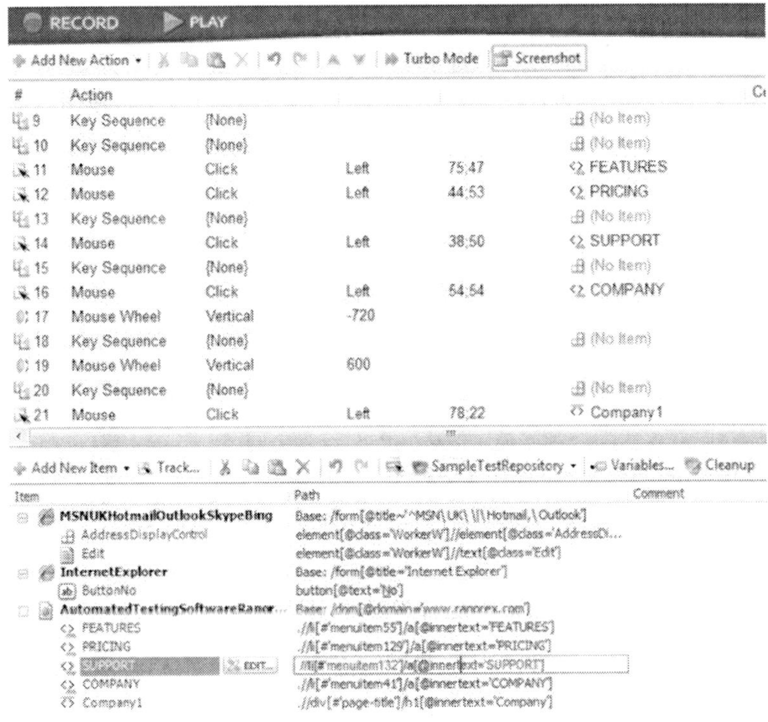

Right click on the actions and select 'view code':

Ranorex Sample Code

//This section is similar to any other C++ scripting on using the different libraries required for the project:

```
using System;
using System.Collections.Generic;
using System.Text;
using System.Text.RegularExpressions;
using System.Drawing;
using System.Threading;
using WinForms = System.Windows.Forms;
//Ranorex Libraries are listed in this section:
using Ranorex;
using Ranorex.Core;
using Ranorex.Core.Testing;
using Ranorex.Core.Repository;

namespace SampleTest
{
  /// <summary>
  ///sample test project
  /// </summary>
        [TestModule("fb61d5f3-f5a1-4f62-b19e-48dfd3e7a009",
ModuleType.Recording, 1)]
   public partial class Recording2: ITestModule
   {
     /// <summary>
    ///This is an Instance of the SampleTestRepository repository.
     /// </summary>
   public static SampleTestRepository repo = SampleTestRepository.
Instance;

      static Recording2 instance = new Recording2();
```

```
/// <summary>
/// Constructs a new instance in this section.
/// </summary>
public Recording2()
{
}

/// <summary>
/// Gets a static instance of this recording.
/// </summary>
public static Recording2 Instance
{
   get { return instance; }
}

#region Variables

#endregion

/// <summary>
/// Starts the replay of the static recording <see cref=”Instance”/>.
/// </summary>
   [System.CodeDom.Compiler.GeneratedCode(“Ranorex”,
“5.2.4”)]
public static void Start()
{
   TestModuleRunner.Run(Instance);
}

/// <summary>
/// Performs the playback of actions in this recording.
/// </summary>
/// <remarks>You should not call this method directly, instead
pass the module
```

```
/// instance to the <see cref="TestModuleRunner.Run(ITestModule)"/> method
/// that will in turn invoke this method.</remarks>
[System.CodeDom.Compiler.GeneratedCode("Ranorex", "5.2.4")]
void ITestModule.Run()
{
    Mouse.DefaultMoveTime = 300;
    Keyboard.DefaultKeyPressTime = 100;
    Delay.SpeedFactor = 1.0;

    Init();

    Report.Log(ReportLevel.Info, "Keyboard", "Key sequence '{None}'.", new RecordItemIndex(0));
    Keyboard.Press("{None}");
    Delay.Milliseconds(0);

    Report.Log(ReportLevel.Info,"Mouse","Mouse Left Click item 'MSNUKHotmailOutlookSkypeBing.AddressDisplayControl' at 198;8.", repo.MSNUKHotmailOutlookSkypeBing.AddressDisplayControlInfo, new RecordItemIndex(1));
    repo.MSNUKHotmailOutlookSkypeBing.AddressDisplayControl.Click("198;8");
    Delay.Milliseconds(200);

    Report.Log(ReportLevel.Info, "Keyboard", "Key sequence '{None}'.", new RecordItemIndex(2));
    Keyboard.Press("{None}");
    Delay.Milliseconds(0);

    Report.Log(ReportLevel.Info, "Mouse", "Mouse Left Click item 'AutomatedTestingSoftwareRanorexT.Company1' at 78;22.",
```

```
repo.AutomatedTestingSoftwareRanorexT.Company1Info, new
RecordItemIndex(20));
            repo.AutomatedTestingSoftwareRanorexT.Company1.
Click("78;22");
        Delay.Milliseconds(200);

    }

#region Image Feature Data
#endregion
  }
}
```

VB Scripting Excel Macro Automation

Visual Basic Scripting is a wide used scripting language for automation tools such as HP Unified Functional Testing (formerly Quick Test Professional) and TestComplete (which supports five scripting languages including VB script!).

VB Script is a light version of Microsoft's programming language Visual Basic and default scripting language for ASP (Active Server Pages). Projects which need custom automation frameworks due to unavailability of front end systems or the projects where SOAP/REST messages have to be automated, excel based automation frameworks are designed using vb script in order to overcome the challenges! This Excel Macro based automation is a most important automation skillset in which most of the leading banks, telecommunication and public sector companies look forward to have technical specialist with Excel VBA (Macro) automation expertise. In this section, the introduction to excel macro based VB script automation is discussed.

Excel Macro Based Automation

Excel macros are designed with set of commands and functions which are required to execute and run the automation tests for the testing projects. MS Excel provides a built in functionality known as Excel Formulas (build in macros) which are available for scripting through macros.

	A	B	C	D	E
1	2				
2	3				
3	4				
4	=sum				
5	SUM		Adds all the numbers in a range of cells		
6	SUMIF				
7	SUMIFS				
8	SUMPRODUCT				
9	SUMSQ				
10	SUMX2MY2				
11	SUMX2PY2				
	SUMXMY2				

Type values in each cells and navigate to an empty cell, type =SUM and then drag to select the data to see the sum of the selected data. This is an example of a built in macro of MS Excel.

Creation of Macro

Microsoft VB Editor is the environment used to create or edit macros and VB Scripts. The complete automation script and the logic of automation framework can be updated at Microsoft VB Editor.

Following are the steps to be followed to create automation framework with sub-routines/macros:

- Open an excel sheet (latest version)
- Press Alt+F11 (shortcut key to open MS VB Editor) or alternatively select Developer Tab, click on Visual Basic Button.

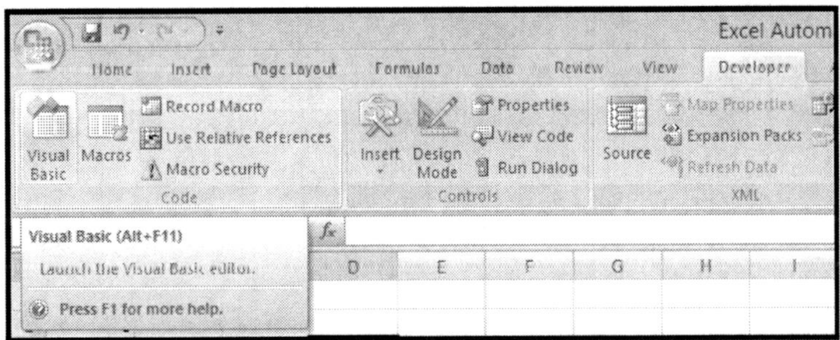

Enable Excel Macros

The scripts and sub routines can be saved in macros only when it is enabled at Macro security. In order to enable it, user has to click on Developer, select Macro Security and choose the option of 'Enable all macros' as mentioned below

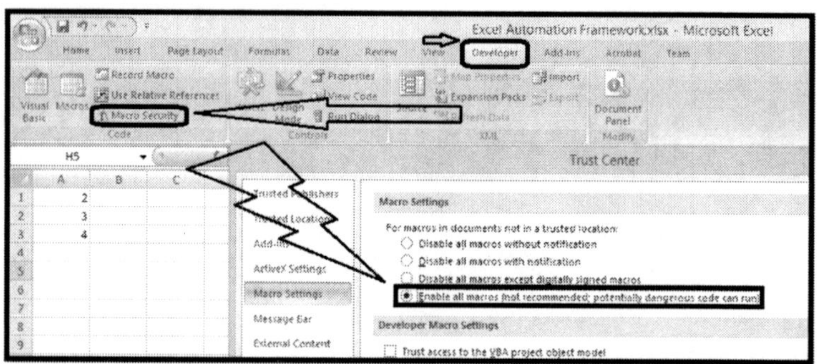

Sample script at Visual Basic Editor

Follow the steps below to create a Macro:

1) Open a Excel file
2) Press Alt + F11
3) Verify Microsoft Script Editor is getting opened
4) Create a sub-routine as:

```
Public Sub welcome()
    MsgBox "Welcome to Excel Macro Automation Framework"
End Sub
```

5) Save the Excel File

Follow the below steps to execute the macro created above:

1) Open a Excel file
2) Press Alt + F8

3) Verify Macro is getting opened

4) Select the Macro Name (which is saved earlier) and click on Run button

5) The message box should be displayed as designed in the script.

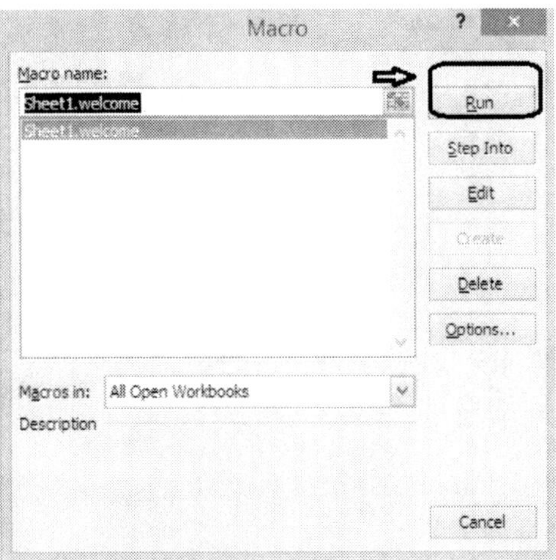

Message Box:

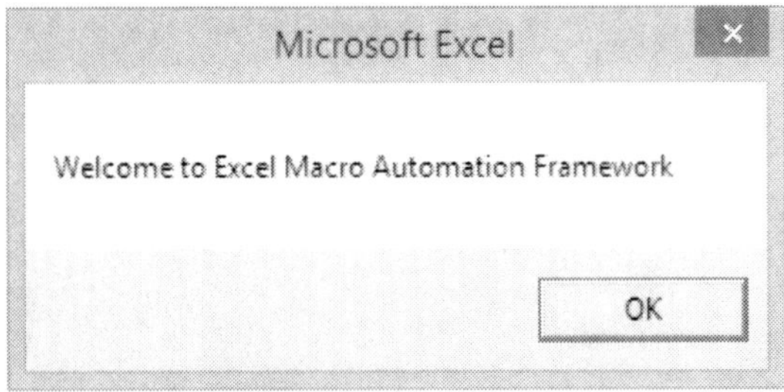

Sample script to access the data from the excel sheet

Often it is highly recommended to take the test data from excel sheet and use it as part of automation test execution. For an example, if the set of HTTP requests has to be sent, the message can be designed by parameterize the values in the columns of the excel sheet. If hundred users has to login to the particular page, the login functionality is common. So this can be scripted in excel macro and the login credentials of hundred users can be listed in the excel and referred while running the script.

Access/Read the text present in the Excel file through a Macro Function, follow the following steps:

1) Create a Macro
2) Be clear about the Row-number and Column-number from where the text is to be accessed.
3) Use the syntax: Cells(Row-index, Column-index).value
4) The text captured by this step can stored in a variable
5) Then it can be displayed through a MsgBox

```
Public Sub welcome ()

    MsgBox "Excel Macro Automation Framework"

    strLoginID = Cells(2, 1).Value

    MsgBox "The LoginID is: "& strLoginID

    strPwd = Cells(2, 2).Value

    MsgBox "The Password is: "& strPwd

End Sub
```

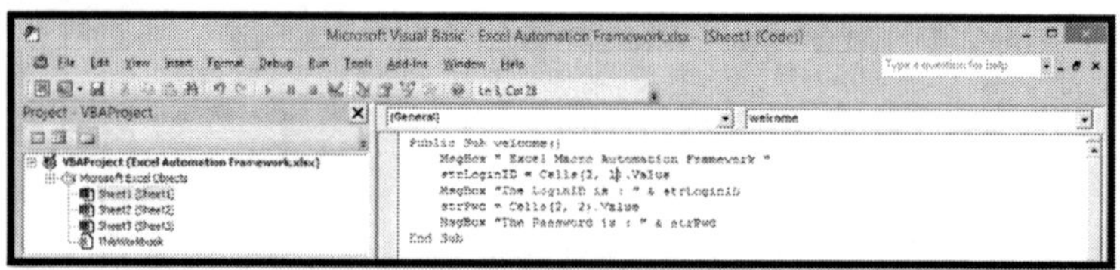

Result:

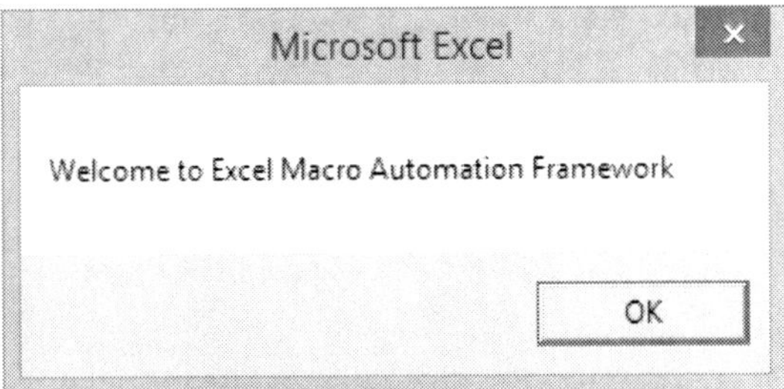

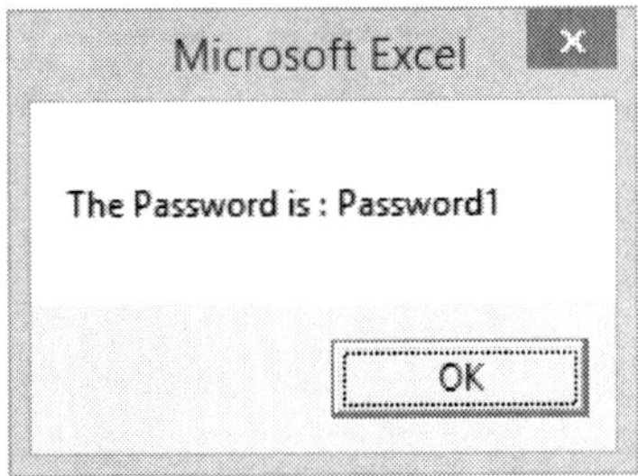

Manipulation of the string through Excel Macros enables the users to

1) copy the text,
2) modify the text and/or
3) delete the text

Steps to perform any String Manipulations

1) Obtain the text which is to be manipulated.
2) Decide the Text operation like Append, Delete or modify… which is to be performed.

3) Decide whether the new-text is to be displayed in Msgbox or inside the Excel file.

Script:

```
Public Sub welcome()
   MsgBox "Excel Macro Automation Framework"
   strLoginID = Cells(2, 1).Value
   strPwd = Cells(2, 2).Value
     Cells(2, 3).Value = strLoginID & "is the user id and " &
strLoginID & " is the password."
End Sub
```

Result:

	A	B	C
1	Login ID	Password	Result
2	User1	Password1	User1is the user id and User1 is the password.
3	User2	Password2	

Example Script for Case based conditional loop

Assume that the browser has to be selected for each test automation script and it has to be recognized by entering the number in the excel sheet.

Following is the script designed for Browser selection:

```
Public Sub welcome()
 For Row = 2 To 6
   Dim str1 As String
   Dim n As Integer
   Var = Cells(Row, 1).Value

  'This is the sample of CASE statement
  Select Case Var
```

```
        Case 1: result = “Chrome”
        Case 2: result = “Firefox”
        Case 3: result = “Internet Explorer”
        Case 4: result = “Safari”
        Case 5: result = “Opera”

    End Select

    If Cells(Row, 1) <= 5 Then
        Cells(Row, 2).Value = “The Browser selection is ” & result
        Else
       MsgBox “Enter right number for the browser and continue”
    End If
Next
End Sub
```

Press Alt+F8 to execute this script:

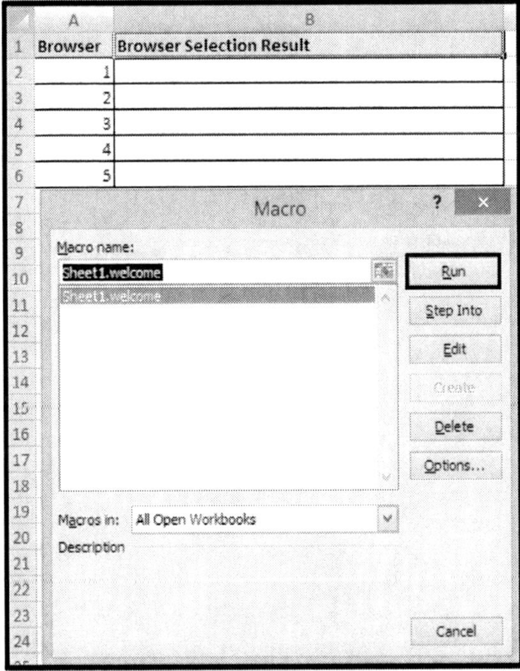

Valid Result:

	A	B
1	Browser	Browser Selection Result
2	1	The Browser selection is Chrome
3	2	The Browser selection is Firefox
4	3	The Browser selection is Internet Explorer
5	4	The Browser selection is Safari
6	5	The Browser selection is Opera

Instead the value from 1 to 5, enter 7 in one of the rows and validate the result as follows:

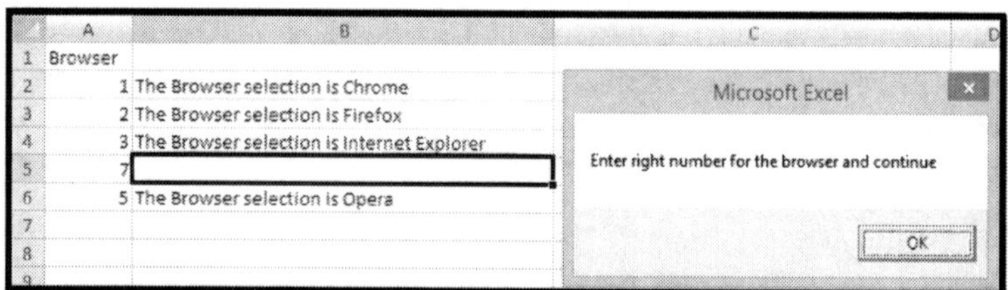

Commonly used VB Script functions are listed for reference:

String - Accepts a number and a character. Returns a string created with the character repeated the given number of times.

Len - Returns the number of characters in a given string.

InStr - Accepts two strings and returns whether the second is contained within the first or not.

Left, Right - Accepts a string and a length, and returns a substring of the given length from the beginning or the end of the original string. Returns the original string if the given number is larger than the actual length of the string.

Mid - Accepts a string, a starting point, and a length. Returns a substring of the given length from the starting point of the original string.

Split - Accepts a string and a delimiter character, and returns an array of substrings.

Date - returns the current system date. Time returns the current system time. Now returns the system date and time.

DateAdd - Adds the specified number of years, months, weeks, days, hours, minutes, or seconds to the given date.

DateDiff - Returns the number of years, months, weeks, days, hours, minutes, or seconds between the two given dates. The return value is negative if the first date is after the second date.

Day, Month, Year, Weekday-Accepts a date and returns just the desired portion of the date.

GUI Form Control in Excel VBA

With the help of VB Form UI objects, Excel VBA automation frameworks are designed with available objects to utilize functions like RUN, COMPILE and other functions:

1) Text Box
2) Button
3) Label
4) ComboBox
5) ListBox
6) CheckBox
7) OptionBox (RadioButton)
8) ToggleButton
9) Frame
10) TabStrip
11) Multi-page
12) ScrollBar

13) Spin button

14) Image

15) RefEdit

These objects can be inserted by selecting Developer tab, click Insert button and choose the object:

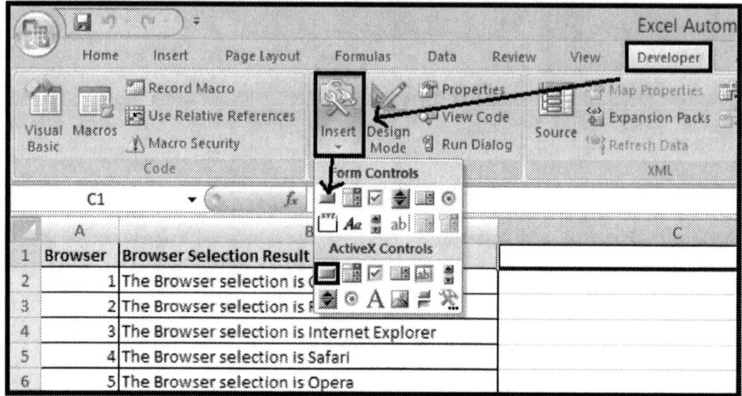

Choose the button and change the name to RUN:

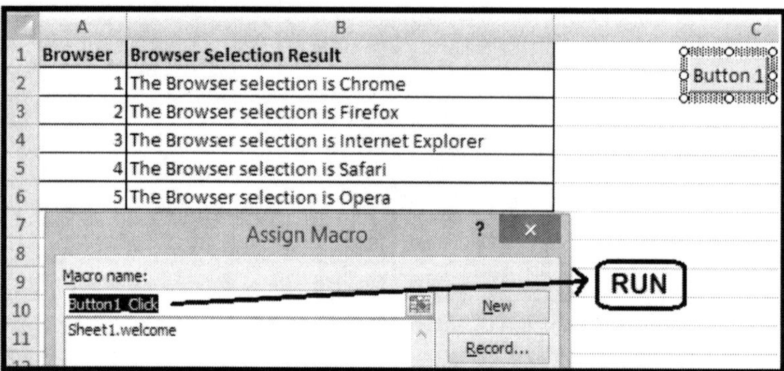

How to Edit the Name?

Right click on the button and click on Edit Text as follows:

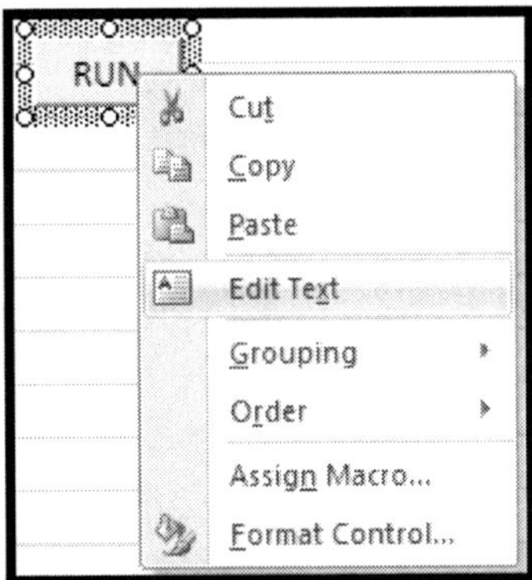

Assign the script to the button

Once the script is assigned to the button, no need to execute every time by pressing Alt+F8. So all user need is to click on the button RUN to execute!

This can be done by right click on the button, choose 'Assign Macro', Select the sub routine developed for the automation framework and click on OK.

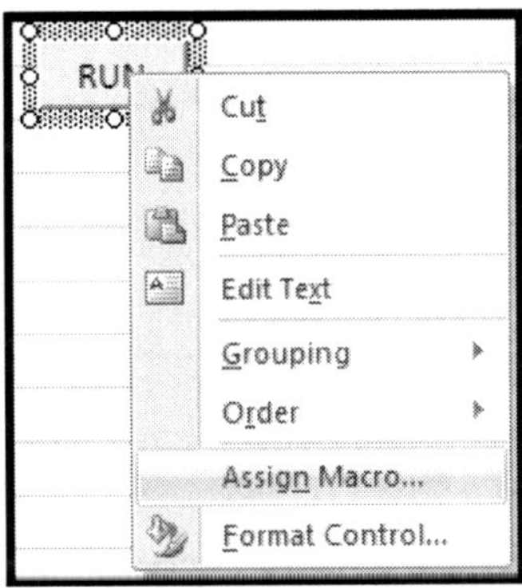

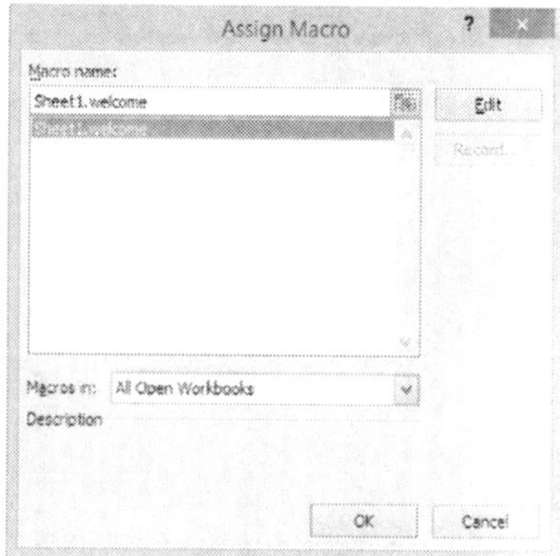

Once the sub routine is assigned, just click on the RUN button to get the results :

Step1: Click on RUN button

	A	B	C
1	Browser	Browser Selection Result	
2	1		RUN
3	2		
4	3		
5	4		
6	5		

Step2: Validate the Results

A	B	C
Browser	Browser Selection Result	
1	The Browser selection is Chrome	RUN
2	The Browser selection is Firefox	
3	The Browser selection is Internet Explorer	
4	The Browser selection is Safari	
5	The Browser selection is Opera	

Control Form in Excel VBA

Click Insert and select UserForm to create a new form for data inputs

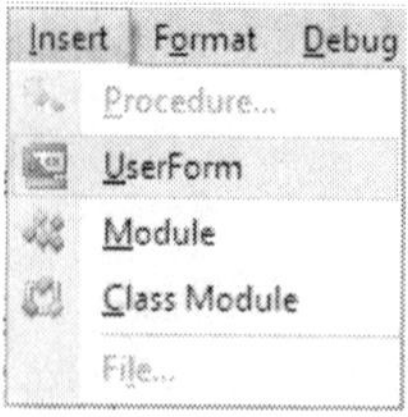

Create a form with following labels, text boxes and button:

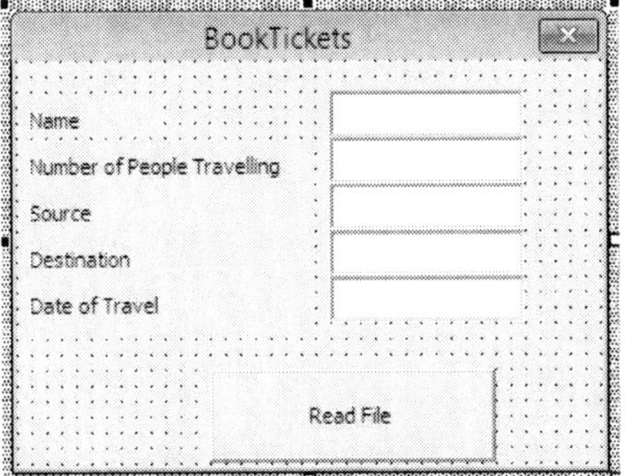

Write the script for sheet1 as follows:

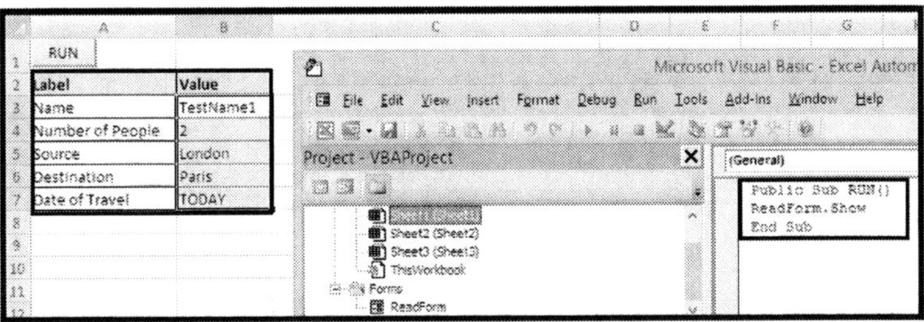

Script for the form:

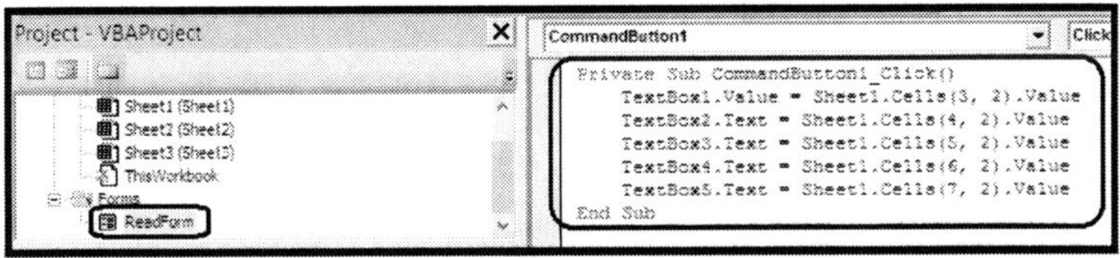

Basically clicking on the RUN button open the form as below:

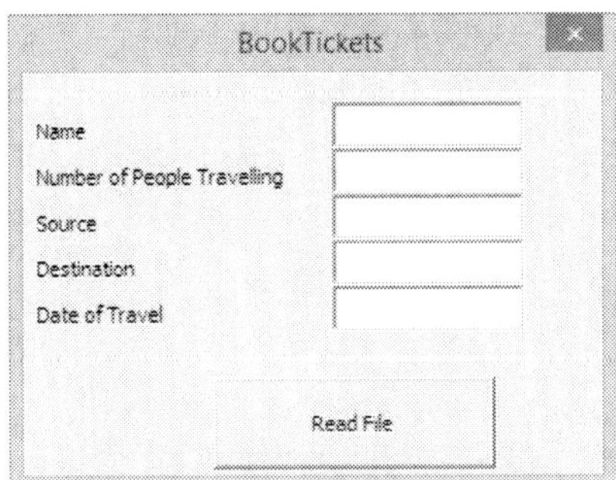

Click on the ReadFile button and see the data updated in the sheet:

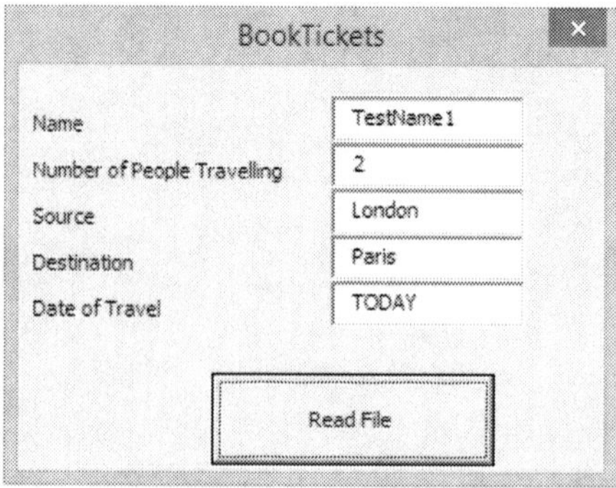

Similarly, Introduce a new button with the name Write File to write back to the same location in excel is possible through the below script:

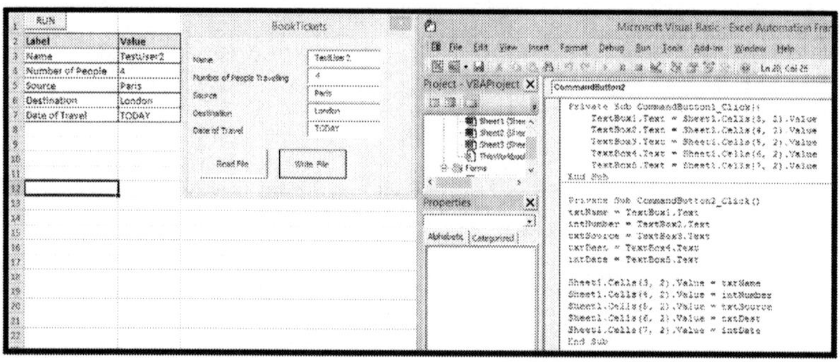

Script:

In ReadForm:

```
Private Sub CommandButton1_Click()
   TextBox1.Text = Sheet1.Cells(3, 2).Value
   TextBox2.Text = Sheet1.Cells(4, 2).Value
   TextBox3.Text = Sheet1.Cells(5, 2).Value
   TextBox4.Text = Sheet1.Cells(6, 2).Value
   TextBox5.Text = Sheet1.Cells(7, 2).Value
End Sub

Private Sub CommandButton2_Click()
```

```
txtName = TextBox1.Text
intNumber = TextBox2.Text
txtSource = TextBox3.Text
txtDest = TextBox4.Text
intDate = TextBox5.Text

Sheet1.Cells(3, 2).Value = txtName
Sheet1.Cells(4, 2).Value = intNumber
Sheet1.Cells(5, 2).Value = txtSource
Sheet1.Cells(6, 2).Value = txtDest
Sheet1.Cells(7, 2).Value = intDate
End Sub
```

In Sheet1:

```
Public Sub RUN()
ReadForm.Show
End Sub
```

Nature of the Automation Frameworks in Excel VBA

Test Data sheets are integrated with automation frameworks using Excel VBA and the framework runs the test automation tool in the background by clicking on the RUN button or the similar button in the Excel sheet. This is the most important technology in automation frameworks which is expected to grow large in the next couple of years.

Example 1: Capture the test data in Sheet1, Click on Run button which leads to test execution through Selenium Web-driver

Example 2: Capture the test data in Sheet1, Click on Run button which leads to test execution through HP UFT

Example 3: Capture the test data in Sheet1, Click on Run button which leads to test execution through SOAP Messages.

Sample Project on Excel VBA Data Comparison:

Step1- Create a tab 'Source' with Data in three columns 'Employee ID, Name, Address' along with Compare button:

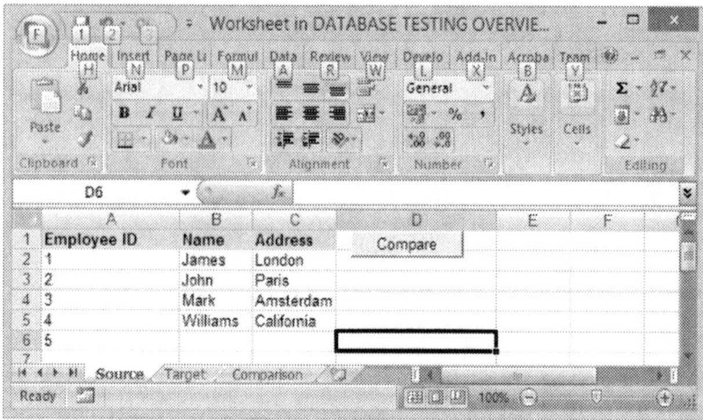

Step2- Create a tab 'Target' with Data in three columns 'Employee ID, Name, Address'

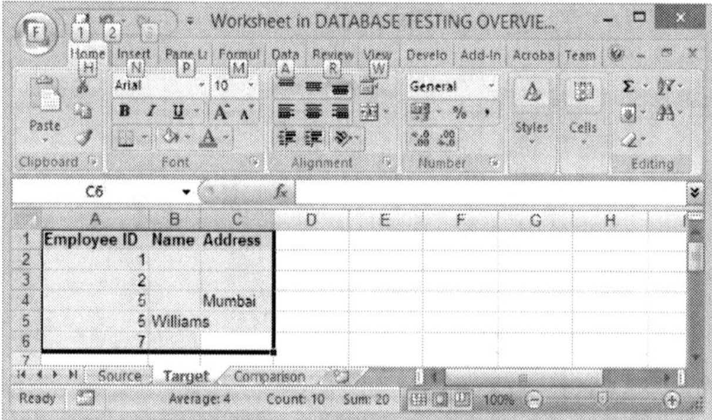

Step3- Create a blank tab 'Comparison':

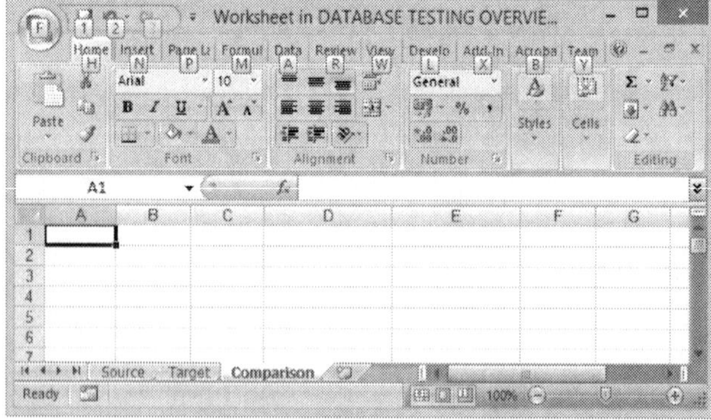

Step4-Test Script in ThisWorkbook:

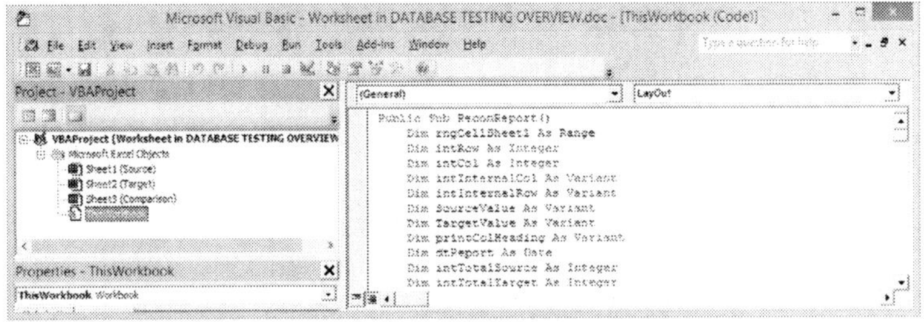

Write the sample scripts given below to understand the Excel VBA Code:

```
Public Sub ReconReport()
    Dim rngCellSheet1 As Range
    Dim intRow As Integer
    Dim intCol As Integer
    Dim intInternalCol As Variant
    Dim intInternalRow As Variant
    Dim SourceValue As Variant
    Dim TargetValue As Variant
    Dim printColHeading As Variant
    Dim dtReport As Date
    Dim intTotalSource As Integer
    Dim intTotalTarget As Integer
    Dim strRange As Variant

    Worksheets(1).Name = "Source"
    Worksheets(2).Name = "Target"
    Worksheets(3).Name = "Comparison"

    dtReport = Now()

    Worksheets("Comparison").Range("A1:D1").MergeCells = True
    Worksheets("Comparison").Cells(1, 1).Font.ColorIndex = 5
    Worksheets("Comparison").Cells(1, 1).Font.Bold = True
```

```
Worksheets("Comparison").Cells(1, 1) = "Report Generated
On : " & dtReport

intRow = 3
intCol = 1

Call LayOut(intRow, intCol)
Worksheets("Comparison").Cells(intRow, intCol) = "DB"
Worksheets("Comparison").Cells(intRow, intCol).
ColumnWidth = 8
Call LayOut(intRow, intCol + 1)
Worksheets("Comparison").Cells(intRow, intCol + 1) = "Column"
Call LayOut(intRow, intCol + 2)
Worksheets("Comparison").Cells(intRow, intCol + 2) = "Row"
Worksheets("Comparison").Cells(intRow, intCol + 2).
HorizontalAlignment = xlRight

Call LayOut(intRow, intCol + 3)
Worksheets("Comparison").Cells(intRow, intCol + 3) = "Source
Value"
        Worksheets("Comparison").Cells(intRow,    intCol    +
3).ColumnWidth = 15
        Worksheets("Comparison").Cells(intRow,    intCol    +
3).HorizontalAlignment = xlRight

Call LayOut(intRow, intCol + 4)
Worksheets("Comparison").Cells(intRow, intCol + 4) = "Target
Value"
        Worksheets("Comparison").Cells(intRow,    intCol    +
4).ColumnWidth = 15
        Worksheets("Comparison").Cells(intRow,    intCol    +
4).HorizontalAlignment = xlRight

intRow = intRow + 1
```

```
Worksheets("Comparison").Cells(intRow, intCol) = "Source"
 Worksheets("Comparison").Cells(intRow, intCol).Font.Bold =
True
intRow = intRow + 1

intTotalSource = 0
intInternalCol = 1
Do While (intInternalCol <= Worksheets("Source").UsedRange.
Columns.Count)
    intInternalRow = 1
    printColHeading = "N"
        Do While (intInternalRow <= Worksheets("Source").
UsedRange.Columns(intInternalCol).Rows.Count)
      SourceValue = Worksheets("Source").Cells(intInternalRow,
intInternalCol)
      TargetValue = Worksheets("Target").Cells(intInternalRow,
intInternalCol)
     If Not SourceValue = TargetValue Then
       If printColHeading = "N" Then
         Worksheets("Comparison").Cells(intRow, intCol + 1) =
Worksheets("Target").Cells(1, intInternalCol)
        printColHeading = "Y"
        intRow = intRow + 1
       End If
         Worksheets("Comparison").Cells(intRow, intCol + 2) =
intInternalRow
         Worksheets("Comparison").Cells(intRow, intCol + 3) =
SourceValue
         Worksheets("Comparison").Cells(intRow, intCol + 4) =
TargetValue
       intRow = intRow + 1
       intTotalSource = intTotalSource + 1
     End If
     intInternalRow = intInternalRow + 1
```

```
      Loop
      intInternalCol = intInternalCol + 1
    Loop

    intRow = intRow + 1


    strRange = "A" & intRow & ":D" & intRow

    Worksheets("Comparison").Range(strRange).MergeCells = True
    Worksheets("Comparison").Cells(intRow,1).Font.ColorIndex=5
    Worksheets("Comparison").Cells(intRow, 1).Font.Bold = True
    Worksheets("Comparison").Cells(intRow, 1) = "Total Number of
    Difference: " & intTotalSource


    intTotalTarget = 0
    intRow = intRow + 3
    Worksheets("Comparison").Cells(intRow, intCol) = "Target"
    Worksheets("Comparison").Cells(intRow, intCol).Font.
    Bold = True
    intRow = intRow + 1
    intInternalCol = 1
    Do While (intInternalCol <= Worksheets("Target").UsedRange.
Columns.Count)
      intInternalRow = 1
      printColHeading = "N"
            Do While (intInternalRow <= Worksheets("Target").
UsedRange.Columns(intInternalCol).Rows.Count)
        TargetValue = Worksheets("Target").Cells(intInternalRow,
intInternalCol)
        SourceValue = Worksheets("Source").Cells(intInternalRow,
intInternalCol)
        If Not SourceValue = TargetValue Then
```

```
            If printColHeading = "N" Then
              Worksheets("Comparison").Cells(intRow, intCol + 1)
= Worksheets("Source").Cells(1, intInternalCol)
              printColHeading = "Y"
              intRow = intRow + 1
            End If
             Worksheets("Comparison").Cells(intRow, intCol + 2) =
intInternalRow
             Worksheets("Comparison").Cells(intRow, intCol + 3) =
SourceValue
             Worksheets("Comparison").Cells(intRow, intCol + 4) =
TargetValue
            intRow = intRow + 1
            intTotalTarget = intTotalTarget + 1
          End If
          intInternalRow = intInternalRow + 1
        Loop
      intInternalCol = intInternalCol + 1
    Loop

    intRow = intRow + 1

    strRange = "A" & intRow & ":D" & intRow

    Worksheets("Comparison").Range(strRange).MergeCells = True
    Worksheets("Comparison").Cells(intRow, 1).Font.ColorIndex =
5
    Worksheets("Comparison").Cells(intRow, 1).Font.Bold = True
    Worksheets("Comparison").Cells(intRow, 1) = "Total Number of
Difference: " & intTotalTarget

End Sub

Public Sub LayOut(ByVal row As Integer, ByVal col As Integer)
```

```
    Worksheets("Comparison").Cells(row, col).Font.Bold = True
     Worksheets("Comparison").Cells(row, col).Interior.ColorIndex
= 3
    Worksheets("Comparison").Cells(row, col).Font.ColorIndex = 0
    Worksheets("Comparison").Cells(row, col).Font.Bold = True
End Sub
```

Step5-Right click on the Compare Button in Source Tab and assign following macro:

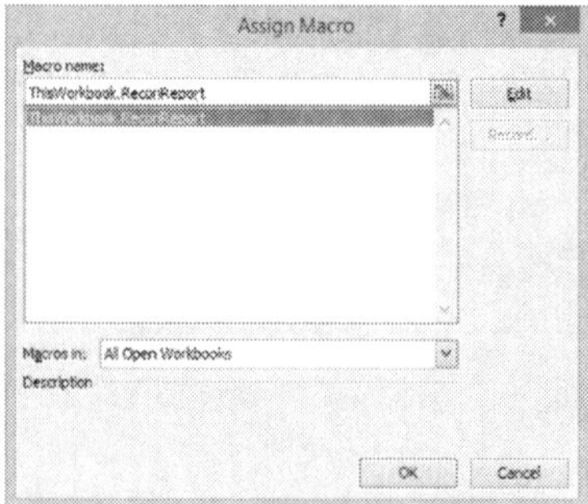

Step 6 Test Execution-Click on Compare button and see the result in comparison tab:

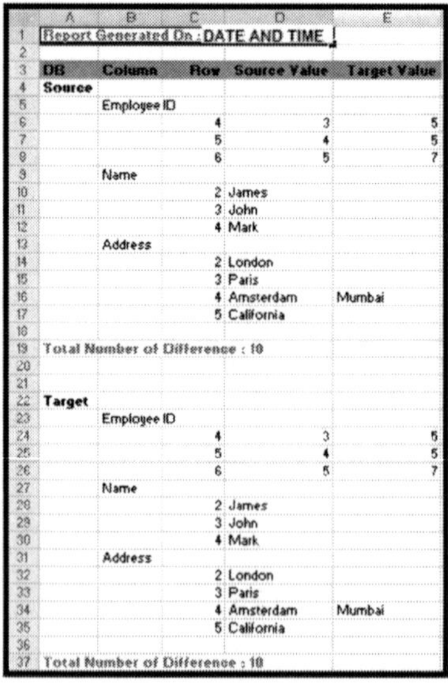

	A	B	C	D	E
1	Report Generated On : DATE AND TIME				
2					
3	DB	Column	Row	Source Value	Target Value
4	Source				
5		Employee ID			
6			4	3	5
7			5	4	5
8			6	5	7
9		Name			
10			2	James	
11			3	John	
12			4	Mark	
13		Address			
14			2	London	
15			3	Paris	
16			4	Amsterdam	Mumbai
17			5	California	
18					
19	Total Number of Difference : 10				
20					
21					
22	Target				
23		Employee ID			
24			4	3	5
25			5	4	5
26			6	5	7
27		Name			
28			2	James	
29			3	John	
30			4	Mark	
31		Address			
32			2	London	
33			3	Paris	
34			4	Amsterdam	Mumbai
35			5	California	
36					
37	Total Number of Difference : 10				

How to Test Excel Sheet?

The most manual tests completed with the help of excel sheets for test cases and test execution in small and medium level companies. But testing the Excel itself as an Application Under Test (AUT) is a different task and it can be achieved with automation tools like HP UFT (formerly QTP).

Solution for the Excel Testing using HP UFT

Following is the sample script to compare the excel files and its objects as part of HP UFT Automation Framework.

We need two excel files to test this script at the folder C:\excelfolder\ File Names: *excelfile*1.xls and *excelfile*2.xls

Paste this script in HP UFT or Excel VBA macro to get worked:

Mismatch=0
Set myxl = **createobject**(«excel.application»)

'To make Excel visible
myxl.Visible = **True**

'Open a workbook "excelfile1.xls"
Set Workbook1= myxl.Workbooks.Open("C:\excelfolder\excelfile1.xls")

'Open a workbook " excelfile2.xls"

```
Set Workbook2= myxl.Workbooks.Open("C:\excelfolder\
excelfile2.xls")

Set mysheet1=Workbook1.Worksheets("Sheet1")
Set mysheet2=Workbook2.Worksheets("Sheet1")

'Compare two sheets cell by cell
For Each cell In mysheet1.UsedRange
'Highlights the cell if cell values not match
    If cell.Value <>mysheet2.Range(cell.Address).Value Then
      'Highlights the cell if cell values not match
      cell.Interior.ColorIndex = 3
        mismatch=1
    End If
  Next
If Mismatch=0 Then
   Msgbox "No Mismach exists"
End If
'close the workbooks
Workbook1.close
Workbook2.close

myxl.Quit
set myxl=nothing
```

For further reading and practice, download the projects at https://github.com/narayananpalani/testautomation

IBM Rational Functional Test

RFT use Java (primary) and VB scripting as programming language and it consists of following features:

Projects
Test Object Inspector
Test Object Map
Recording test scripts
Replay test scripts
Debug scripts
Java Scripting
Create Verification points – GUI, Bitmap, Menu
Databases sample scripts
Data Pool the test cases
Suite (Batch Run)

Following menus are available on top level:
File
Edit
Navigate
Search
Project
Script
Configure
Run
Window
Help

How to Create a Project in IBM RFT?

Test project has to be created to automate the application and maintain the test scripts. Also it is suggested to have unique project name as per the project title to remember them during the test execution.

Click on File Menu, select New and click on Project...

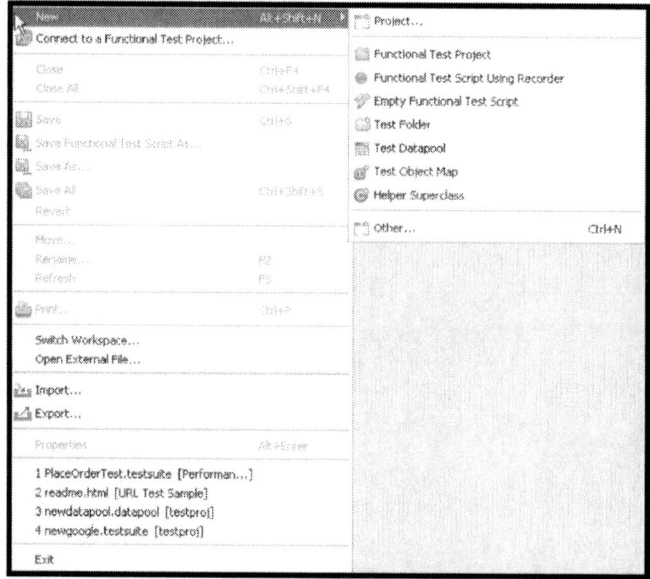

How to delete a project?

Click on Edit and select Delete as follows

How to navigate to different projects in IBM RFT?

Testing teams can align different projects in IBM RFT. If a user need to navigate to different test project, click on Navigate menu and select Go to as follows

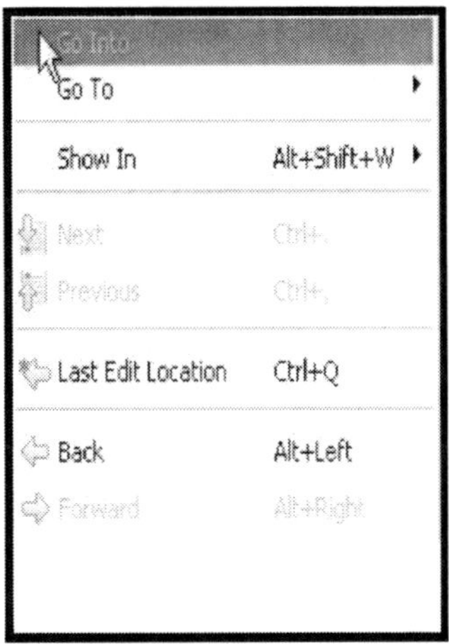

How to Search for the particular script?

Click on Search in menu and select Search

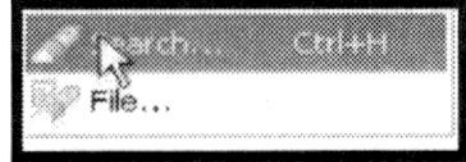

How to Run the scripts in IBM RFT?

Click on Script in menu items and select Run button

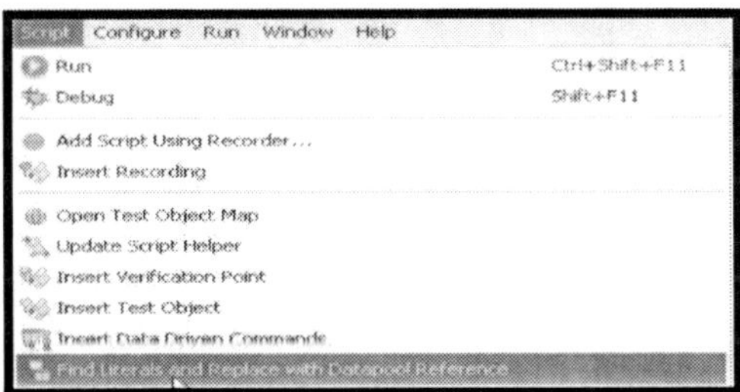

How to create a test automation project using IBM RFT?

Step1: Test Application needs to be configured in order to automate using IBM RFT. Navigate to configure tab

How to configure the menu and applications in IBM RFT?

Click on Configure and select 'Configure Applications for Testing'

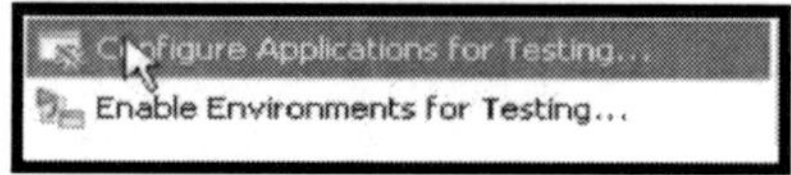

Set up the path of the test application:

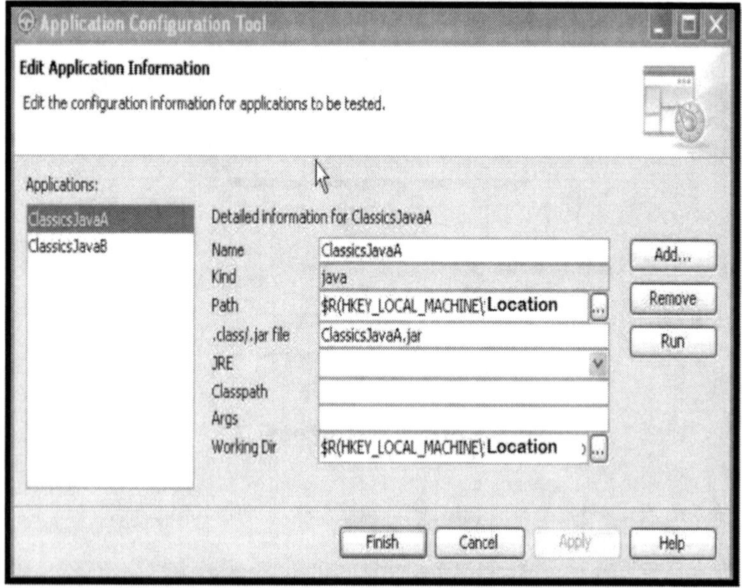

If the test application is a web browser, this has to be configured in Configure>Enable Environment

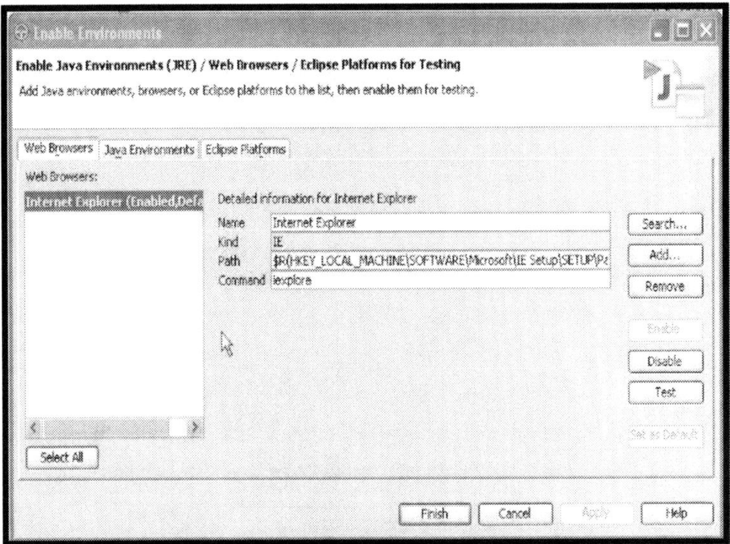

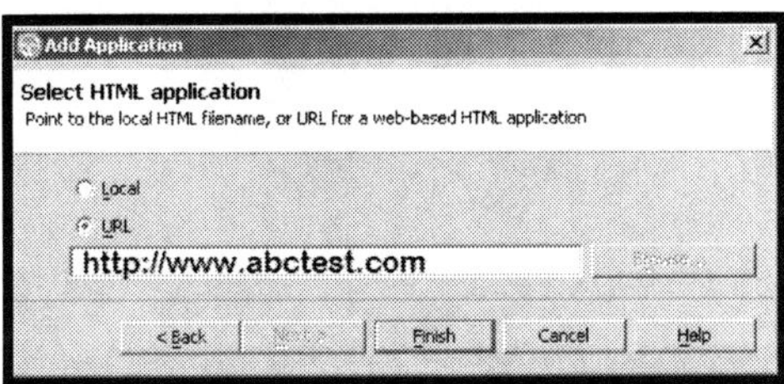

Step2: Test Object Inspector-Click on Run in menu and select Test Object Inspector:

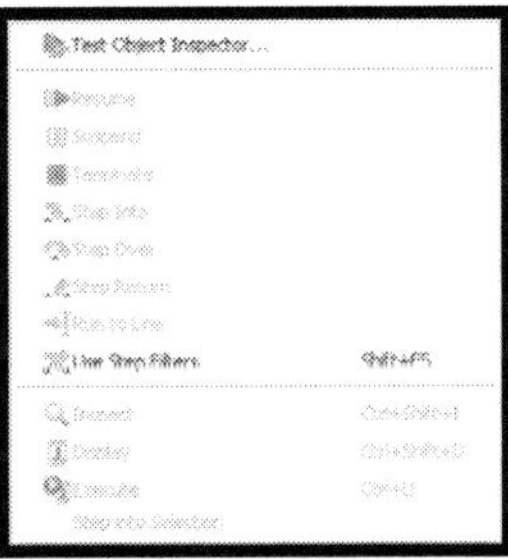

Test objects are viewed using this feature and information such as parent hierarchy, inheritance hierarchy, test object properties, non value properties, and method that can be used for those objects. Windows objects are also captured from test object inspector!

Best Practice:

Evaluate the tool by testing the sample application and analyzing the test object capturing method in order to perform Proof of Concept for Test Automation Readiness.

Parent Hierarchy details explored through Test Object Inspector:

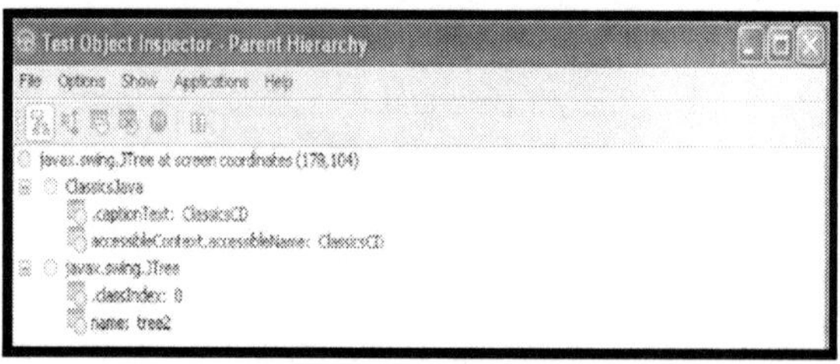

Step3-Preferences: Set the Recognition Level and Warning Level of objects based on the observation from PoC (Proof of Concept):

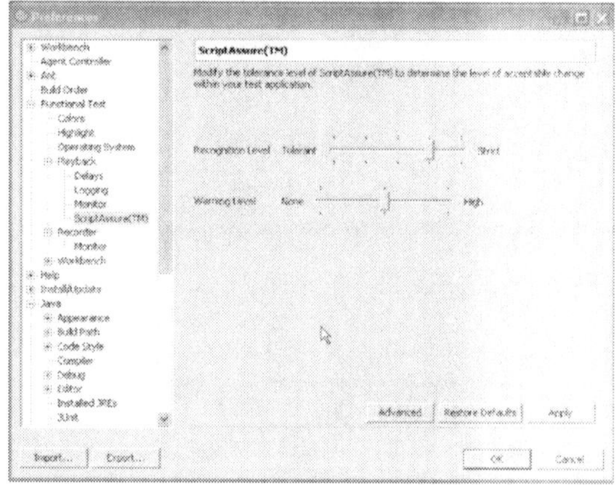

Step4-Record the script:

During the recording of test script, the script commands are appear as object.action() format for example: object.select("item") or object. click(). All commands are based on GUI (Graphical User Interface) objects and test object map plays key role as a repository to all the test objects.

Most used commands are listed below for reference:

edit box, list box, check button, radio button, push button, tab, grid, scroll bar, window, menu, toolbar, edit box

Click on Add Script using Recorder and record the script

Types of common RFT commands

Action Commands: Commands which trigger the events such as click, edit, open such as object.click()

Get Commands: Commands returning the information or the property of the particular element such as object. getProperty("PropertyName")

Verification Point based Commands: Verify object attributes such as objectVP.performtest()

Wait for Existance based Commands: Wait for certain seconds until the appearence of the object and then move on to the next command line such as object.waitforexistance("Test Object ")

Step5-Identify how the objects are mapped for each test script:

Once the test script is recorded, recognized mappings of logical to physical names of classes and objects in the application are stored in following format:

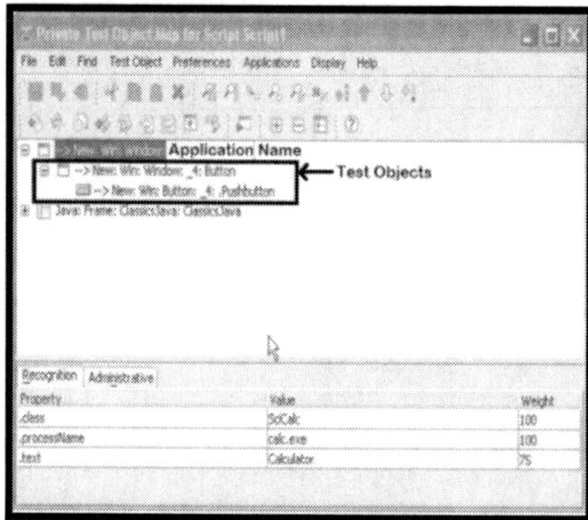

Sample Test Script

```
/*
* Description: Test Automation Sample Script
*/
import resources.order1Helper;
import com.rational.test.ft.*;
import com.rational.test.ft.object.interfaces.*;
import com.rational.test.ft.object.interfaces.SAP.*;
import com.rational.test.ft.object.interfaces.siebel.*;
import com.rational.test.ft.script.*;
import com.rational.test.ft.value.*;
import com.rational.test.ft.vp.*;

public void sampletestMain(Object[] args)
{
// Frame: Order Request System
jmb().click(atPath("Order"));
jmb().click(atPath("Order->Place New Order..."));
// Frame: Member Logon
newCustomer().click();
ok().click();
```

```
// Frame: Place an Order
cardNumberIncludeTheSpacesText().click(atPoint(24, 11));
placeAnOrder().inputChars("Music iPod Buy");
nameText().click(atPoint(27, 13));
placeAnOrder().inputChars("Sell");
phoneText().click(atPoint(17, 12));
placeAnOrder().inputChars("Purchase");
placeOrder().click();
}
```

For further reading and practice, download the projects at https://github.com/narayananpalani/testautomation

Cucumber BDD (Behavior Driven Development)

Cucumber (e.g: Specflow) are wide used automation framework to generate the test scenarios as feature files which are directly influenced by Testable Requirements.

Example Cucumber Project

Requirement

Zoo website should provide the capability to check for animals availability

Feature File

Feature: Proof of concept of the cucumber framework

Scenario: My first test

Given I navigated to zoo website

When I click on the link

Then I check to see that no animals are available

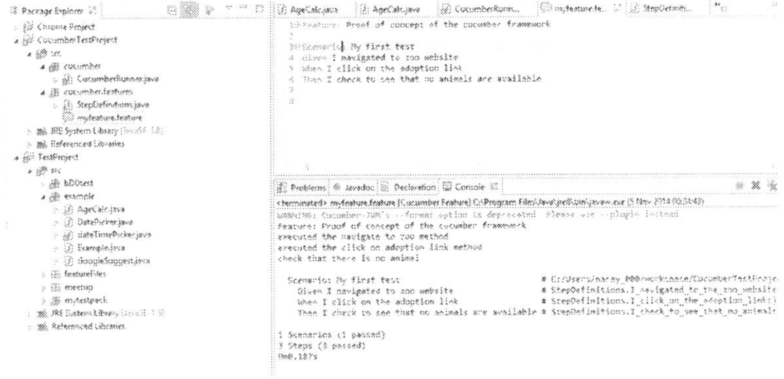

Step Definitions

Each feature files Given, When and Then contains a step definition as follows:

```
package cucumber.features;
import cucumber.api.PendingException;
import cucumber.api.java.en.Given;
import cucumber.api.java.en.Then;
import cucumber.api.java.en.When;

public class StepDefinitions {
        @Given(“^I navigated to zoo website$”)
        public void I_navigated_to_the_zoo_website() throws
Throwable{
        System.out.println(“executed the navigate to zoo method”);
        }

        @When(“^I click on the adoption link$”)
        public void I_click_on_the_adoption_link() throws
Throwable{
                System.out.println(“executed the click on
adoption link method”);
        }
```

```
        @Then("^I check to see that no animals are available$")
        public void I_check_to_see_that_no_animals_are_
available() throws Throwable{
                System.out.println("check that there is no animal");
        }
}
```

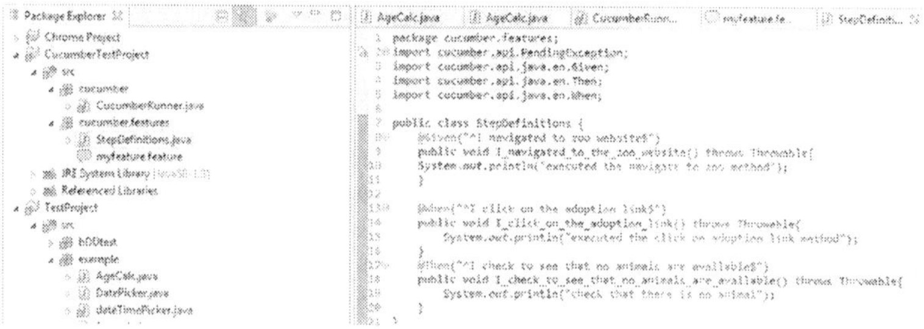

Cucumber Runner

This component help in running the associated feature file with it's step definition:

```
package cucumber;
import org.junit.runner.RunWith;
import cucumber.api.junit.*;
@Runwith(Cucumber.class)
@Cucumber.Option(
                format = {"pretty, "json:target/cucumber.json"}
                features = {"src/cucumber/"}
                )
public class CucumberRunner {

}
```

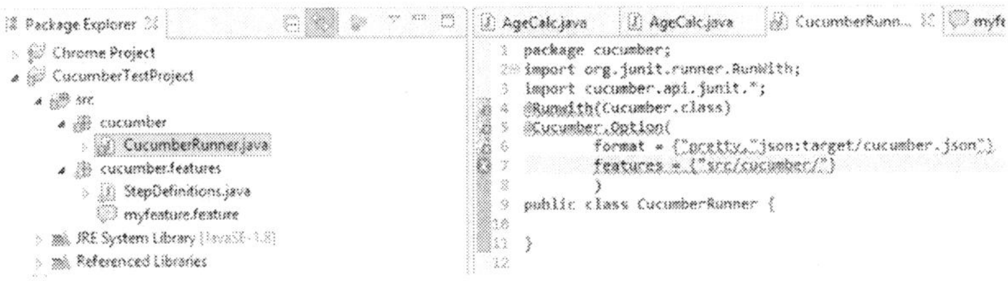
Package Explorer
Chrome Project
CucumberTestProject
src
cucumber
CucumberRunner.java
cucumber.features
StepDefinitions.java
myfeature.feature
JRE System Library [JavaSE-1.8]
Referenced Libraries
AgeCalc.java
AgeCalc.java
CucumberRunn...
package cucumber;
import org.junit.runner.RunWith;
import cucumber.api.junit.*;
@RunWith(Cucumber.class)
@Cucumber.Option(
format = {"pretty","json:target/cucumber.json"},
features = {"src/cucumber/"}
)
public class CucumberRunner {
}

For further reading and practice, download the projects at https://github.com/narayananpalani/testautomation

SOA Test Automation

Service Oriented Architecture (SOA) Testing is an evolving testing domain which is expected grow rapidly in the next twenty years with multiple new implementations. SOA is an architecture overall to build the business applications based on the requirements. It consists of loosely couple black box components orchestrated to provide a well defined/established service by connecting the business processes into one umbrella.

SOA is a collection of services that communicates within, perform data transfer, co-ordinate the activities together for the business requirements!

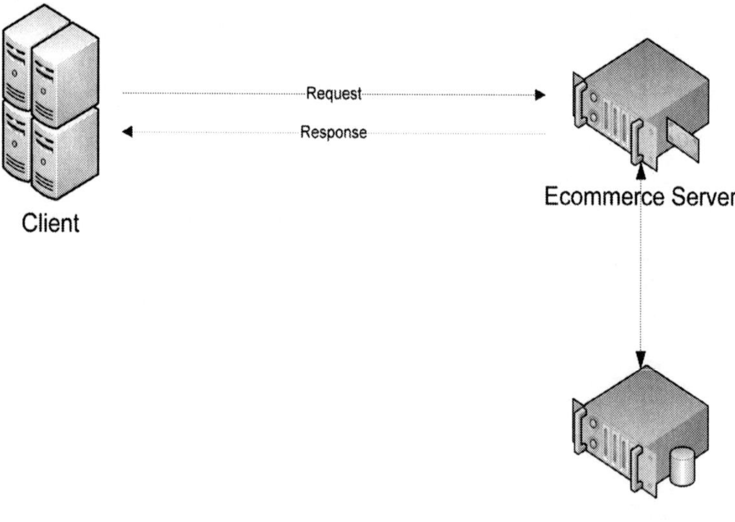

Typical request and response of a eCommerce Server Client Model is described above. If a customer buying a product from eCommerce website, the client computer/device or mobile talks to the server of eCommerce System as a Request and receives the Response in order to process the purchase.

Purchasing of a product from eCommerce SOA-An Example

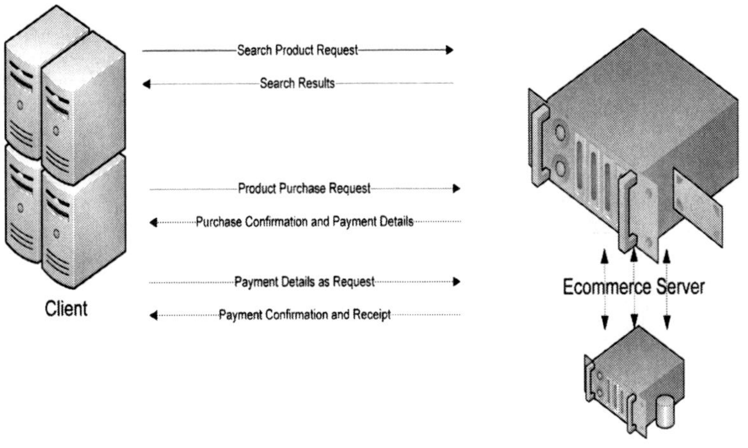

When customers purchase products over the eCommerce portals, they interact with eCommerce servers to get the response and all the request and response are getting stored in Database server in order to track the orders. Verifying requests and responses of these eCommerce transactions need a strong expertise over test automation on the Requests push over the server and verification over the Responses what customers get is typical testing example in SOA model.

What is called 'Service' in SOA?

Any repeatable task in business transaction is considered as service. Request for a exchange rate over the foreign exchange transfer website which is a request and the ideal response is the exchange rate and fee for the particular amount of transfer.

What is 'Service Orientation' in SOA?

When different services are providing similar process results, the better approach in the business is to integrate the related services together. For example, if eCommerce platform integrated to bank payments and shipment systems, the entire workflow get integrated in one login and the user can book the service, pay for the service and use the shipment system till the end of the service which is the integration of the complete services.

What are the types in SOA Testing?

SOAP UI Testing, XML Testing, REST Protocol Testing are some types of SOA testing at the moment.

SOAP Messages Automation

Simple Object Access Protocol (SOAP) is a standard protocol specification for message exchange based on XML. XML messages is used for the communication between the web service and client.

SOAP defines the rules for communication for example what are all the tags that should be used in XML and their meaning. An advantage of SOAP, Since HTTP requests are usually allowed through firewalls(will not filtered by Firewall.), programs using SOAP to communicate can be sure that they can communicate with programs anywhere. WSDL Refactoring allows you to automatically update your tests and simulations to be compliant with new versions of your WSDLs

Automation of SOAP messages is one of the key area where the next generation test automation focussing on!

SOAP message has four parts which are Envelope, Header, Body, Fault. Only Envelope and Body are mandatory in order to send the SOAP messages through the URL.

SOAP Sender usually sends the message with format and data in respective tags. SOAP receiver receives the SOAP messages and process it. So SOAP receiver process and send the response back which will be received and validated.

Sample SOAP Input Message


```
<soapenv:Envelope xmlns:soapenv="http://schemas.xmlsoap.org/soap/envelope/" xmlns:b="http://htng.org/2013A"
xmlns:ns="http://www.opentravel.org/OTA/2003/05"
         xmlns:wsu="http://docs.oasis-open.org/wss/2004/01/oasis-200401-wss-wssecurity-utility-1.0.xsd"
         xmlns:xs="http://www.w3.org/2001/XMLSchema">
  <soapenv:Header>
   <To xmlns="http://schemas.xmlsoap.org/ws/2004/08/addressing">http://localhost:63682/Service1.asmx</To>
   <Action
xmlns="http://schemas.xmlsoap.org/ws/2004/08/addressing">http://localhost:63682/Service1.asmx?op=UpdateRoomStatus</Action>
   <ReplyTo xmlns="http://schemas.xmlsoap.org/ws/2004/08/addressing">
    <Address>http://localhost:63682/Service1.asmx</Address>
   </ReplyTo>
   <MessageID xmlns="http://schemas.xmlsoap.org/ws/2004/08/addressing">uuid:ceb2798e-76d9-433b-87de-
2da0e96557d3</MessageID>
   <Security xmlns="http://docs.oasis-open.org/wss/2004/01/oasis-200401-wss-wssecurity-secext-1.0.xsd">
    <UsernameToken  xmlns="http://docs.oasis-open.org/wss/2004/01/oasis-200401-wss-wssecurity-secext-1.0.xsd"
xmlns:ns15="http://schemas.xmlsoap.org/ws/2006/02/addressingidentity" xmlns:ns14="http://docs.oasis-open.org/ws-sx/ws-
secureconversation/200512" xmlns:ns13="http://www.w3.org/2003/05/soap-envelope" wsu:Id="uuid_f794ba10-e1a0-40ae-b184-
909efbd1e2e9">
     <Username  xmlns="http://docs.oasis-open.org/wss/2004/01/oasis-200401-wss-wssecurity-secext-1.0.xsd">IGRUser</Username>
     <Password  xmlns="http://docs.oasis-open.org/wss/2004/01/oasis-200401-wss-wssecurity-secext-1.0.xsd" Type="http://docs.oasis-
open.org/wss/2004/01/oasis-200401-wss-username-token-profile-1.0#PasswordText">*****</Password>
    </UsernameToken>
   </Security>
  </soapenv:Header>
  <soapenv:Body>
   <b:HTNG_HotelRoomStatusUpdateNotifRQ EchoToken="Echo22222" TimeStamp="2014-08-17T09:30:47Z" Version="1.0">
    <b:POS>
     <b:Source>
      <b:RequestorID Type="10" ID_Context="SUPERHOTEL_PMS" ID="PMS1">
       <b:CompanyName>Superhotel</b:CompanyName>
      </b:RequestorID>
     </b:Source>
    </b:POS>
    <b:PropertyInfo ChainCode="HotelChain" BrandCode="HotelBrand" HotelCode="HotelHotel"/>
    <b:Room RoomID="EE12345">
     <b:Devices>
      <b:Device ID="2341ae3c" FriendlyName="MB-12345" Description="Mini Bar" Class="InRoomRefreshmentCenter">
       <b:PriorHealthStatus Value="ERROR" Reason="UNKNOWN"/>
       <b:CurrentHealthStatus Value="OPERATIONAL"
       Reason="POWER_CYCLED">Manual device reset performed</b:CurrentHealthStatus>
      </b:Device>
      <b:Device ID="ef3278ea" FriendlyName="OS-12345" Description="Ceiling Sensor"
      Class="OccupancyDetection">
       <b:PriorHealthStatus Value="ERROR" Reason="LOW_BATTERY"/>
       <b:CurrentHealthStatus Value="OPERATIONAL"
       Reason="BATTERY_REPLACEMENT">Device online.</b:CurrentHealthStatus>
      </b:Device>
     </b:Devices>
    </b:Room>
   </b:HTNG_HotelRoomStatusUpdateNotifRQ>
  </soapenv:Body>
</soapenv:Envelope>
```


The above message is a sample SOAP Input request message for Room Booking Service which sends to respective SOAP Receiver for Processing the message. The next message is the output received after the process. The below Response Message has to be validated in order to make sure that the request and response are matching as expected.

Sample SOAP Output Message


```
<soap:Envelope xmlns:soap="http://schemas.xmlsoap.org/soap/envelope/" xmlns:xsi="http://www.w3.org/2001/XMLSchema-instance"
xmlns:xsd="http://www.w3.org/2001/XMLSchema" xmlns:wsa="http://schemas.xmlsoap.org/ws/2004/08/addressing"
xmlns:wsse="http://docs.oasis-open.org/wss/2004/01/oasis-200401-wss-wssecurity-secext-1.0.xsd" xmlns:wsu="http://docs.oasis-
open.org/wss/2004/01/oasis-200401-wss-wssecurity-utility-1.0.xsd">
  <soap:Header>
    <wsa:Action>http://localhost:63682/Service1.asmx?op=UpdateRoomStatusResponse</wsa:Action>
    <wsa:MessageID>urn:uuid:b567a472-4528-4508-8e98-2c7e530aef6c</wsa:MessageID>
    <wsa:RelatesTo>uuid:ceb2798e-76d9-433b-87de-2da0e96557d3</wsa:RelatesTo>
    <wsa:To>http://localhost:63682/Service1.asmx</wsa:To>
    <wsse:Security>
      <wsu:Timestamp wsu:Id="Timestamp-7f59be89-cb53-4385-a882-3138dc06e253">
        <wsu:Created>2016-04-16T10:54:06Z</wsu:Created>
        <wsu:Expires>2016-04-16T10:59:06Z</wsu:Expires>
      </wsu:Timestamp>
    </wsse:Security>
  </soap:Header>
  <soap:Body>
    <HTNG_HotelRoomStatusUpdateNotifRS Version="0" xmlns="http://htng.org/2013A">
      <Success/>
    </HTNG_HotelRoomStatusUpdateNotifRS>
  </soap:Body>
</soap:Envelope>
```


SOAP Automation Using Excel VBA

SOAP messages can be sent using Excel VBA (Refer the section of Excel VBA Automation to understand the Visual Basic Editor).

Update SERVER Address with valid address for the URL it is getting used below.

```
Option Explicit

'Set Reference to Microsoft XML, v6.0
Sub login()
   Dim responseText As String
   Dim sURL As String
   Dim sEnv As String
   Dim xmlhtp As New MSXML2.XMLHTTP
   Dim xmlDoc As New DOMDocument
   Dim startPos, endPos, openTag, closeTag, startTagPos, sid
As String
   sURL = "[URL="http://<SERVER ADDRESS>:8080/
axis/services/USD_R11_WebService?wsdl"]http://<
```

```
SERVER ADDRESS >:8080/axis/services/USD_R11_
WebService?wsdl[/URL]"
  sEnv = "<?xml version=""1.0"" encoding=""utf-8""?>"
  sEnv = sEnv & "<soap:Envelope xmlns:xsi=""[URL="http://
www.w3.org/2001/XMLSchema-instance"]http://
www.w3.org/2001/XMLSchema-instance[/URL]""
xmlns:xsd=""[URL="http://www.w3.org/2001/XMLSchema"]
http://www.w3.org/2001/XMLSchema[/URL]""
xmlns:soap=""[URL="http://schemas.xmlsoap.org/soap/
envelope/"]http://schemas.xmlsoap.org/soap/envelope/[/
URL]"">"
  sEnv = sEnv & " <soap:Body>"
  sEnv = sEnv & " <login xmlns=""[URL="http://www.
ca.com/UnicenterServicePlus/ServiceDesk"]http://www.
ca.com/UnicenterServicePlus/ServiceDesk[/URL]"">"
  sEnv = sEnv & " <username></username>"
  sEnv = sEnv & " <password></password>"
  sEnv = sEnv & " </login>"
  sEnv = sEnv & " </soap:Body>"
  sEnv = sEnv & "</soap:Envelope>"
  With xmlhtp
    .Open "post", sURL, False
    .setRequestHeader "Host", "webservices.gama-system.
com"
    .setRequestHeader "Content-Type", "text/xml;
charset=utf-8"
    .setRequestHeader "soapAction", "[URL="http://www.
ca.com/UnicenterServicePlus/ServiceDesk"]http://www.
ca.com/UnicenterServicePlus/ServiceDesk[/URL]"
    .setRequestHeader "Accept-encoding", "zip"
    .send sEnv
    xmlDoc.LoadXML .responseText
    responseText = .responseText
```

```
    End With
    openTag = "<loginReturn"
    closeTag = "</loginReturn>"
    startPos = InStr(1, responseText, openTag) + 10
    endPos = InStr(1, responseText, closeTag)
    startTagPos = InStr(startPos, responseText, ">") + 1
    ' Parse xml for returned value
    sid = Mid(responseText, startTagPos, endPos - startTagPos)
    'Call Next Web Service
    getUser
End Sub
```

Sample Test Project on SOAP Excel VBA Automation

Step1:

Capture the sample SOAP Request:

Request:

```
POST http://www.w3schools.com/webservices/tempconvert.asmx HTTP/1.1
Host: www.w3schools.com
Content-Type: text/xml; charset=utf-8
Content-Length: 388
SOAPAction: "http://www.w3schools.com/webservices/CelsiusToFahrenheit"

<?xml version="1.0" encoding="utf-8"?>
<soap:Envelope xmlns:xsi="http://www.w3.org/2001/XMLSchema-instance" xmlns:xsd="http://www.w3.org/2001/XMLSchema" xmlns:soap="http://schemas.xmlsoap.org/soap/envelope/">
  <soap:Body>
    <CelsiusToFahrenheit xmlns="http://www.w3schools.com/webservices/">
```

```
    <Celsius>25</Celsius>
   </CelsiusToFahrenheit>
  </soap:Body>
</soap:Envelope>
```

Response:

```
HTTP/1.1 200 OK
Cache-Control: private, max-age=0, public
Content-Type: text/xml; charset=utf-8
Date: Thu, 04 Jun 2015 20:59:50 GMT
Server: Microsoft-IIS/7.5
X-AspNet-Version: 4.0.30319
X-Powered-By: ASP.NET
Content-Length: 408

<?xml version="1.0" encoding="utf-8"?><soap:Envelope
xmlns:soap="http://schemas.xmlsoap.org/soap/envelope/"
xmlns:xsi="http://www.w3.org/2001/XMLSchema-
instance" xmlns:xsd="http://www.w3.org/2001/XML
Schema"><soap:Body><CelsiusToFahrenheitResponse
xmlns="http://www.w3schools.com/webservices/"><Celsiu
sToFahrenheitResult>77</CelsiusToFahrenheitResult></
CelsiusToFahrenheitResponse></soap:Body></soap:Envelope>
```

Step2:

Analyse what needs to be parameterized?

Answer: Inputs can be parameterized. In the request above:

<Celsius>25</Celsius>

Step3:

Create a new excel file, insert a button and update with Input column and input value:

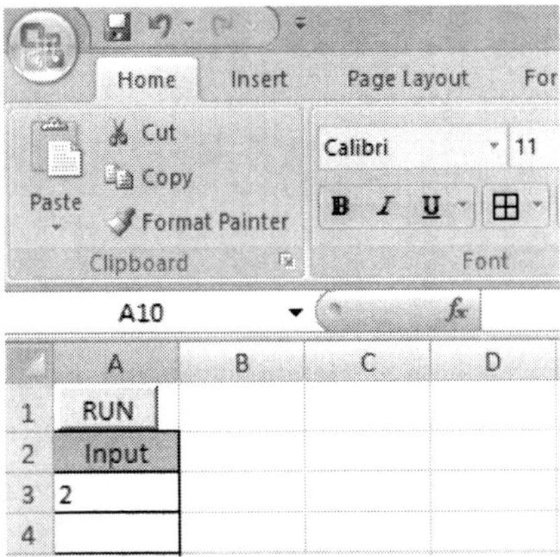

For further reading and practice, download the projects at https://github.com/narayananpalani/testautomation

Data Ware House Testing (DWH)

DWH is one of the highly important and growing sector of software testing industry. The expertise required in DWH/ETL (Extract-Transform-Load) has been very critical for world leading testing projects

Key Advantages of any ETL Tools

As per Ralph Kimball (Author of The Data Warehouse ETL Toolkit), three important area to determine best ETL tools are,

Timeliness of the Tool: How quick the tool performs the ETL process

Data Volume: How much data it is capable of extract, transform and load to process the steps

Response Time: How quick it is to respond back with the results what is required when requested.

Datawarehousing Process Flow

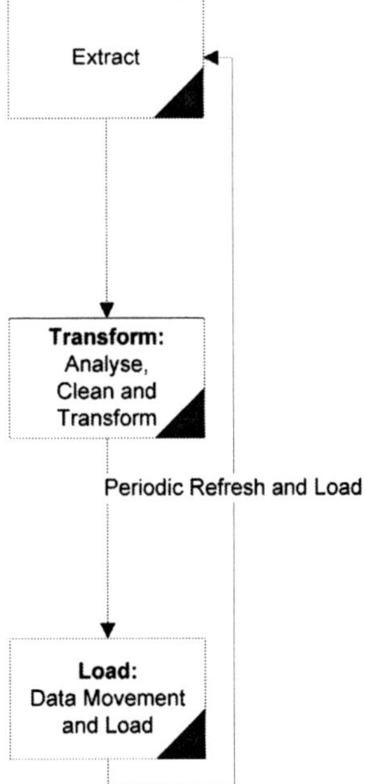

Why Data Transformation is required?

Every business is growing with multiple business transactions which enable to have multiple databases for store the records. Each database have different codification and format requirements based on the business need.

When two business merge, this create a disparity over the data representations. So Merger and Acquisitions provide a gateway to handle ETL process in a structured and more advanced method.

Why The Data Has To Be Transformed?

Operational data of business has to be converted into a consistent, business oriented format which lead to the need of transformation. Which means that the transformation computes the derived information and summarization is carried out to aggregate and pre-compute the summaries.

When The Importance of Load To Be Known?

If multiple data formats are used in different database tables, it is obvious that the load process is tedious in order to maintain the large database systems.

The ETL Process of DWH Testing

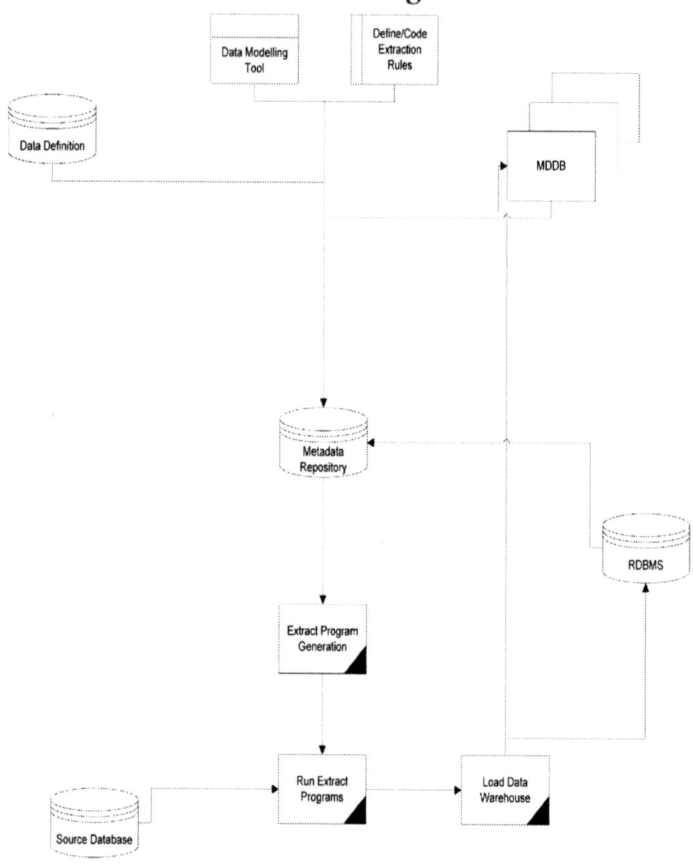

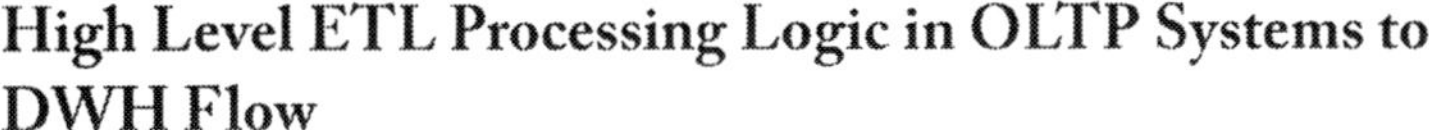

High Level ETL Processing Logic in OLTP Systems to DWH Flow

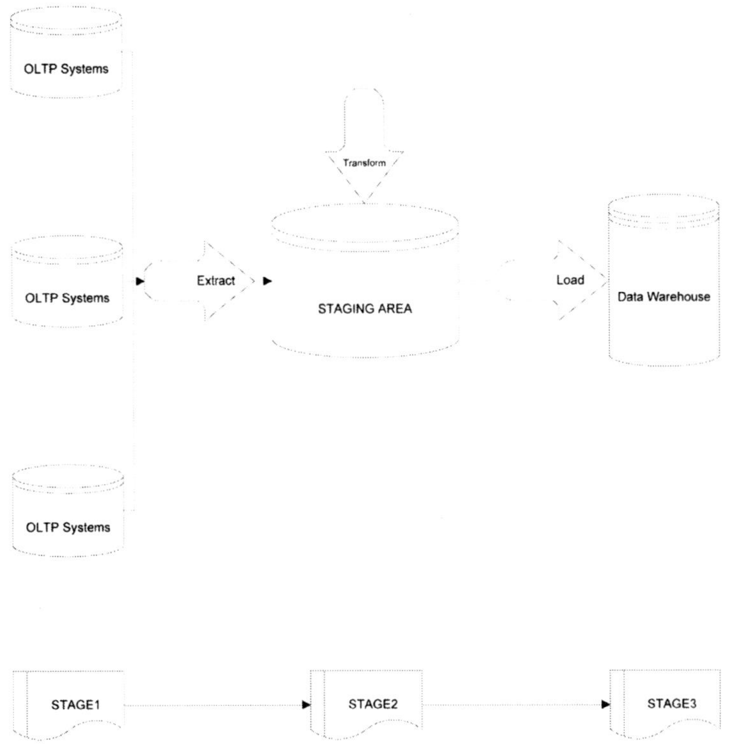

How Organizations Choose Among ETL Products

When big organizations change over a period of time, they adapt either generic solutions which are built in already to serve the market needs or they adapt a custom solution in which specifications are made based on the business needs. In custom solutions RDBMS staging tables and stored procedures are used and programming languages such as C, C++, Perl, Visual Basic are most required skills to perform customization. Building Code Generators are the key tasks of those ETL activities. Either of the ways the testing of data transformation is compulsory to make sure that the ETL process is working as expected.

Why Generic Solutions are Required by Organizations?

Auto generated scripts are major advantage of generic solutions and the limitation due to manual coding across project has been reduced when the solutions are implemented. Especially if the business value has to be quantified in terms of how benefit it is to implement any tool or solution? is something depends on how beneficiary the tool is. With the help of Generic solutions functionality, reliability and viability are no longer considered as major or critical issues by organizations!

ETL Tools

Huge number of transformation rules with a GUI (Graphical User Interface) can be specified by ETL tools. These ETL tools can generate programs to transform data across the database. Multiple data sources can be controlled and data redundancy can be addressed to the greater extent!

Metadata can be generated as output from ETL tools and most of the tools run multi-threaded environment based low-cost servers to benefit the ease of tool usage!

ETL Tool-Classification

Generation 1: Code Generation Oriented Products

Some of the famous first generation tools: Prism, Passport, ETI-Extract, Copy Manager, SAS/Warehouse Administrator

Source code generated through ETL tools in first generation and most of the projects customized the source code to executable code to utilize in projects. GUI interfaces are used to define the process and server or host runs the extract, transform and load process. Most of the tools generate the source code automatically for extract program and it can be compiles, scheduled and run in batch mode. Intermediate files also used and most of the programs were single threaded in first generation with the capability of metadata generation to limited amount of the complete project.

Though the tools were mature and programmers were capable of use their Cobol, C and C++ knowledge to generate code, the training to those ETL tools were complex and expensive. Especially Extract related programs has to be compiled from source and transformation based code has to be customized manually for single execution as parallel execution was not supported in those days! So most of the metadata were manually generated with limited amount of auto generation in place!

Generation 2: Engine Directed Projects

Some of the famous first generation tools: Data Mart Solution, DataStage, PowerCenter/Mart

Executable code can be generated when configuration and customization are set as per the project description and this executable code can directly generate metadata as outputs with the help of Generation 2 tools! All Extraction, Transformation and Load runs can be performed in server machines and data can be directly processed on server from source.

Structured Query Language (SQL) for Software Testing

Functional Testers are expected to hold good knowledge on SQL to get into testing projects as a basic requirement. This is to make sure that the project database has been verified based on the tests performed. In terms of DB verification, basic queries of SQL is highly recommended as a knowledge base for any entry level testers.

For automation testers, Advanced SQL level understanding is highly recommended as the code has to interact with DB to extract the relevant test results and match them with front end results.

What is SQL?

SQL is structured query language for storing, manipulating and retrieving data which stored in relational database. Some relational databases are as follows: MySQL, MS Access, Oracle, Sybase, Informix

Enhance Automation Framework with DB verification Capability

Let us take an example of implementing SQL based tests in selenium. Download the required jar file (mysql-connector-java-3.1.13-bin.jar)from:

http://www.java2s.com/Code/Jar/m/Downloadmysqlconnectorjava3114bingjar.htm

Once downloaded, update to the Reference Libraries as mentioned in the earlier chapters on the Automation Framework Development.

```
//As part of the class file, update the required imports as follows:

import org.TestNG.After;
import org.TestNG.Before;
import org.TestNG.Test;
import java.sql.Connection;
import java.sql.DriverManager;
import java.sql.ResultSet;
import java.sql.Statement;

//This class file is explained in terms of adapting the DB verification within the selenium script
public class DBTesing {
// Database URL has been assigned with DB_URL as a constant
public static String DB_URL="jdbc:mysql://localhost:3306/user";
// Connection object which is assigned to null initially.
static Connection con = null;
// Statement object is assigned as stmt
private static Statement stmt;
// Constant for DB Username
public static String DATABASE_USER = "root";
// Constant for Database Password
public static String DATABASE _PASSWORD = "root";
@Before
public void setUp() throws Exception {
try{
// Database connection is getting established in this line
String dbClass = "com.mysql.jdbc.Driver";
Class.forName(dbClass).newInstance();
// DB Connection is getting estabilished here:
Connection con = DriverManager.getConnection(DB_URL, DATABASE_USER, DATABSE_PASSWORD);
```

```
// Statement object to send the SQL statement to the Database
stmt = con.createStatement();
}
catch (Exception e)
{
e.printStackTrace();
}
}
@Test
public void test() {
try{
//Insert the SQL query within the Selenium Script here:
String query = "select * from table  t where empid=101";
// Get the contents of t table from DB
ResultSet res = stmt.executeQuery(query);
// Print the result untill all the records are printed
// res.next() returns true if there is any next record else returns false
while (res.next())
{
System.out.print(res.getString(1));
System.out.print("\t" + res.getString(2));
System.out.print("\t" + res.getString(3));
System.out.println("\t" + res.getString(4));
}
}
catch(Exception e)
{
e.printStackTrace();
}
}
@After
public void tearDown() throws Exception {
```

```
// Close Database connection
if (con != null) {
con.close();
}
}
}
```

Sample Test Plans

Training Institute-Training Webpage Master Test Plan

Introduction

This is the Master Test Plan for Training Institute-Training who is highly adept in IT field and provides teaching, training and project work. They give individual attention and help throughout the course to help build their skills and market standards.

This plan will address only the items and elements as listed in the test plane. The primary focus of this plan is to ensure that all the functions of the web page is working fine to unable user to find the information they need about training and course and identify any issues or functions that are not working properly.

The project will have five levels of testing, Unit, System, Integration, Performance and Acceptance. The details for each level are addressed in the approach section and will be further defined in the level specific plans

The estimated timeline for this project is very aggressive (Eight (8) months), as such, any delays in the development process or in the installation and verification of the third party software could have significant effects on the test plan. The acceptance testing is expected to take twenty days from the application delivery from system test and is to be done in parallel with the current application process.

Test Items

The following is a list, by version and release, of the items to be tested:

A. About Us

B. Course

C. Learning Methods

D. Schedules

E. FAQ's

F. Careers

The following is a list, by version and release, of the items not to be tested:

A. Contact Us

Software Risk Issues

There are several parts of the project that are not within the control of this project but have direct impact on the process and must be checked as well.

A. Tabs are not working

B. Website is not working on windows or apple base system

C. Website doesn't support chrome or internet explorer version

Features To Be Tested

A. About Us

B. Course

C. Learning Methods

D. Schedules

E. FAQ's

F. Careers

Features Not To Be Tested

A. Contact Us

Approach (Strategy)

Functional Testing is used in this project and there are plans to implement Selenium in later cycles

Item Pass/Fail Criteria

When the Tests meet the requirements: Item Pass

When the Test Results failed to meet the requirements: Item Fail

Suspension Criteria and Resumption Requirements

If the Test Environment is not available, tests has to be suspended and resumed only when the environment is ready

Test Deliverable

Master Test Plan

Test Scenarios High Level

Test Cases

Test Data Sheet

Tools and their inputs

Emulators

Error Logs and Execution Logs

Problem Reports and Corrective Actions

Remaining Test Tasks

Task	Assigned To	Status
Create Test Data Sheet	Test Engineer	
Create Test Framework	Automation Tester	
Verify emulator prototype	Test Lead	
Verify Webpage	Environment Manager	
Verify Test Plan	Test Manager	

Environmental Needs

Wifi-Strong Internet Connection

Server of the AUT

Laptop's Hardware Requirements: Windown 10 X 64 Bit with 8GB Ram

Staffing and Training Needs

Preferred to have exclusive test resource for performance testing.

All testers need to be trained in Eggplant as it is essential to undergo custom based application training before test execution

Responsibilities

Test Execution Signoff: Test Manager

Test Evidences Signoff: Business Analyst

End of Test Report Sign off: Project Manager

Schedule

Test Cycle based schedule is updated in QC for Test Execution. Overall mobile testing assignment is schedule for nine months.

Planning Risks and Contingencies

A. Limited Test Resources for Performance Testing

B. Unavailability of Resources during Regional Holidays

Approvals

Project Sponsor: Baba

Development Management: Training Institute-Training Team

Project Manager: Thakur

Environment Manager: Imran

Sample Mobile Application Test Plan

Note: Following is the sample test plan derived after using the mobile app MobileApp in Android device. Users requested to download this app to understand the below sample test plan format

Test plan identifier: T4245

Reference: App name: MobileApp version:2.2.0(2.0.1-LONG)

- Project plan: Providing a secure app for users example people can share their details such as DOB or bank details without any doubt.
- System Requirement: This app is work just on the latest version of IOS in iPhone and latest version of android.
- Low Level Requirement: This app is only work in latest version of iPhone and HTC or any other phone BUT if it won't be latest version then your phone may be can get hacked.
- Design : This app design is very simple. you can add a person just by phone number and then later it will come up in activity.

Introduction

This is the test plan for MobileApp mobile application. This document explains the testing methodology for a mobile application, and is to be used as a guide for the testing activity. The scope of testing as explained in the document is to test the operating characteristics of an application that runs on mobile devices supporting Android and iOS.

This plan will address the items and elements as listed in the test items. The primary focus of this plan is to ensure that all the functions of MobileApp mobile application version 2.2.4.1028.ff8c9c9 (1028) is working fine, identifying any faults with the application, report it back to the developer team, carry out regression testing and close the testing when everything is fixed.

The estimated timeline for this project is 2 weeks, as such, any delays in the development process could have significant effects on the test plan.

Test Items

MobileApp App, version 2.2.0 in Emulator

MobileApp App for IOS

MobileApp App for Android

MobileApp website

Software Risk Issues

The following may impact the test cycle:

- Device availability – Android and iOS
- Any new feature addition/modification to the application which is not communicated in advance.
- Any delay in the software delivery schedule including defect fixes. Any changes in the functional requirements since the requirements were signed-off/formulated

Existing Software Risk Identified and needs to be investigated as part of testing in this release.

Features to be Tested

The following are the features to be tested that will be performed to the MobileApp mobile application version 2.2.4.1028.ff8c9c9 (1028).

A. Application Characteristics (AC) – Information about the application is provided to help the testing team in the testing work.

B. Stability (ST) – Focusing on the application being stable on the device.

C. Application Launch (AL) – Once an application is loaded it must start (launch) and stop correctly in relation to the device and other applications on the device.

D. User Interface (UI)

E. Operating Characteristics (OP) - of an application that runs on mobile devices supporting Android and iOS.

F. Functionality (FN) - Documented features are implemented in the application and work as expected. Sources for the information are user manuals, formatted application specification documents and online documentation.

G. Connectivity (CO) – the application must demonstrate its ability to communicate over a network correctly. It must be capable of dealing with both network problems and server-side problems.

H. Personal Information Management (PI) - The application accessing user information needs to be able to do it in an appropriate manner and not to destroy the information.

I. Security

Test Estimation

Following are the test estimation in MANDAYS:

Product	Resources	Test Design	System Testing	Integration Testing	UAT	Total Duration
MobileApp App, version 2.2.0 in Emulator	1	5	3	2	1	11
MobileApp App for IOS	1	2	3	2	1	8
MobileApp App for Android	1	2	3	2	1	8
MobileApp website		2	3	2	1	8
						35

Features not to be Tested

Network Security and Service Layer Access

Hardware Assembly (Mobile Phone itself)

Approach strategy

MobileApp app is planned to be tested in following mobiles types: Iphone and Samsung as per IEEE standards

Pass/Fail Conditions

It is expected that test cases must pass all the tests in each test category to be successful.

A retest needs to be performed on any test that have failed.

Suspension Criteria/Resumption Requirements

Resumption

- Development of the application is complete
- Successful completion of unit testing for the applications
- Release of software to the test environment
- Dedicated resources are allocated
- Test Cases have been reviewed
- Test environment is up and working
- Build is complete and smoke test has been done.

Suspension

The Following is the criteria when the testing will be stopped for this module:

- The test cases have all been executed.
- At least 95% have passed successfully and The remaining 5% that have failed do not impact critical functionality
- The test results have been evaluated reviewed and accepted.
- There are no showstoppers or high criticality defects unresolved or outstanding

Remaining Test Tasks

Task	Assigned To	Status
Create Mobile Test Framework	Automation Tester	
Verify the Mobile Test Resource Plan	Test Manager	
Create Test Data Sheet	Test Engineer	
Verify emulator prototype	Test Lead	
Verify Cloud Computing Environment	Environment Manager	

Environmental Needs

The following elements are required to support the overall test at all levels within the mobile project:

- Access to both development and production based emulators and mobile applications.
- An exclusive test environment for performance testing as it should impact the regular test executions of other test cycles.

Staffing and Training Needs

Preferred to have exclusive test resource for performance testing.

All testers need relevant training as it is essential to undergo custom based application training before test execution.

Responsibilities

Responsibilities of the testing team for the project are as follows:

Test Execution Signoff: Test Manager

Test Evidences Signoff: Business Analyst

End of Test Report Sign off: Project Manager

Schedule

Overall mobile testing schedule will be decided with the project manager.

Planning Risks and Contingencies

When mobile devices are not available for testing, emulators should be used

If there is an immediate deployment required for the patch, functional testing need to be conducted on the fly to make sure all the major functionalities are working fine.

As a contingency plan, when the mobile application is failing as part of the testing, earlier version of call sign app needs to be considered for testing

Approvals

Test Plan Approval-CTO

Mobile Testing-Tips

"Entry Criteria for Mobile Testing

Requirements should be delivered successfully to enter into the Testing Assignment. Stable mobile application should be ready for testing and test plan should have been reviewed and approved.

Task

Set of tasks to be performed as part of mobile testing like test scenario preparation, test case design, test data preparation, test case review, uploaded reviewed test pack to test execution tools as per the test execution activities.

Validation

Validation of the mobile products and application are taken care in this phase.

Validation: Are we testing the right product?'

Verification: Verification: Are we testing the product right?

Exit Criteria

Some of the major exit criteria are like relevant test cases should have been executed as part of test execution. Designed documents like test data, test results documents should have got approved. Test log and defect log are properly mapped to the test execution results. Review and sign off approvals of End of Test Report is one of the primary criteria to exit from the mobile testing projects

Constraints and Challenges over the Mobile Test Automation Projects

Mobile devices have been expanding across the platforms and browsers and rendering different offerings across the globe. Hence the device diversity is pretty much high comparing to any other product types, it requires an exclusive expertise over particular product type specialization. Expertise resource utilization over the latest technology and application is a major challenge in this automation projects. Multiple network operators and networks are used like GSM, GPRS, Wi-Fi, Wi-Max and connectivity speed vary across the region. So simulating the exact customer like scenario in the tests are bit challengeable in test automation. Because limitations over the processing speed and mobile memory size are tough to simulate in the emulators or the test environment. "

-From the book *'Mobile Software Testing'* by author

Quick Recap of Software Testing Fundamentals

Basics	Examples
Requirement - is a functionality that anyone expects from the system.	A customer shall be able to pay the rent online to the council
Scenario - is any condition that could possibly happen in production while the requirement executed.	Verify a customer is able to log in to his/her rent account Verify a customer is able to make the payment Verify customer receive the rent payment receipt confirmation Verify rent system shows no outstanding debit on his/her rent account

Test Case - Input + Pre-conditions > Post-conditions + Output	Council online domain should be up and running. A customer should have valid user name and password and account set up.
Test Set - A group of tests similar test cases that require the same steps to be executed	1. Open a browser and type www.company.co.uk 2. Enter user name and password 3. Log in to rent account and check outstanding rent balance 4. Make payment and submit 5. Receive payment confirmation 6. Check system is updated and shows nil outstanding rent
Test Data	A customer is required to have online rent account A customer is required to have user name and password

Basics of Software Testing

1. Requirement:

The Requirement is needed to design a test. Requirement can be described as any functionality(task) expects out of system. A Single requirement can have number of scenarios.

Example :

1. Customers must be able to place orders online.
2. Downloading or Uploading documents or videos online.

2. Test Scenario :

High level of requirements can be deal through with concepts of scenarios, it could be any condition that could happen in production. Each requirement can have number of scenarios, the more scenarios one can think and test, the more reliable and more predictable the system is going to be.

Example :

1. Someone try to cancel the order which does not exists Or which has been already cancelled Or not has been cancelled before Or can cancels the order which is refundable or non-refundable.. any one condition

2. Someone try to upload a document but not logged in Or not registered on the site Or trying to upload a document which is exceeding the uploading document size limit.

3.Test Cases :

Test cases are described as set of pre-conditions (they are all the conditions that exists before the test) and input, which would produce a set of post-conditions and output. A scenario can have number of test cases. There is a one too many relationship between scenarios and test cases.

Example :

1. Customer cancels a refundable order...then the test case would be Mr. A cancelling the order no. 1234 and that order is refundable one and was paid by credit card and the credit card is still available, the order now been cancelled.

In the above example the order number is the input (i.e.1234) and pre-conditions are the all those facts about order(not cancelled before, it has been paid by credit card, credit card is still valid and it has not been chipped).

For this test case Post-conditions would be: order cancelled, credit card is debited with right amount, inventory reflected back with cancellation. And output would be some sort of confirmation of cancellation of order message.

Difference between one test case to another would be the difference between the input and pre-conditions and as a result a difference in the post-conditions or in the output. This way one can create large number of test cases for the same scenario.

4. Test Set :

A group of similar test cases that require the same steps to be executed for e.g. cancellation of order would be cancellation of order regardless of it has been cancelled before or whether its refunded or non refunded one.

Example:

You can have 40 or more test cases that have to do with cancellation of orders.

5. Test Script :

Test Script is a set of steps needed to execute similar test cases, be it a manual or automated. For each test set you have one test script. Test cases that require same step to be executed again and again, Test Script is attached to the test set. There is one too many relationship from Test Set to Test Cases because each Test Set consists of a number of similar Test Cases.

Sample Test plan for the Online shopping mall Web Application

Test Plan Identifier: OSM-01

Introduction:

This Master TEST PLAN is to test the OSM Web Application (the online shopping) and to verify the application is running efficiently and reliably for the End users. So we are going to Test all the items and features in the application. We make sure the application is defect or fault free, however the Functional testing execution raised up with the fault or failure of application, we will then create a new defect lifecycle to programmer.

After the issues fixed up the Unit testing will be taken and transfer to the re testing for final follow up before reaching UAT. This test execution needs a latest version of browser and a Internet connection to processed a good Testing environment.

Test Items:

- OSM webpage
- Category
- Search
- Checkout and cart

- Login for users, Administrator, vendors
- Registration for visitors, Shop vendors
- Requesting for shop
- Customer care
- Status
- Feedback with Book entry
- Add, remove, update categories/Items
- Sales report

Software Risk issues:

The test cycle will get delayed in the following issues.

1. Any delay in the network, may slow down the testing process
2. Version of the web browser, may cause delay in opening the webpage
3. Display session expires and re attempt for the login

Features to be tested:

The following features to checked are:

- Lunching the webpage should display the Home page with the logo, Menus, tabs, sub tabs.
- The Home page should display the search button, View category menu item which as the several check box like Apparel, Kitchen, accessories, Bath accessories, Food items.
- When clicking each any every check box it should direct the new page with relevant products items and also it must show the Most purchased product.

- By giving the valid username and password in the login section should open the user Account.
- By giving the invalid entry it should display the error massage with the cancel and new user registration button
- After the login attempt it shows View my profile button, by clicking this should navigate the new page with all information.
- After selecting the products the page should allow the user to add the items in cart, or to proceed the checkout directly.
- The product page should contains the customer care button, So while clicking this should navigate the page down to seller information and a customer care details.
- The Cart should allow the user to add n number of items for purchase. Minimum rage will be 1 item.
- If the product is out of stock then by clicking the buy or add to cart should show the error message and followed by other best selling products, customer care, and product updating alert.
- After the conformation the page should directs to a new page which as users profile information and buying history
- By clicking check out after selecting the items, should enables the users to add or remove items before payment method.
- In the null purchase state, clicking the order status, cancel order should shows error message. If the item as been purchased then by clicking Order status, Cancel order, give feedback, should opens new page with all needed information
- When the administrator get login the new page with following menus should appears, Manage employees,

Approve/ reject shop creation request, add/ remove categories, view guest book. By clicking these should navigate the new page with all information.

- When the shop vendor get login then it directs to a new page with following menus, Maintain shop, Advertise product, ,Add/ remove, update items, create sales reports, discontinue shop.

Features not to be tested:

Not such item listed.

Approach strategy:

The OSM web application is planned to tested in the windows 8 with the updated chrome browser as per the IEEE standard.

In this it is will be functional testing.

Pass/ Fail conditions:

It is expected that all test cases must pass all the tests execution in each test category to be successful.

A re- test needs to be performed on any test that have failed and re fixed.

Suspension criteria/ Resumption requirements:

Suspension:

- Test execution may get interrupt due to poor Internet connection
- The old version of browser can cause delay in process
- The delay in developing

Resumption:

- The Development of the Application is completed
- The test cases have been reviewed
- The release the application to Test environment

Reaming task:.

Test case, test execution, end report.

Environment needs:

The elements required to support the test are as follows:

- Internet
- System with windows 8 or more updated version
- Web browser with newly updated

Staffing and training needs:

Need training in web application

Responsibilities:

Test manager

Schedule:

5days for the developing and 2day execution

Sample Test Requirement-Functional Requirements for Pay.co.uk(sample site)

Functional Requirements-

A. System should display homepage when launched

B. System should allow users to register and create account (Personal or business)

C. Existing users must be able to sign in

D. System should allow user to view available balance, completed and pending balance.

E. System must allow existing users with credit to pay and send money up to available balance.

F. System must allow users with a positive balance withdraw funds up to available balance to bank account on profile.

G. System should allow users create and manage invoices.

H. System should allow user see and view a dashboard of account activities.

I. System should allow users to create and edit profile

J. System must allow user to add a bank account registered to users name.

K. System must allow user to link a credit card registered to users address.

L. System should allow user to link personal verified phone number.

M. System should allow user to view transactions. Historical transaction of a maximum of 3yrs should be available when requested.

N. System should allow user to link account to ebay.

O. System must be able to process payment while prompted from 3rd party's website.

A. System should display homepage when launched

I. The website www.pay.co.uk(sample site) is entered and queried.

Input=www.pay.co.uk(sample site) PreConditions- Internet, browser, website is valid. Post Condition- website successfully loads. Output-Page successfully displays the homepage.

II. Incorrect address is typed and queried.

Input= www.pay.co.uk or any site other than www.pay.co.uk(sample site). Pre-conditions-Internet browser, internet, invalid website. POST CONDITION- Website tries to load. OUTPUT- Page displays an error message.

B. System should allow users to register and create account (Personal or business)

I. User creates an account with acceptable data

Input= DRTAYO. PreCondtions-Username has not been chosen by another user. User name is acceptable. PostCondition- Account is created successfully. Output-Confirmation of successful account is displayed and user details are displayed.

II. User creates an account with unacceptable data.

Input= Paypal. Preconditions- Username has been chosen by paypal. Username is not allowed for public use. PostCondition- Account creation is denied. Output- Unsuccessful account message is displayed to user.

III. User creates multiple accounts on same profile.

INPUT- DRTAYO. Preconditions-Username not available to choose. POSTCONDITION- Account creation is denied. OUTPUT- Account is not created and an unsuccessful message is displayed

IV. User creates a personal and business account

INPUT- Drsmith. Precondition-username is available and not chosen by someone else. POSTCONDITION- Account is created. OUTPUT- Successful creation of account and confirmation.

V. User creates an account with data already chosen by another user.

Input- DrManoharran. Precondition-Username is not available to choose. POSTCONDITION- Username is rejected. Output- Rejection message and reason is displayed for user (account not created)

C. Existing users must be able to sign in

I. User signs in with valid credentials

INPUT- DrPatel (Valid). Precondition-Username is valid entered correctly. POSTCONDITION-Username is accepted. Username is verified and validated. OUTPUT- successful login and entry into account is granted.

II. User signs in with invalid credentials

INPUT- Drt=patel (Invalid). PRECONDITION- Username is invalid and unacceptable characters. POSTCONDITION- Details are rejected and not acceptable by system. OUTPUT- Rejection message is displayed and the reason stated on screen to user.

III. Non existing/unregistered user signs in with credentials

INPUT-DRzimzim. PRECONDITION- Username does not exist in database. POSTCONDTION-Details cannot be verified and validated in database. OUTPUT. Rejection message shows on users screen, thus details are not accepted

D. System should allow user to view available balance, completed and pending balance

I. User tries to view available balance

INPUT- Available balance. PRECONDITION- Balance is available to view. User is verified. POSTCONDITION- Balance displays. OUTPUT- Successful display of balance on screen.

II. User tries to view unavailable balance

INPUT- Balance. PRECONDITION- Balance is not available to view. User is verified. POSTCONDTION- Balance unavailable to display. OUTPUT- No figures/ balance is displayed.

E. System must allow existing users with credit to pay and send money up to available balance.

I. User tries to pay/send money within available limit .Eg £100

INPUT- £30. PRECONDITION- Amount is within and less than available limit (£100). POSTCONDITION- Balance has been adjusted. Amount sent has been deducted.

OUTPUT- The amount of £30 has been successfully sent. Confirmation displayed.

II. User tries to pay/send amount that exceeds what is available in balance. Eg £100

INPUT- £110. PRECONDITION- Amount exceeds available balance. (£100). POSTCONDTION-Balance has not been adjusted. No amount has been deducted. OUTPUT- Error message informing user that amount exceeds available balance

III. User tries to send money with a zero or minus balance. Eg (£2)

INPUT - £10. PRECONDTION- Amount is within and less than available limit. No amount has been deducted. POSCONDITION- Balance has not been affected. OUTPUT—Error message informing user that the amount exceeds available balance.

F. System must allow users with a positive balance withdraw funds up to available balance to bank account on profile.

I. User tries to withdraw funds that are below available balance into bank account. Eg £600

INPUT- £60. PRECONDITION- Amount is within and less than available limit (£600). POSTCONDITION- Balance has been adjusted. Amount sent has been deducted. OUTPUT- The amount of £60 has been successfully sent. Confirmation displayed.

II. User tries to withdraw funds that are greater than what is available in balance to bank account. Eg £300

INPUT- £330. PRECONDITION- Amount exceeds available balance. (£300). POSTCONDTION-Balance has not been adjusted. No amount has been deducted.

OUTPUT- Error message informing user that amount exceeds available balance

III. User tries to withdraw funds into a different account than what is available on file.

INPUT - £20. New unverified bank account. PRECONDITION- Amount is valid and within withdrawal limit. A new unverified bank account selected. POSTCONDITION- Balance has not been adjusted. No funds withdrawn. OUTPUT- Error message, informing user of discrepancies in banking details.

G. System should allow users create and manage invoices

I. User tries to create and send invoice.

INPUT- Amount entered, email address of recipient entered. PRECONDITION- Valid email address. Valid amount. POSTCONDITION-Invoice is successfully created. Amount accepted, invoice successfully sent. OUTPUT-Invoice is successfully sent and confirmation message is displayed.

II. User tries to view invoice

INPUT- Select invoice to view. PRECONDITION- Invoice is selected. Invoice is valid. Invoice has not been cancelled. POSTCONDITION- Invoice is successfully viewed. Invoice displays. OUTPUT- Invoice displays on screen.

III. User tries to edit invoice.

INPUT- Amount or information on invoice is edited. PRECONDITION- Invoice is still valid. Invoice is available. POSTCONDITION- Invoice is edited. OUTPUT- Invoice is changed and edited successfully.

IV. User tries to cancel invoice. (Eg invoice 562)

INPUT- Invoice no 562. PRECONDITION- Invoice 562 is available. Invoice has not been cancelled. POST CONDITION- Invoice is cancelled. OUTPUT- Confirmation of cancellation shown.

H. System should allow users to create and edit profile.

I. User tries to create new profile.

INPUT- Name, DOB, address, phone number. PRECONDITION-Valid name, dob, address and phone number combination. POSTCONDITION- Profile is created. OUTPUT- Confirmation of successful profile creation.

II. User tries to edit profile

INPUT-Name,DOB,Phonenumber.PRECONDITION-Acceptable data (Name, DOB, Address and phone number). POSTCONDITION-Details are edited in profile. OUTPUT- Successful and confirmation of edited profile.

III. User tries to delete profile

INPUT- Delete functionality. PRECONDITION-Profile is available, Profile is valid. Profile is selected. POSTCONDITION- Profile is deleted. Profile is unavailable after deleting. OUTPUT- Successfully deleted profile.

I. System must allow user to add a bank account registered to users name.

I. User tries to add bank account registered to users' name.

INPUT- Bank Account number and sort code, name on bank card. PRECONDITION-User profile still exist. User does not have existing bank account on file. POSTCONDITION-Bank account is accepted. Profile updated. OUTPUT- Bank account is successfully added.

II. User tries to add multiple bank account registered to users name.

INPUT- Bank account number and sort code, name on bank card. PRECONDITION- User profile exist, user has existing bank account on file. POSTCONDITION- Bank account is not accepted. OUTPUT- Rejection notice. User is informed about an existing bank account.

III. User tries to add bank account registered to a name other than user's name.

INPUT- Bank account number and sort code, name on bank card. PRECONDITION- User profile exist, bank account holder is different from account holder. POSTCONDITION- Bank account is not accepted. OUTPUT- Rejection notice. User is informed about discrepancies in account holders.

IV. User tries to add bank account not issued in the UK.

INPUT- Bank account number and name on bank card. PRECONDITION- User profile exist. Card issuer is not within the UK. POSTCONDITION- Bank account is not accepted. OUTPUT- Rejection notice. User is informed that only UK cards are accepted.

J. System must allow user to link a credit card registered to users address.

I. User tries to link credit card registered to users address.

INPUT- Credit card details. PRECONDITION-Valid credit card, valid address. POSTCONDITION—Credit card is successfully linked to address. OUTPUT- Credit card confirmed and successfully linked.

II. User tries to link credit card not registered to his address.

INPUT- Credit card details. PRECONDITION-Valid credit card, invalid address. POSTCONDITION—Card cannot be linked due to difference in address. OUTPUT- Unsuccessful/unacceptable link.

III. User tries to link invalid/expired credit card to his address.

INPUT- Credit card details. PRECONDITION-Invalid credit card, valid address. POSTCONDITION- Invalid/ unacceptable credit card. OUTPUT- Unsuccessful due to invalid card message.

K. System should allow user to link personal verified phone number.

I. User tries to link personal verified phone number

INPUT- UK Telephone number. PRECONDITION- Valid UK telephone number. Available profile. POSTCONDITION- Telephone number is accepted. Telephone number is stored and added to profile. OUTPUT- Successfully linked telephone number.

II. User tries to link unverified phone number.

INPUT- UK Telephone number. PRECONDITION- Valid UK telephone number. Not available and not verified. POSTCONDITION- Telephone number is rejected. System prompts user to verify number before adding. OUTPUT- Error message and number not linked. User is prompted to go through verifying number process.

III. User tries to link a non UK (International) number.

INPUT- Non UK telephone number. PRECONDITION- Invalid telephone number. POSTCONDITION- Telephone number is rejected. System prompts user to check telephone number. OUTPUT- Error message and number not linked. User is told to check number.

L. System should allow user to view transactions. Historical transaction of a maximum of 3yrs should be available when requested.

I. User tries to view transactions within a 3 year period.

INPUT- A year old transaction is selected. PRECONDITION- User is signed in. There are transactions of 3yrs present. POSTCONDITION- Transaction is displayed. Output- A years transaction history is displayed.

II. User tries to view transactions over a 3 year period.

INPUT- 4 year's old transaction. PRECONDITION- User is signed in. POSTCONDITION- Only 3yrs old transactions are available. OUTPUT- Only transaction as far back as 3yrs are available.

M. System must be able to process payment while prompted from 3rd party's website.

I. Customer tries to pay with paypal with sufficient funds after checking out on 3rd party's website.

INPUT- User name and password. PRECONDITION- Third party's website has directed user to paypal. Paypal page displays and prompts user to login. POSTCONDITION- Payment is processed successfully. OUTPUT- User is directed back to sellers website after successful payment.

II. Customer tries to pay with paypal hence insufficient credit

INPUT- User name and password. PRECONDITION- Third party's website has directed user to paypal. Paypal page displays and prompts user to login. POSTCONDITION- Payment is unable to process due to insufficient funds. OUTPUT- Order is unsuccessful and user directed back to sellers website.

III. Customer tries to make payment with paypal on a zero or minus balance.

INPUT- User name and password. PRECONDITION- Third party's website has directed user to paypal. Paypal page displays and prompts user to login. POSTCONDITION- Payment is unable to process due to insufficient funds. OUTPUT- Order is unsuccessful and user directed back to sellers website.

Sample Test Case

Test Case Number	Test Case Name	Test Case Description	Test Case Designed By	Pre-condition	Requirement	Test Scenario	Test Step Number	Step Description	Expected Result	Actual Result	Test Execution Status
1	Verify ticket booking on www.nationalrail.co.uk	Verify ticket booking on www.nationalrail.co.uk	Trish Bhatt	1) Windows and Apple Mac operating system with internet connection should be available. 2) www.nationalrail.co.uk should be up and running	Verify ticket booking on www.nationalrail.co.uk	Verify ticket booking on www.nationalrail.co.uk	1	Open web browser and type www.nationalrail.co.uk	A home page should be displayed showing Train Times & Tickets option		

Test Case Number	Test Case Name	Test Case Description	Test Case Designed By	Pre-condition	Requirement	Test Scenario	Test Step Number	Step Description	Expected Result	Actual Result	Test Execution Status
							2	Type Edinburgh in the box From destination under Train Times & Tickets option	Drop down menu should be displayed showing city & station names		
							3	Choose the city name or station name	Should be able to choose the city or station and should appear in the from destination box		

Test Case Number	Test Case Name	Test Case Description	Test Case Designed By	Pre-condition	Requirement	Test Scenario	Test Step Number	Step Description	Expected Result	Actual Result	Test Execution Status
							4	Type London in to the box To destination	Drop down menu should be displayed showing city names		
							5	Click on the drop down menu next to the box called When	Four option should be displayed 1. Leaving 2. Arriving 3. First Train 4. Last Train		
							6	Select the option 1. Leaving	Should be able to choose option 1		

Test Case Number	Test Case Name	Test Case Description	Test Case Designed By	Pre-condition	Requirement	Test Scenario	Test Step Number	Step Description	Expected Result	Actual Result	Test Execution Status
							7	Click on the next box to enter the date and type the date or choose thee date from the calendar	User should be able to type the date or should be able to choose the date for the travel.		
							8	Click on the drop down menu next to the calendar and choose the time to travel	User should be able to choose the time		

Test Case Number	Test Case Name	Test Case Description	Test Case Designed By	Pre-condition	Requirement	Test Scenario	Test Step Number	Step Description	Expected Result	Actual Result	Test Execution Status
							9	Click on the little box before Return and tick the box	Boxes to choose the place, date and time should appear for the user to make selection		
							10	Click on the drop down menu next to Return	Four option should be displayed 1. Leaving 2. Arriving 3. First Train 4. Last Train		
							11	Select the option 1. Leaving	Should be able to choose option 1		

Test Case Number	Test Case Name	Test Case Description	Test Case Designed By	Pre-condition	Requirement	Test Scenario	Test Step Number	Step Description	Expected Result	Actual Result	Test Execution Status
							12	Click on the next box to enter the date and type the date or choose thee date from the calendar	User should be able to type the date or should be able to choose the date for the travel.		
							13	Click on the drop down menu next to the calendar and choose the time to travel	User should be able to choose the time		

Test Case Number	Test Case Name	Test Case Description	Test Case Designed By	Pre-condition	Requirement	Test Scenario	Test Step Number	Step Description	Expected Result	Actual Result	Test Execution Status
							14	Click on yellow button called Go	User should be directed to next page where train departure and arrival time, from and to, duration of the journey, changes and fare porices should bee displayed		
							15	Click on the blue button on the right called Select and choose the third journey option for outbound journey	User should bee able to choose the journey option and it should change to Selected from Select when clicked on		

Test Case Number	Test Case Name	Test Case Description	Test Case Designed By	Pre-condition	Requirement	Test Scenario	Test Step Number	Step Description	Expected Result	Actual Result	Test Execution Status
							16	Click on the blue button on the right called Select and choose the fourth journey option for return journey	User should bee able to choose the journey option and it should change to Selected from Select		
							17	Verify the blue box below called Tickets shows the ticket information and fare prices for the selected journies	It should show only two journies information for example fare type and fare price		

Test Case Number	Test Case Name	Test Case Description	Test Case Designed By	Pre-condition	Requirement	Test Scenario	Test Step Number	Step Description	Expected Result	Actual Result	Test Execution Status
							18	Click on the yellow button called Buy Now	Button should be working and should take the user to next page third party domain where user can buy the tickets and should be able to pay for the journey		

For further reading and practice, download the projects at https://github.com/narayananpalani/testautomation

Object Recognition

In earlier chapters, the topics are covered on how the tools are used along with sample document format for test plan, test cases and other test team document methods.In this chapter, important topic on how automation tools capturing the human usability using object properties recognition!

When user manually operates the functions on the web pages or the applications, the same steps are automated using the object capturing method of automation tools. This is a process of pattern recognition algorithm using feature based or the properties based techniques by every automation tool.

HP UFT (Formerly HP QTP)-Test Object Model

Objects of the applications are captured and used from Object Repository (.tsr files) in the 'Test Object Model'.

Two types of supported repository in QTP are: Local and shared object repository. During the recognition of the objects (using Object Spy tool within QTP or Descriptive Programming-Manually update the script with properties), QTP try to use a 'human' like technology for identification. During test execution, the tool compares the stored object repository with actual properties available on the application. If the Run Time-Objects matches to the stored objects, it perform the actions, events instructed by the script and complete the test execution.

Ranorex-Ready to use GUI Objects

Objects of the applications are captured and used from Ranorex Object Repository to manage GUI/Application based objects and represents the file based mapping information. Ranorex Spy is used to identify the object properties (likeXpath of the properties). The advantage of the tool is on 'Ready to use GUI objects' as each Ranorex Repository automatically generates a source code file in DotNet file in which all the elements of Ranorex adapters are located. Thus the automation scripts are simplified by reusing these auto-generated scripts based on the objects.

Selenium IDE-Locators

Selenium IDE is an add-on to Firefox at the moment and following are the most common object locaters within Selenium IDE: ID, ClassName, Name, TagName, LinkText, PartialLinkText, Xpath, CSS Selector, DOM. After capturing the scripts through Record mode, clicking on Target listbox drop down, it gives the option of picking selective/right object properties for the test. Please refer the Selenium IDE section to understand more with example programs.

Selenium Web Driver-Object Properties

The advantage of Selenium Web Driver is to customize the script by creating the object repository in a separate .properties file and list all the xpath properties of the GUI over the properties file location. Following Locators most used Industry best practice on Selenium web driver: ID, ClassName, Name, TagName, LinkText, PartialLinkText, Xpath, CSS Selector, DOM. Please refer Selenium Web Driver section to understand how to call the properties file within the automation script (class file)

Object Recognition Technology-Automation Testing

In earlier chapters, the topics are covered on how the tools are used along with sample document format for test plan, test cases and other test team document methods. Previous chapter talk about object recognition; In this chapter the key challenges of automation testing in objection recognition is discussed.

XPath of the objects are completing trusted to build the automation frameworks across the organizations. Especially if the automation framework is made up of Selenium or UFT (formerly QTP) or Ranorex or any other automation tool, the core logic of capturing the object is through XPath should be the most common way of automation frameworks.

If the frameworks are depends on XPath or the object properties, the need for changes over a period of time result in automation framework failures. This is one of the main reason why most of the automation framework show Return On Investment only in Long Term! When the project exist for more than five years, it is obvious that the objects travel across many changes. So the automation framework has to be maintained as per the changes made to the objects across the test projects.

Alternative Solutions for the XPath or Object Property Challenges

Multiple XPath Capturing Technology

Instead capturing one particular xpath object property and list it out into the automation framework, it is ease of use to pick atleast three properties of the object within the same line of code and suggest automation framework to pick most relevant object by comparing the object properties.

Selenium Code-For example:

```
driver.findElement(By.name("j_namefield")).click();
```

As per this solution, this line should be altered to:

```
driver.findElement(By.name("j_namefield") || By.ID("j_001")|| By.linkText("FirstName")).click();
```

When more than one object property are captured, even when the changes are made to two different object properties, it won't affect the test execution through the automation framework and the framework still be in a position to run without any maintenance efforts!

Object Property Reference Tables in an Exclusive Database

To avoid rewriting the automation framework scripts and editing the xpath property details frequently, it is useful to list the entire properties and the object details in database which can be controlled by developers and testers for their testing purposes! For example, developers use xpath properties for their unit testing as part of BDD (Behavior Driven Development) and testers use the properties for Regression Testing. So the need of the common xpath referencing table is of right approach-so that the changes to the objects are getting notified by both the stakeholders by implementing this approach!

If the existing code in selenium written in this model:

driver.findElement(By.name("j_namefield")).click();

It has to be upgraded to the below format to adapt this solution:

driver.findElement(By.name (**select object_property from table Ref where test_name= 'Regression'**)).click();

When the database is connected to the framework in initial steps, the ongoing scripts can call the respective line of data and extract the needed object details from DB to perform the test automation. Whenever the object properties are getting changed, this can be updated to the Database to keep the References up-to-date.

File Upload Method:

Automation Framework can display message to upload the object properties csv file or excel file in order to perform the automation execution for the latest object properties uploaded. In this way, any latest changes can be updated to the csv file by developers or testers and it can be used during test execution.

Understanding Selenium through 'Machine Learning Technology'

Pattern recognition and computational learning of automation testing tools are the best way to look ahead on near future to have strong and potential browser automation tools (such as Selenium). Basically machine learning is the expert way of learning and observe how the automation tools are built and how the model work to capture and perform the tests for us.

Let us take the example of Selenium and understand what are the current challenges with the tool and how the model work in terms of automation.

Step1 - Open Questions with Selenium v2

Selenium Web Driver doesn't support HTTP Status Code at the moment. Issue 141 [2]is open with Selenium on this case. Various blogs[3] explain the reasons on why HTTP Status Code is not exposed. Similarly System Level Dialogs like File Upload (Operating System Level Dialogues). This is something expected to get implemented in future by companion projects[4].Due to performance issues, redesign of the Selenium Grid, Redesign of Selenium web-page has been planned[5].

---

[2] http://code.google.com/p/selenium/issues/detail?id=141

[3] http://jimevansmusic.blogspot.co.uk/2012/07/webdriver-y-u-no-have-http-status-codes.html

[4] https://www.youtube.com/watch?v=y3qhb9nsN8Y

[5] https://www.youtube.com/watch?v=y3qhb9nsN8Y

Step2 - Selenium Web Driver-Extract Files

Download the latest jar files from Selenium Web Page. selenium-java-2.47.1.jar and selenium-java-2.47.1-srcs.jar are downloaded (from selenium web page) to explain in this section.

Perform the below command line command to extract the jar file selenium-java-2.47.1.jar:

jar xf selenium-java-2.47.1.jar

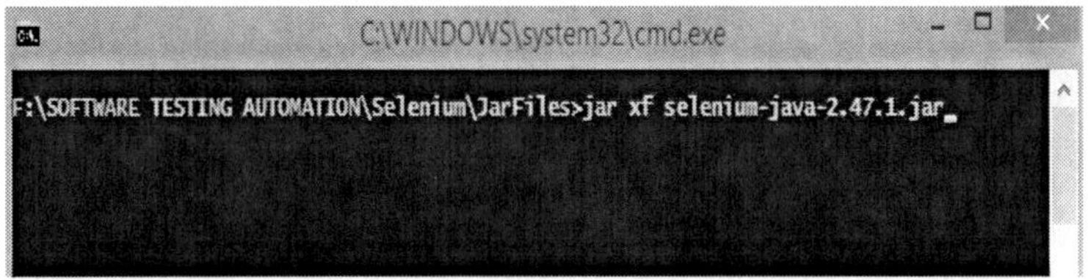

Verify that three folders extracted and listed in the local machine as follows:

Name	Date modified	Type	Size
com	29/07/2015 22:51	File folder	
META-INF	29/07/2015 22:56	File folder	
org	29/07/2015 22:51	File folder	

Similarly Extract the selenium-java-2.47.1-srcs.jar and find folders as follows:

Name	Date modified	Type	Size
com	29/07/2015 23:03	File folder	
org	29/07/2015 23:03	File folder	

Once extracted, navigate to the folder path of selenium-java-2.47.1-srcs.jar:

com\thoughtworks\selenium\webdriven\commands

Make sure that the following list of files are displayed:

AddLocationStrategy.java
AddSelection.java
AlertOverride.java
AllowNativeXPath.java
AltKeyDown.java
AltKeyUp.java
AssignId.java
AttachFile.java
CaptureScreenshotToString.java
Check.java
Click.java
ClickAt.java
Close.java
ControlKeyDown.java
ControlKeyUp.java
CreateCookie.java
DeleteAllVisibleCookies.java
DeleteCookie.java
DeselectPopUp.java
DoubleClick.java
DragAndDrop.java
DragAndDropToObject.java
FindFirstSelectedOptionProperty.java
FindSelectedOptionProperties.java
FireEvent.java
FireNamedEvent.java
GetAlert.java
GetAllButtons.java
GetAllFields.java
GetAllLinks.java
GetAllWindowNames.java
GetAllWindowTitles.java
GetAttribute.java
GetAttributeFromAllWindows.java
GetBodyText.java
GetConfirmation.java
GetCookie.java
GetCookieByName.java
GetCssCount.java
GetElementHeight.java
GetElementIndex.java
GetElementPositionLeft.java
GetElementPositionTop.java
GetElementWidth.java
GetEval.java
GetExpression.java
GetHtmlSource.java
GetLocation.java
GetSelectOptions.java
GetTable.java
GetText.java
GetTitle.java
GetValue.java
GetXpathCount.java
GoBack.java
Highlight.java
IsAlertPresent.java
IsChecked.java
IsConfirmationPresent.java
IsCookiePresent.java
IsEditable.java
IsElementPresent.java
IsOrdered.java
IsSomethingSelected.java
IsTextPresent.java
IsVisible.java
KeyDownNative.java
KeyEvent.java
KeyPressNative.java
KeyState.java
KeyUpNative.java
MetaKeyDown.java
MetaKeyUp.java
MethodDeclaration.java
MouseEvent.java
MouseEventAt.java
NoOp.java
Open.java
OpenWindow.java
Refresh.java
RemoveAllSelections.java
RemoveSelection.java
RunScript.java
SelectFrame.java
SelectOption.java
SelectPopUp.java
SelectWindow.java
SeleniumSelect.java
SetNextConfirmationState.java
SetTimeout.java
ShiftKeyDown.java
ShiftKeyUp.java
Submit.java
Type.java
TypeKeys.java
Uncheck.java
UseXPathLibrary.java
WaitForCondition.java
WaitForPageToLoad.java
WaitForPopup.java
WindowFocus.java
WindowMaximize.java

This is the core command base of Selenium Web Driver and Selenium understand the program (of automation tester) and runs the tests using these in-built command based java files.

Let us understand more on how selenium recognizes each commands when the script is scripted through the automation frameworks.

Step3 Understand the Pattern in which the automation tool work

Following are the files involved in the source logic:

com\thoughtworks\selenium\DefaultSelenium.java
This is the primary Interface of Selenium and end user interact with this interface

com\thoughtworks\selenium\BrowserConfigurationOptions.java

Browser configuration details such as single window, multiple window, executable path and time out details are handled and controlled

com\thoughtworks\selenium\CommandProcessor.java
New Selenium Testing Sessions are controlled (including killing the web browser to stop the tests)

com\thoughtworks\selenium\DefaultRemoteCommand.java
This is the RemoteCommand interface of Selenium

com\thoughtworks\selenium\HttpCommandProcessor.java
This is the logic in which Selenium sends commands and retrieves expected results via HTTP

com\thoughtworks\selenium\RemoteCommand.java
Single remote action has been controlled in the logic of this class

com\thoughtworks\selenium\ScreenshotListener.java
ITestResult has been used in this class to capture the screenshot and save with extension .png

com\thoughtworks\selenium\Selenium.java
This is the core logic where selenium defines an object that runs Selenium's commands to find objects

List of commands supported by Selenium and respective class files:

Command	Related Logic in File
AddLocationStrategy	com\thoughtworks\selenium\ webdriven\commands\ AddLocationStrategy.java
AddSelection	com\thoughtworks\selenium\ webdriven\commands\AddSelection. java

Command	Related Logic in File
AlertOverride	com\thoughtworks\selenium\webdriven\commands\AlertOverride.java
AllowNativeXPath	com\thoughtworks\selenium\webdriven\commands\AllowNativeXPath.java
AltKeyDown	com\thoughtworks\selenium\webdriven\commands\AltKeyDown.java
AltKeyUp	com\thoughtworks\selenium\webdriven\commands\AltKeyUp.java
AssignId	com\thoughtworks\selenium\webdriven\commands\AssignId.java
AttachFile	com\thoughtworks\selenium\webdriven\commands\AttachFile.java
CaptureScreenshotToString	com\thoughtworks\selenium\webdriven\commands\CaptureScreenshotToString.java
Check	com\thoughtworks\selenium\webdriven\commands\Check.java
Click	com\thoughtworks\selenium\webdriven\commands\Click.java
ClickAt	com\thoughtworks\selenium\webdriven\commands\ClickAt.java
Close	com\thoughtworks\selenium\webdriven\commands\Close.java
ControlKeyDown	com\thoughtworks\selenium\webdriven\commands\ControlKeyDown.java
ControlKeyUp	com\thoughtworks\selenium\webdriven\commands\ControlKeyUp.java
CreateCookie	com\thoughtworks\selenium\webdriven\commands\CreateCookie.java
DeleteAllVisibleCookies	com\thoughtworks\selenium\webdriven\commands\DeleteAllVisibleCookies.java

Command	Related Logic in File
DeleteCookie	com\thoughtworks\selenium\webdriven\commands\DeleteCookie.java
DeselectPopUp	com\thoughtworks\selenium\webdriven\commands\DeselectPopUp.java
DoubleClick	com\thoughtworks\selenium\webdriven\commands\DoubleClick.java
DragAndDrop	com\thoughtworks\selenium\webdriven\commands\DragAndDrop.java
DragAndDropToObject	com\thoughtworks\selenium\webdriven\commands\DragAndDropToObject.java
FindFirstSelectedOptionProperty	com\thoughtworks\selenium\webdriven\commands\FindFirstSelectedOptionProperty.java
FindSelectedOptionProperties	com\thoughtworks\selenium\webdriven\commands\FindSelectedOptionProperties.java
FireEvent	com\thoughtworks\selenium\webdriven\commands\FireEvent.java
FireNamedEvent	com\thoughtworks\selenium\webdriven\commands\FireNamedEvent.java
GetAlert	com\thoughtworks\selenium\webdriven\commands\GetAlert.java
GetAllButtons	com\thoughtworks\selenium\webdriven\commands\GetAllButtons.java
GetAllFields	com\thoughtworks\selenium\webdriven\commands\GetAllFields.java
GetAllLinks	com\thoughtworks\selenium\webdriven\commands\GetAllLinks.java
GetAllWindowNames	com\thoughtworks\selenium\webdriven\commands\GetAllWindowNames.java

Command	Related Logic in File
GetAllWindowTitles	com\thoughtworks\selenium\webdriven\commands\GetAllWindowTitles.java
GetAttribute	com\thoughtworks\selenium\webdriven\commands\GetAttribute.java
GetAttributeFromAllWindows	com\thoughtworks\selenium\webdriven\commands\GetAttributeFromAllWindows.java
GetBodyText	com\thoughtworks\selenium\webdriven\commands\GetBodyText.java
GetConfirmation	com\thoughtworks\selenium\webdriven\commands\GetConfirmation.java
GetCookie	com\thoughtworks\selenium\webdriven\commands\GetCookie.java
GetCookieByName	com\thoughtworks\selenium\webdriven\commands\GetCookieByName.java
GetCssCount	com\thoughtworks\selenium\webdriven\commands\GetCssCount.java
GetElementHeight	com\thoughtworks\selenium\webdriven\commands\GetElementHeight.java
GetElementIndex	com\thoughtworks\selenium\webdriven\commands\GetElementIndex.java
GetElementPositionLeft	com\thoughtworks\selenium\webdriven\commands\GetElementPositionLeft.java
GetElementPositionTop	com\thoughtworks\selenium\webdriven\commands\GetElementPositionTop.java
GetElementWidth	com\thoughtworks\selenium\webdriven\commands\GetElementWidth.java
GetEval	com\thoughtworks\selenium\webdriven\commands\GetEval.java

Command	Related Logic in File
GetExpression	com\thoughtworks\selenium\webdriven\commands\GetExpression.java
GetHtmlSource	com\thoughtworks\selenium\webdriven\commands\GetHtmlSource.java
GetLocation	com\thoughtworks\selenium\webdriven\commands\GetLocation.java
GetSelectOptions	com\thoughtworks\selenium\webdriven\commands\GetSelectOptions.java
GetTable	com\thoughtworks\selenium\webdriven\commands\GetTable.java
GetText	com\thoughtworks\selenium\webdriven\commands\GetText.java
GetTitle	com\thoughtworks\selenium\webdriven\commands\GetTitle.java
GetValue	com\thoughtworks\selenium\webdriven\commands\GetValue.java
GetXpathCount	com\thoughtworks\selenium\webdriven\commands\GetXpathCount.java
GoBack	com\thoughtworks\selenium\webdriven\commands\GoBack.java
Highlight	com\thoughtworks\selenium\webdriven\commands\Highlight.java
IsAlertPresent	com\thoughtworks\selenium\webdriven\commands\IsAlertPresent.java
IsChecked	com\thoughtworks\selenium\webdriven\commands\IsChecked.java
IsConfirmationPresent	com\thoughtworks\selenium\webdriven\commands\IsConfirmationPresent.java
IsCookiePresent	com\thoughtworks\selenium\webdriven\commands\IsCookiePresent.java
IsEditable	com\thoughtworks\selenium\webdriven\commands\IsEditable.java

Command	Related Logic in File
IsElementPresent	com\thoughtworks\selenium\webdriven\commands\IsElementPresent.java
IsOrdered	com\thoughtworks\selenium\webdriven\commands\IsOrdered.java
IsSomethingSelected	com\thoughtworks\selenium\webdriven\commands\IsSomethingSelected.java
IsTextPresent	com\thoughtworks\selenium\webdriven\commands\IsTextPresent.java
IsVisible	com\thoughtworks\selenium\webdriven\commands\IsVisible.java
KeyDownNative	com\thoughtworks\selenium\webdriven\commands\KeyDownNative.java
KeyEvent	com\thoughtworks\selenium\webdriven\commands\KeyEvent.java
KeyPressNative	com\thoughtworks\selenium\webdriven\commands\KeyPressNative.java
KeyState	com\thoughtworks\selenium\webdriven\commands\KeyState.java
KeyUpNative	com\thoughtworks\selenium\webdriven\commands\KeyUpNative.java
MetaKeyDown	com\thoughtworks\selenium\webdriven\commands\MetaKeyDown.java
MetaKeyUp	com\thoughtworks\selenium\webdriven\commands\MetaKeyUp.java
MethodDeclaration	com\thoughtworks\selenium\webdriven\commands\MethodDeclaration.java
MouseEvent	com\thoughtworks\selenium\webdriven\commands\MouseEvent.java
MouseEventAt	com\thoughtworks\selenium\webdriven\commands\MouseEventAt.java

Command	Related Logic in File
NoOp	com\thoughtworks\selenium\webdriven\commands\NoOp.java
Open	com\thoughtworks\selenium\webdriven\commands\Open.java
OpenWindow	com\thoughtworks\selenium\webdriven\commands\OpenWindow.java
Refresh	com\thoughtworks\selenium\webdriven\commands\Refresh.java
RemoveAllSelections	com\thoughtworks\selenium\webdriven\commands\RemoveAllSelections.java
RemoveSelection	com\thoughtworks\selenium\webdriven\commands\RemoveSelection.java
RunScript	com\thoughtworks\selenium\webdriven\commands\RunScript.java
SelectFrame	com\thoughtworks\selenium\webdriven\commands\SelectFrame.java
SelectOption	com\thoughtworks\selenium\webdriven\commands\SelectOption.java
SelectPopUp	com\thoughtworks\selenium\webdriven\commands\SelectPopUp.java
SelectWindow	com\thoughtworks\selenium\webdriven\commands\SelectWindow.java
SeleniumSelect	com\thoughtworks\selenium\webdriven\commands\SeleniumSelect.java
SetNextConfirmationState	com\thoughtworks\selenium\webdriven\commands\SetNextConfirmationState.java
SetTimeout	com\thoughtworks\selenium\webdriven\commands\SetTimeout.java
ShiftKeyDown	com\thoughtworks\selenium\webdriven\commands\ShiftKeyDown.java

Command	Related Logic in File
ShiftKeyUp	com\thoughtworks\selenium\webdriven\commands\ShiftKeyUp.java
Submit	com\thoughtworks\selenium\webdriven\commands\Submit.java
Type	com\thoughtworks\selenium\webdriven\commands\Type.java
TypeKeys	com\thoughtworks\selenium\webdriven\commands\TypeKeys.java
Uncheck	com\thoughtworks\selenium\webdriven\commands\Uncheck.java
UseXPathLibrary	com\thoughtworks\selenium\webdriven\commands\UseXPathLibrary.java
WaitForCondition	com\thoughtworks\selenium\webdriven\commands\WaitForCondition.java
WaitForPageToLoad	com\thoughtworks\selenium\webdriven\commands\WaitForPageToLoad.java
WaitForPopup	com\thoughtworks\selenium\webdriven\commands\WaitForPopup.java
WindowFocus	com\thoughtworks\selenium\webdriven\commands\WindowFocus.java
WindowMaximize	com\thoughtworks\selenium\webdriven\commands\WindowMaximize.java

Following are the list of action related classes help in performing respective actions described in the selenium script:

Type of Interactions using Selenium Script	Logic Location
Action	org\openqa\selenium\interactions\Action.java
ActionChainExecutor	org\openqa\selenium\interactions\ActionChainExecutor.java

Type of Interactions using Selenium Script	Logic Location
Actions	org\openqa\selenium\interactions\Actions.java
ButtonReleaseAction	org\openqa\selenium\interactions\ButtonReleaseAction.java
CanPerformActionChain	org\openqa\selenium\interactions\CanPerformActionChain.java
ClickAction	org\openqa\selenium\interactions\ClickAction.java
ClickAndHoldAction	org\openqa\selenium\interactions\ClickAndHoldAction.java
CompositeAction	org\openqa\selenium\interactions\CompositeAction.java
ContextClickAction	org\openqa\selenium\interactions\ContextClickAction.java
DoubleClickAction	org\openqa\selenium\interactions\DoubleClickAction.java
HasInputDevices	org\openqa\selenium\interactions\HasInputDevices.java
HasTouchScreen	org\openqa\selenium\interactions\HasTouchScreen.java
internal	org\openqa\selenium\interactions\internal
InvalidCoordinatesException	org\openqa\selenium\interactions\InvalidCoordinatesException.java
Keyboard	org\openqa\selenium\interactions\Keyboard.java
KeyDownAction	org\openqa\selenium\interactions\KeyDownAction.java
KeyUpAction	org\openqa\selenium\interactions\KeyUpAction.java
Mouse	org\openqa\selenium\interactions\Mouse.java
MoveMouseAction	org\openqa\selenium\interactions\MoveMouseAction.java
MoveTargetOutOfBoundsException	org\openqa\selenium\interactions\MoveTargetOutOfBoundsException java

Type of Interactions using Selenium Script	Logic Location
MoveToOffsetAction	org\openqa\selenium\interactions\MoveToOffsetAction.java
PauseAction	org\openqa\selenium\interactions\PauseAction.java
SendKeysAction	org\openqa\selenium\interactions\SendKeysAction.java
touch	org\openqa\selenium\interactions\touch
TouchScreen	org\openqa\selenium\interactions\TouchScreen.java

Following are the list of files supports selenium to Find certain objects through the script:

org\openqa\selenium\lift\find\BaseFinder.java
org\openqa\selenium\lift\find\DivFinder.java
org\openqa\selenium\lift\find\Finder.java
org\openqa\selenium\lift\find\HtmlTagFinder.java
org\openqa\selenium\lift\find\ImageFinder.java
org\openqa\selenium\lift\find\InputFinder.java
org\openqa\selenium\lift\find\LinkFinder.java
org\openqa\selenium\lift\find\PageTitleFinder.java
org\openqa\selenium\lift\find\TableCellFinder.java
org\openqa\selenium\lift\find\TableFinder.java
org\openqa\selenium\lift\find\XPathFinder.java

Following are the list of files supports selenium to Match certain objects through the script:

org\openqa\selenium\lift\match\AttributeMatcher.java
org\openqa\selenium\lift\match\DisplayedMatcher.java
org\openqa\selenium\lift\match\NumericalMatchers.java
org\openqa\selenium\lift\match\SelectionMatcher.java
org\openqa\selenium\lift\match\TextMatcher.java

org\openqa\selenium\lift\match\ValueMatcher.java

Following are the list of files supports selenium in logging the issues and information while test execution:

org\openqa\selenium\logging\CompositeLocalLogs.java
org\openqa\selenium\logging\HandlerBasedLocalLogs.java
org\openqa\selenium\logging\LocalLogs.java
org\openqa\selenium\logging\LogCombiner.java
org\openqa\selenium\logging\LogEntries.java
org\openqa\selenium\logging\LogEntry.java
org\openqa\selenium\logging\LoggingHandler.java
org\openqa\selenium\logging\LoggingPreferences.java
org\openqa\selenium\logging\LogLevelMapping.java
org\openqa\selenium\logging\Logs.java
org\openqa\selenium\logging\LogType.java
org\openqa\selenium\logging\NeedsLocalLogs.java
org\openqa\selenium\logging\profiler
org\openqa\selenium\logging\SessionLogHandler.java
org\openqa\selenium\logging\SessionLogs.java
org\openqa\selenium\logging\StoringLocalLogs.java
org\openqa\selenium\logging\profiler\EventType.java
org\openqa\selenium\logging\profiler\HttpProfilerLogEntry.java
org\openqa\selenium\logging\profiler\ProfilerLogEntry.java

Network Connection and Interfaces are controlled in following java based class files:

org\openqa\selenium\mobile\NetworkConnection.java
org\openqa\selenium\net\DefaultNetworkInterfaceProvider.java
org\openqa\selenium\net\EphemeralPortRangeDetector.java
org\openqa\selenium\net\FixedIANAPortRange.java
org\openqa\selenium\net\LinuxEphemeralPortRangeDetector.
java
org\openqa\selenium\net\NetworkInterface.java
org\openqa\selenium\net\NetworkInterfaceProvider.java

org\openqa\selenium\net\NetworkUtils.java
org\openqa\selenium\net\OlderWindowsVersionEphemeralPortDetector.java
org\openqa\selenium\net\PortProber.java
org\openqa\selenium\net\UrlChecker.java
org\openqa\selenium\net\Urls.java
org\openqa\selenium\opera\OperaDriver.java
org\openqa\selenium\opera\OperaDriverService.java
org\openqa\selenium\opera\OperaOptions.java
org\openqa\selenium\os\CommandLine.java
org\openqa\selenium\os\ExecutableFinder.java
org\openqa\selenium\os\Kernel32.java
org\openqa\selenium\os\OsProcess.java
org\openqa\selenium\os\ProcessUtils.java
org\openqa\selenium\os\UnixProcess.java
org\openqa\selenium\os\WindowsProcessGroup.java
org\openqa\selenium\os\WindowsRegistryException.java
org\openqa\selenium\os\WindowsUtils.java

Machine Learning based Orthogonal Array Tests (ML-OATs)

The present issues of testing projects such as failure of test automation, expensive tool licenses causing less or negative ROI (Return on Investments), useless and extracted test cycles are the result of poor test planning. This can be avoided by systematically reducing or removing the three wastes of automation test cycles which is explained in this chapter.

Test Suites play key-role across the test life cycle! But designing test suite need a clever methodology where in worthy addition and waste deletion has to be updated in structural cycles.

As a first step, test suite has to be designed by referring to requirements. When 'General Abstract Test Suites' are made in initial stage of the project, the list of test combination has to be analysed in detail. Once decision tree has been made with tree nodes and leafs of primary and secondary test combinations,

When the test suites are made as abstracts, first level of wastes are produced in the test project! That is none other than the list of test suite abstracts which are designed for unsure test requirements and deferred defects! There is no use by designing tests and executing till the end while the requirement is not going to be implemented or deferred! Even if the project management is not sure on what are the requirements or defects going to be deferred, this has to be taken seriously while designing the test suites. So periodic reviews

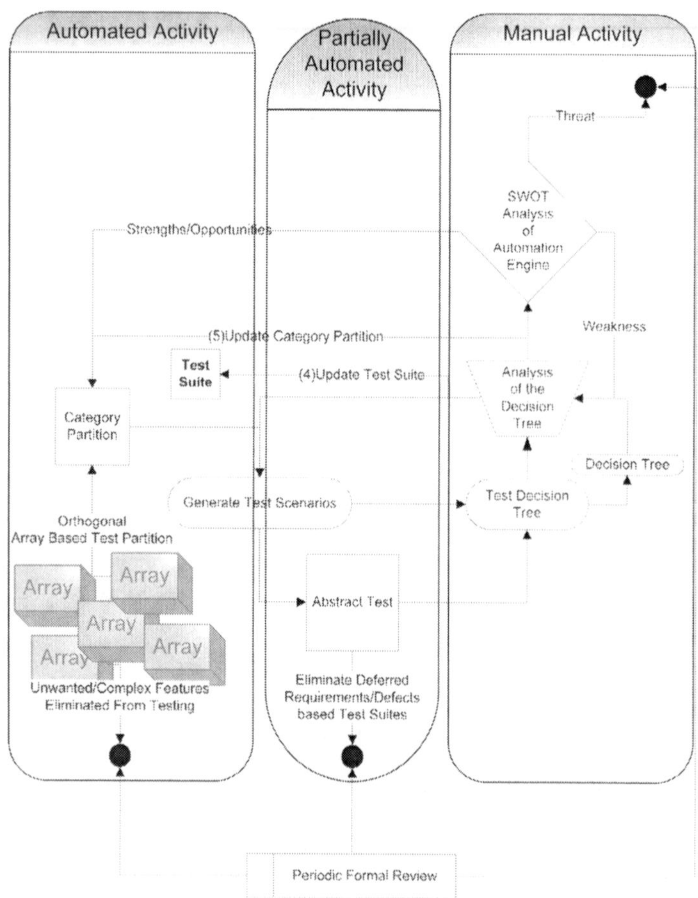

Reference: 'Novel Applications of Machine Learning in Software Testing' by Lionel C. Briand

has to be scheduled by test managers to analyse this primary waste hence huge number of automation scripts can be reduced in the test project!

After eliminating unnecessary test suites through first set of wastes, Decision Tree method should be used to design the tree of test combinations. Here comes the need of SWOT Analysis (Strength, Weakness, Opportunities, Threat) to find out the automation capability of the testing team. Strength is the automation test resources availability within the team and Opportunity is the percentage of possible automation conversion of the project where as Weakness and Threat are all the possible constraints to the test projects inclusive of incorrect review or no intervention from test directors on reviewing the automation frameworks and failure to review on knowledge sharing process between automation and manual testing resources etc.

When the list of threats are identified, they are the next set of wastes in the test project. As an example, test suite which takes endless time to automate, if it is proved to be low priority, it can be identified or classified as threat since automation meant to bring Return On Investment (ROI) and the goal is not to automation each and everything of the test project (assuming not all the project items are belongs to critical or high priority category). The important question arise here as why low priority or expensive automatable item considered as threat? Yes-this may lead to termination of automation project without achieving proper returns. Think that the automation project is to reduce the time and effort. If it ten times of manual testing effort to automate the test items and twenty times of same manual testing efforts to maintain them, it is of absolutely no use to build such automation implementations

After reducing the wastes from the steps above, Category Partition can be best implemented by using Orthogonal Array (Orthogonal Array [in short OA] is used to arrive at set of possible test combinations to deliver complete test coverage).

Using OA, complete test combinations and types are derived and business arrives at a decision point to use a sub test set from OA combinations to accomplish the test execution. *(My earlier book on Advanced Test Strategy explains about OA with some examples)*

Once OA is implemented, unnecessary test combinations can be reduced and revised automation test pack can be implemented in the test project hence performing the same workflow every cycle of the project help in reviewing the project elements and reducing the wastes!

As a final step, formal periodic review has to be done on the machine learning based automation test approach and eliminate the wastes with approval from each stakeholders.

Final Words...

As a part 1, this book has been best analysed and revised to bring a short note on each important automation tools in software testing industry. Especially topics such as test scheduling, Selenium based examples are written after implementing them in sample projects. To benefit readers, these sample frameworks and projects are updated in GIT for referencing them whenever required. Overall it took six years to understand the entire platform of automation tools and one entire year to write the concepts down to a complete book. If the readers are expected to see complete information of a particular tool, it may have not experienced in this book as the objective of this book is to analyse the available automation tools in panoramic view and pick best suited tools to projects. So readers are requested to read the books or manuals of respective tools to understand detailed instructions on how they have been designed and used for the testing projects.

In some of the chapters, it is meant to be disconnected from the flow of the book and intentionally the chapters are written in this perspective as the connection between the chapters can be best understand only after practising the sample projects from GIT! This book is concentrating on providing the hands-on experience to readers on test automation -not only reading experience! So if the intention of the readers is just to read the book like any other automation book, then it is not going to benefit much on the career in automation testing.

After reading each chapter, if readers are spending good time on practicing the sample projects then it gives the blend of reading knowledge and benefits of experiencing the same basics in automation implementations. It takes few days to read the whole book-but it reaches at-least three months to read and practice the entire set of sample projects along with all the chapters.

Feedback

If you are not happy with this book, feel free to write to me at my linkedin page-so I can understand and try to help you in most possible way. You can reach my linkedin page by entering 'Narayanan Palani' in Google search.

If you are benefited from this book and happy, please navigate to Amazon page and don't forget to comment in 'Review Comments' by searching 'software automation testing secrets revealed' in Amazon search or the page where the book has been purchased. Your comments are valuable more than anything else and your one line of comment will definitely help other job seekers, test engineers to take decision on purchasing this book and get benefited. Thank you!

References

[1] https://github.com/narayananpalani/testautomation

[2] http://www.seleniumhq.org/

[3] http://software-testing-tutorials-automation.blogspot.co.uk

[4] http://software-testing-tutorials-automation.blogspot.co.uk/p/selenium-webdriver.html

[5] http://software-testing-tutorials-automation.blogspot.co.uk/2014/07/create-data-driven-framework-for.html

[6] https://code.google.com/p/selenium/wiki/GettingStarted

[7] https://github.com/techtalk/SpecFlow/wiki/Unit-test-providers

[8] http://www.specflow.org/getting-started/#InstallSetup

[9] http://phantomjs.org/download.html

[10] http://stackoverflow.com/questions/7000251/how-schedule-build-in-jenkins

[11] http://reportunit.relevantcodes.com/

[12] http://www-03.ibm.com/software/products/en/functional

[13] http://www8.hp.com/uk/en/software-solutions/unified-functional-automated-testing/

[14] http://www.borland.com/en-GB/Products/Software-Testing/Automated-Testing/Silk-Test

[15] http://www.groovy-lang.org/

Index

Author's Book on Mobile Testing is available in the market now:

CPSIA information can be obtained at www.ICGtesting.com
Printed in the USA
LVOW08s1456060316

477992LV00005B/409/P